E-Business Innovation and Change Management

Mohini Singh
RMIT University, Australia

Dianne Waddell
Edith Cowan University, Australia

IDEA GROUP PUBLISHING
Hershey • London • Melbourne • Singapore

658.406
E16

Acquisitions Editor:	Mehdi Khosrow-Pour
Senior Managing Editor:	Jan Travers
Managing Editor:	Amanda Appicello
Development Editor:	Michele Rossi
Copy Editor:	Ingrid Widitz
Typesetter:	Amanda Appicello
Cover Design:	Michelle Waters
Printed at:	Integrated Book Technology

Published in the United States of America by
　　　Idea Group Publishing (an imprint of Idea Group Inc.)
　　　701 E. Chocolate Avenue, Suite 200
　　　Hershey PA 17033
　　　Tel: 717-533-8845
　　　Fax: 717-533-8661
　　　E-mail: cust@idea-group.com
　　　Web site: http://www.idea-group.com

and in the United Kingdom by　　Cav
　　　Idea Group Publishing (an imprint of Idea Group Inc.)
　　　3 Henrietta Street
　　　Covent Garden
　　　London WC2E 8LU
　　　Tel: 44 20 7240 0856
　　　Fax: 44 20 7379 3313
　　　Web site: http://www.eurospan.co.uk

Library of Congress Cataloging-in-Publication Data

E-business innovation and change management / Mohini Singh, editor.
　　　　p. cm.
　　ISBN 1-59140-138-0 -- ISBN 1-59140-139-9 (ebook)
　1. Electronic commerce--Management. 2. Organizational effectiveness.
I. Singh, Mohini.
　　HF5548.32.E1773 2003
　　658.4'06--dc22

　　　　　　　　　　　　　　　　　　　　　　　　　　2003014948

British Cataloguing in Publication Data
A Cataloguing in Publication record for this book is available from the British Library.

All work contributed to this book is new, previously-unpublished material. The views expressed in this book are those of the authors, but not necessarily of the publisher.

E-Business Innovation and Change Management

Table of Contents

Preface

Organizations around the world are capitalizing on new technologies such as the Internet and the World Wide Web to develop e-business. Evolving e-business models, integrated solutions and improved technological infrastructure are continuously changing the way business is conducted. For example, e-business is a revolution that brings with it new ways of dealing with customers and business partners, new revenue streams, new ways of processing information, new organization structures, new skill sets, electronic supply chains, new standards and policies, new collaborations and the need for adaptable business strategies. To attain and maintain success with e-business, effective management of associated changes is also essential. However, e-business and change management have often been addressed as separate issues by practitioners and academics alike, often leading to disappointing results. An acceptance and thorough understanding of the interdependence and synergy that a holistic approach can offer is imperative for organizations to survive in this new economy and achieve a competitive advantage.

The objective of this book is to introduce e-business innovations and provide an extensive discussion on change management issues, tools and models for implementing and successfully managing the transition to digital business. It specifically focuses on innovative business models and processes, technology innovation, human resource considerations, leadership styles and skills for managing e-business organizations, business partner and customer relationship management issues and e-business strategy development. All chapters included in this book include useful change management issues pertinent to e-business.

Mohini Singh, in her chapter, *Innovation and Change Management*, addresses e-business as digital transformation of business processes and management issues critical for the implementation of innovations. A discussion of issues from the inception of the idea to performance evaluation of the innovation implemented has been included. A comprehensive and complete set of issues addressing strategic, financial, technological, organizational, sociotechnical and the environment in which the organization operates has been presented.

Owen Cope and Dianne Waddell discuss the notion of developing a new and unique leadership style to manage change as a result of e-business adaptation, in the chapter *Leadership in E-Business.* The chapter is based on research carried out in the Australian manufacturing industry and determines the extent of e-business change and the required leadership styles for managing in an e-business environment. The outcome of the research clearly highlights the value of a consultative, rather than a coercive, leadership style for e-business change management.

Valerie Baker, Tim Coltman and Joan Cooper have highlighted the importance of executive judgement on decisions in *Executive Judgement and the e-Business Advantage.* They have discussed the similarities between e-business and information technology, and illustrated the impact of judgement on Information Technology strategies. The chapter introduces a tool for evaluating judgement on IT strategy and associated changes. Implications of judgement for e-business (an offshoot of IT) strategies are accordingly examined.

Sushil Sharma presents a framework for managing change in the chapter *A Change Management Framework for E-Business Solutions.* The chapter is divided into three parts: the first describes e-business and change management process; the second focuses on e-transformation and the third outlines how the framework can be applied as a tool to manage e-business transformation.

Resistance: A Medium for the Successful Implementation of Technological Innovation by Dianne Waddell discusses the positive impact of resistance during the implementation of e-business. The discussion in the chapter is an emphasis on understanding resistance, non-adversarial effects of resistance on innovations, and strategies for managing resistance. She also highlights the fact that strategies for managing resistance for e-business are the same as those for any innovation.

Building Effective Online Relationships by Byron Keating, Robert Rugimbana and Ali Quazi introduces traditional customer relationship management, discusses at length online customer relationship strategies and illustrates with diagrams the relationship profitability and management model. Dimensions of quality relationships and services identified from literature have been discussed at length.

Fang Zhao, in the chapter, *E-Partnership and Virtual Organizations: Issues and Options*, emphasizes partnerships and communication in virtual organizations. Management issues addressing challenges and risks of e-partnerships, productivity and revenue sharing in virtual organizations, and sharing core competencies and the need for effective communications have been discussed with recommendations.

Paul Hawking, Susan Foster and Andrew Stein introduce the innovation in managing people and management relationship in the chapter *A B2E Solution: Change Management Perspectives*. B2E solutions are Intranet-based people management solutions increasingly adopted by large organizations in Australia and New Zealand. Change management issues in relation to people management, business processes and innovations have been discussed, including two case studies.

Ramanie Samaratunge and Dianne Waddell, in their chapter, *E-Government in Developing Countries: A Sri Lankan Experience*, discuss the gradual change from traditional government services and data management to technology-based government records management and services. Although e-government in developed countries is generally Internet-based with online government service deliveries and payments, this chapter presents applications of basic technology to government services in Sri Lanka as e-government initiatives, and change management issues with technology reforms.

Arthur Tatnall and Stephen Burgess describe the adoption of e-business by small and medium enterprises in the chapter *Using Actor-Network Theory to Identify Factors Affecting the Adoption of E-Commerce in SMEs*. Actor-Network theory and innovation translation is discussed at length, and case studies have been included to further qualify the discussion and application to SME's.

An important and evolving innovation in e-business is the application of mobile technologies, resulting in mobile-commerce. Nabeel Al-Qirim, in the chapter *The Application of the Innovative Mobile Technologies in the Business Environment: Challenges and Implications*, introduces mobile business and discusses the application of mobile technologies, protocols, examples and change management issues.

Pauline Ratnasingam, in the chapter *The Evolution of Technology Innovation at Dakin Farms*, establishes management and change management issues with innovation implementations using a case study. The impact of innovation, lessons learned from it and the whole systems development cycle have been carefully outlined in this chapter.

Mohini Singh and Betty Zoppos, in the chapter *From Cash to E-Money: Payment System Innovations in Australia*, explore the change and developments in payment system instruments in Australia in the last decade. Numerous relevant retail payment instruments, trends and developments in payment systems, innovations in payment methods and e-payment risks form the gist of this chapter.

In the chapter *Security Management in an E-Business Environment*, Mohini Singh looks at the change in security management from a physical environment to a networked online environment. Basic online security concepts, risks, issues, challenges and the importance of security policies and procedures are presented and explicated.

This book concludes with a chapter from Dianne Waddell, *Ethics and E-Business: An Oxymoron?*, discussing numerous e-business ethical dilemmas, governance of ethical e-business issues and the nature of ethics and trust in e-business. Communication predicaments in the electronic world and their implications are presented with examples and literature discussions.

This book contains substantive evidence that no longer can we separate the issues of e-business and change management. The authors of these chapters have highlighted the crucial need to have an integrative approach to managing technology, innovations and e-business.

We wish to thank all the authors for their collaboration and contribution to this book. Their creative ideas and outstanding scholarships have added value in making this a useful and interesting publication.

Mohini Singh and Dianne Waddell

Chapter I

Innovation and Change Management

Mohini Singh
RMIT University, Australia

ABSTRACT

E-business is an innovation that modern day organisations cannot do without. It is based on technology, evolves with technological developments, digitises and automates business processes, is global and leads to improved competitiveness, efficiencies, increased market share, and business expansion. E-businesses models include business-to-business, business-to-consumer, government-to-government, government-to-business, government-to-consumer and numerous others that evolve with new developments. Technological developments applied to e-business results in new issues in the organisation, in dealing with business partners and customers, requires new laws and regulations and automated business processes. Conducting business electronically is a change from traditional ways of doing things, leading to large scale transformation of existing business. To attain business efficiencies from e-business, it is imperative that organisations effectively manage the e-business environment, and all associated changes to digitize and maintain the environment. This chapter discusses management paradigms essential for e-business change management.

INTRODUCTION

E-business innovations are digital transformation of business processes which results in a profound effect upon existing business practices (Patel & McCarthy, 2000). The business press often focuses on the success stories of e-businesses with reports or case studies mostly biased to successful implementations. However, with all the state-of-the-art 'hype and glitter', e-business in some organisations has produced largely disappointing results. Research (Singh, 2000) shows that the problem lies not so much in the technologies and e-business models as in the misperception of managers that a patchwork of 'e' applications handled by technicians or consultants will turn the existing business into e-business. Patel and McCarthy (2000, p. 3) emphasised that e-business is about changing everything in an organisation and not just 'suturing on an e-commerce appendage to the body corporate'. Technical adjustments such as integration, debugging and effective web sites are necessary, but managerial and organisational adjustments requiring planning, allocation of responsibilities, coordination between different groups and departments, negotiation, and human resource initiatives are also essential to develop the appropriate culture for e-business. Diese et al. (2000) suggest that e-business is not about technology; it is about organisational change management and people applying technology to work with business partners and customers. E-business change is a large-scale change within the organisation and its partners (Chaffey, 2000). Common errors associated with e-businesses identified from research (Singh, 2000) are that organisations get all wrapped up with technology, the software modules, and transaction and processing speeds that enormous amounts of staff time, mental energy and dollars are devoted to working on technology and relatively less time is devoted to people and business processes. E-business innovations are about embracing change and changing rapidly. E-business implementations also call for a change in company culture, which has been generally described as a system of shared meaning within an organisation determining the way employees act (Singh, 2000).

This chapter discusses management issues pertinent to the implementation and management of innovations such as e-business and new technologies. The issues discussed in this chapter have been adopted from earlier research (Singh, 1997, 1998, 2000) and literature on managing change with e-business and other new technology based innovations.

E-BUSINESS
CHANGE MANAGEMENT ISSUES

The issues discussed in the following section include variables that can be modified, adjusted and combined so that they can be practically applied to organisations of different sizes, and are particularly relevant to those operating as traditional businesses adopting new information technologies to become 'bricks and clicks'.

Identifying the Strategic Opportunities of E-Business Innovation

E-business in organisations is linked with the Internet and the growth in the use and application of computers. The identification and establishment of strategic opportunities of e-business for the firm will lead to an understanding of the innovation and its justification for improved business, competitiveness and customer service. Hackbarth and Kettinger (2000) suggest a four stage 'strategic breakout' model addressing initiation, diagnosis of the industry environment, breakout to establish a strategic target and transition or plotting a migration path, emphasising the need to innovate away from traditional strategic approaches by using the term 'breakout' to show the need for new marketplace structures and business revenue models. UK Institute of Directors (2000) illustrates the difference between traditional business strategy and e-business strategy by suggesting a short *planning horizon* for e-business projects, an iterative strategic *planning cycle* to incorporate the pace of technological change, an informational power base for access, control and manipulation of critical information instead of a positional power base and the *core focus* to be on customers rather than the factory and production of goods. Deise et al. (2000) emphasise that the focus of e-business strategy will vary according to the evolutional stage of e-business, suggesting that the focus will transform from selling channels (sell-side e-commerce) to value-chain integration (buy-side e-commerce) and creation of value networks. Venkataraman's (2000) 'dot-com strategy' for existing businesses looking to make use of digital media include five questions: What is your strategic vision?; How do you govern dot-com operations?; How do you allocate key resources for the dot-com operations?; What is your operating infrastructure for the dot-com operations?; and Is your management team aligned for the dot-com agenda?

The strategic importance of e-business should be analysed on the basis that it contributes positively to the competitive edge of a company through the benefits it offers. The speed at which change may occur in e-business is indicated by the speed at which new access technologies are adopted (Chaffey, 2002). Although top management may have a strategic plan to introduce e-business and associated changes, the responsibility for the choice of implementation and financial evaluation of e-business innovation is invariably given to technical staff, who sometimes fail to perceive e-business as part of company strategy. Other issues to consider are the financial position of the organisation for the required investment, the ability of a company in terms of resources to accommodate e-business, and if the innovation will conform to the business strategy of the organisation. Human resource strategies of employee attitudes, morale, safety and ergonomics and upgraded skills should be positively related.

Companies compete on cost and customer-focused performance factors such as quality, delivery reliability, design lead times and flexibility. E-business processes allow for increased accuracy, flexibility and uniformity, making a firm's operations more competitive by increasing productivity, decreasing costs and leading to increased market share. It also enables a company to respond quickly to customer demand and evaluate e-business benefits as strategic opportunities.

Justification of E-Business

Other reasons for e-business in a company are reaching out to customers at greater geographic distances, having a shop front 24 hours a day, seven days a week, acquiring a new channel of business and integrated business processes (Singh, 2000). E-business promotes a better company image, requires less floor space, leads to increased accuracy of data and brings with it opportunities for more challenging responsibilities and training (Whinston et al., 1998). However, these benefits are not easy to quantify and are referred to as non-financial benefits (Zhuang & Lederer, 2003). An emphasis on cost benefit analysis to justify e-business projects tends to ignore these as positive outcomes of innovations. Changing traditional business to e-business usually requires large expenditure and involves the whole organisation; thus a well-conceived methodology for its justification is required to ensure that the decision to implement is based on sound business strategies which are developed to serve the long and short term interests of the company. The first step would be to recognise the potential benefits of e-business that will be derived from successful implementation. Tangible benefits may include increased revenue from new customers acquired on-line, acquisition of new business partners for discounted or cheaper raw materials and savings resulting from reduced errors. Intangible benefits are non-quantifiable, such as improved customer satisfaction and improved morale of employees. Intangible benefits should be taken into account as well and for evaluation converted to quantifiable benefits wherever possible. For example, customer satisfaction can be converted to increased sales and less need to employ people to deal with customer complaints. An improved morale of employees could be equated to the reduced costs of sick leave taken by employees. It was noted from earlier research (Singh, 1997) that companies did not pay much attention to non-quantifiable benefits because they relied on a pure and tangible cost/benefit analysis for the justification of innovations.

It is important to take into account the costs of technology, software, networking requirements, fees paid to consultants and experts hired to run the project and training expenses for the existing employees. If benefits exceed costs then e-business becomes an option, but according to traditional methods of cost/benefit analysis rarely do benefits exceed costs in the short term. Many of the benefits are realised in the long term; therefore justification of innovations suggested by Singh (1997) needs an evaluation method that will consider that such investments require a longer period for returns, and strategic advantages such as improved quality, improved flexibility, image and business efficiencies of automated business processes and data management are taken into account. Far reaching impacts of e-business on the overall operation of the organisation should be considered in order to capture its full cost and benefits.

Communication

After accepting and justifying e-business innovation, it should be communicated to the employees because as explained by Saraph and Sabastian (1992), a well-planned communications program is vital in the introduction of new technologies. Devaraj and Kohli (2002) emphasise that most initiatives fail to have the desired effect because of lack of timely, complete and meaningful communication. Early communication will prepare the employees for change, and feedback from them should be noted, as the employees recognise the specific needs of the organisation better than most outside consultants (Rao & Deshmukh, 1994). Communication of the technology idea should not only be a process of telling or informing but a mutual process of exchanging ideas, thoughts, and sharing of anxieties, fears and reservations (Zairi, 1992). Early and honest communication of the innovation and its impact on the company's operations is essential to create a culture that will allow an easier diffusion of e-business within the organisation. An emphasis on the benefits that will affect employees will readily obtain their acceptance, whereas doubts and negative impacts will lead to resistance. Communication will reduce the information gap and erase the anti-technology feeling (De & Huefner, 1995).

Top Management Support

That top management support is required to make things happen is accepted wisdom for almost any change. There would seem to be a number of factors that make it particularly necessary with the introduction of innovations and e-business technologies. Innovations such as e-business are cross-functional. Top management support is needed to ensure that a cross-functional approach is taken to overcome the problems of opposition from any functional group within the organisation. If employees believe that top management fully supports a new project or technology, they will be more likely to cooperate with the implementation (Ettkin et al., 1990). Innovation implementations require adequate resources including money, but more importantly, people and time. Without top management support these often evaporate. Top management support is essential for the project since it is they who allocate the funds which turn the wheels of change in the organisation. At all stages of implementation, management must monitor and alter the process if necessary. Delays may have to be addressed, problems resolved, or further progress modified as the learning process continues during the entire implementation cycle (Noori, 1990; Gold, 1992). The choice of technology must be matched to a company's business requirements and it is top management which can ensure that this happens in their organisation. Erickson et al. (1990) are of the opinion that management of technology must be purposeful rather than hopeful and must always be connected with the firm's overall business strategy to gain and sustain competitive advantage.

Beatty and Gordon (1988) describe the role of top management as that of a 'godfather' who watches over, protects the project from interference, and convinces other executives of its value. They have also suggested that to encourage motivation, top management should be rewarded for taking risks, encouraged to acquire technical literacy, and given the time for planning and the liberty to promote some technically literate people to the executive level. Innovation implementations require comprehensive rethinking and readjustment of job descriptions, information systems, organisational structure incentives and decision making process. To the extent that the status quo represents a barrier to such changes, the role of top management is critical for successful implementation.

Project Leader and Project Team

The project leader's role has been described by Noori (1990) as the engine that keeps the project moving forward until it is completed. Whether the project leader will be chosen from within the company or appointed from outside, the need for a committed project champion is required. The project leader will be a person who will assume responsibility for the success and failure of the project. He or she will spot and track trends in the market environment, develop and exploit a corporate knowledge base, sponsor opportunities for knowledge sharing and organisational learning and build a corporate culture that fosters creative and entrepreneurial input from employees. Creating organisational learning opportunities for employees to learn from one another through tacit methods such as mentoring programs, or through explicit methods such as documentation of and training in best practices is another important role of the technology champion.

A committed and skilled person, usually at the middle management level, is required to lead e-business projects. A project leader who is competent and who can make good decisions about e-business, knows what the company is looking for from the innovation, determines who has expertise and who can be involved in decision making, does not get confused by technical and computer jargon, and gets the right information from the technical people is required to champion the project.

According to Kramer et al. (1992), the champion serves as a leader to whom other managers look for assurance and vision. The champion, by confidently taking ultimate responsibility for the decision, motivates other stake-holders to willingly and enthusiastically accept the changes and risks associated with innovations. Meredith (1986) outlined the role of the technology champion as the creative originator of technology idea, entrepreneur who sells the idea, sponsor and coach of the project and project manager who takes charge of operational planning. The project leader should be a person who clearly understands the company functions both internally and externally, and should have the ability and authority to implement the system and be able to sell the idea, benefits and requirements of technology to superiors, subordinates and peers (Carter, 1991). This person will be someone from the middle management level and will possess technical, interpersonal and project management skills.

In a large firm, representation from each functional area may be desirable, whereas in a smaller firm a few people with cross-functional knowledge may be sufficient. Cross-functional teams permit cross-pollination of ideas and techniques, and allow for mutual education of domain experts. Cross-functional teams will allow project leaders to analyse problems through the eyes of the workers in their sections. It is important to consider how work will be organised during implementation and who will be involved. Planning for e-business must be seen as a critical step, specifying replacement of employees who will be trained and those who will form the project team. New recruits and new responsibilities should be put in place to avoid disruptions, opposition and misunderstandings.

E-Business Infrastructure Requirements

Once the e-business concept is accepted, it is essential to define an adequate e-business infrastructure for the organisation. E-business infrastructure refers to the combination of hardware such as servers and client PCs in an organisation, the network used to link this hardware and software applications to deliver services to customers, business partners and employees (Chaffey, 2002). E-business, although hosted on the Internet, requires and includes CRM technologies, ERP systems, JAVA platforms, intranets and extranets. Technology specifications can be attained from vendors, the Internet, management consultants, and user and professional organisations. Compatibility of hardware, software and integration with existing and incremental technologies requires careful analysis.

The most obvious thing to look at in selecting the e-business infrastructure is whether the technologies will support and enhance business processes. The level of utilisation, flexibility in setups, the capacity of technology, its capability and potential for integration with existing and incremental technologies, as well as the integration of the front end and back end systems for seamless processing of information should be assessed. It is useful to address re-engineering of business processes for e-business requirements at the same time infrastructure decisions are made. The degree of effort required to implement e-business applications should be a good indication of the personnel and training needs of the company for the technology to be viable. The costs of any modifications required to existing technology before e-business is adopted should also be assessed. Feasibility of technology is an important issue to consider in avoiding cost overruns. Technology vendors, Internet service providers, and legal contracts for ongoing support are essential considerations, with proper coordination in case of multi-vendor equipment and software.

E-Business Planning

Creative planning of the project, incorporating decisions to determine the sequence of pre- and post-implementation events, is essential prior to implementation. Failure to create the proper environment for e-business may produce negative results. The role of senior and middle management in managing technological change, creating the right environment and organisational culture, and keeping abreast of the progress of the project team will ascertain their commitment to the project. The plans for implementation, organisational changes and sociotechnical issues in relation to e-business and their association with the strategic objectives established earlier are critical for managing the innovation.

Organisation Structure

With innovations such as e-business the organisational form is fluid, flexible and information-based (Farhoomand & Lovelock, 2001). Complex equipment, highly skilled employees and a dynamic external environment propel the organisation design toward an adaptable structure that facilitates innovation and rapid change, and encourages input from employees who are familiar with the problems but would not normally be contributing to decision making. Existing organisational arrangements need to be examined so that an accurate picture of the synergistic potential of e-business can be realised. For e-business innovation each department within the organisation needs to assess its operations to exploit its strategic potential. If the electronic data processing potential of the innovation is to be fully exploited then it must be integrated into all aspects of the firm's activities.

E-business requires integrated business processes which diminish the separation between functions, breaking down traditional department barriers, resulting in a flatter organisation structure. Adaptable and flatter organisation structures lead to employee empowerment, free flow of information and transparency of data to all employees in the organisation. It will also result in the integration of functional areas and expertise, making it easy for teamwork across disciplines, and multiskilling. Multiskilled workers enable the company to deal with absenteeism, provide a better upkeep of work schedules and require fewer persons to handle several functions simultaneously. Adoption of e-business leads to a networked organisation eliminating 'command and control' structure with fewer layers resulting in rapid information flow both vertically and horizontally (Farhoomand & Lovelock, 2001). Effective management of information, people, business processes and technology necessitates proper planning of the organisation structure and successfully managing the change to the resulting new arrangement and culture.

Sociotechnical Issues

It is essential to consider people factors right from the onset of e-business innovation and not after implementation, as it usually happens. Zairi (1992) suggested that human resource justification needs should be considered alongside technological justification. Proper planning of staffing, new job design, training, reward system, gain sharing, security issues and access to data, and employee management relationship is required before implementing e-business. Important sociotechnical issues to consider include training, staffing and new job designs, technology integration, project team and leader.

a) Training

Education and training act as the catalyst for changes that accompany new technologies and innovations. It also constitutes an essential basis for employee empowerment. Trained employees are significantly better problem solvers and problem presenters (Kumar & Motwani, 1995). Training and development programs for e-business projects should be aimed at developing all those affected by it in the organisation. Senior and top management should be educated about e-business so that they can comprehend the benefits of the application and its requirements providing the resources to effectively implement and manage the innovation. As suggested by Abdul-Gader and Kozar (1995), if the decision makers are alienated from technology they will be reluctant to support the purchase of newer evolving technologies. For IT managers, e-business leaders, software engineers or system analysts, an appreciation of the production process, business attributes (for example, accounting, marketing, inventory management), ergonomics and psychology will be helpful in designing integrated systems. Managers and supervisors also require training to cope with changes and forge allied relationship with their subordinates as a result of e-business. Their roles are sometimes changed to team leaders for which they require appropriate training in motivation, communication and appraisal techniques. Appropriate training will provide employees with the technical, conceptual, analytical and problem-solving skills enabling them to adapt to uncertainties with unanticipated changes. The cost of training can be justified by the long-term expected contribution of skilled employees to the productivity of the company.

b) Health and Safety

Health and safety of employees is another important consideration at the planning stage. The intense computerisation that accompanies business imposes risks of VDU (video display unit) exposure, radiation, risks to vision, stress related problems and physical injury such as RSI (repetitive strain injury). E-business implementation will require planning for proper ergonomics so that risks associated with computer-based technologies are avoided. Addressing ergonomics issues will result in methods of designing machines, operations, workstations and environments so that they match human capabilities and limitations. Information on safety issues can be incorporated in the training programs.

c) Staffing, Reward System and New Job Designs

A series of staffing issues regarding redeployment, retrenchment, higher salaries, improved benefits or recruitment of additional staff is an important consideration before e-business is implemented. New job designs can be reinforced with appropriate rewards. Rewards encourage employees to accept change, take up training and new or additional responsibilities. The reward system will need to be carefully designed because as suggested by Gerwin and Kolodny (1992), they elicit strong feelings with respect to fairness and equity.

Technology Integration

Detailed aspects of technology implementation and its integration with the back end system should be considered to avoid the high costs of islands of technology, duplication of work and for seamless processing of information. Islands of technology with strong and protective organisational setup usually make integration a political as well as technical problem. To tackle this problem effectively, it is important to identify the requirements of technology upgrades and integration possibilities within the organization and with business partners.

Supplier of Technology

Assessing e-business infrastructure requirements will identify potential Internet service providers, suppliers of technology and integrated solutions. Proper coordination of all stakeholders is required in the case of multi-vendor equipment and operations control software. As suggested by Mikulski (1993), the financial stability of the vendor and the quality of management within its organisation should be determined before a technology agreement is established between the company and the vendor. Another issue to consider while assessing suppliers is capability of the vendor to respond to the request in the time frame required by the company. The availability of the right kind of expertise from the supplier to provide modifications to the technology/software if required by the company is also an important consideration. Forming a strategic alliance with the supplier for quality documentation, updates, installation, training and maintenance on a regular basis is essential for continued support.

Installation and Commissioning of E-Business

Proper planning of the issues discussed above will result in e-business being installed within the time and resources allocated. Successful implementation will depend on the quality of decisions made regarding resources, impact of e-business on people, training, and integration of e-business with the existing business. Clear-cut responsibilities and action plan of the project team, management and employees must be established for the implementation. Four implementation strategies are suggested in the next section. The strategy most appropriate to the situation can be selected. These are familiar implementation strategies for computer-based technologies suggested by practitioners and scholars such as Martin et al. (1994), Alter (1992), Laudon and Laudon (1993) and Dayton (1987).

- Direct Cutover, sometimes referred to as cold turkey. This strategy is used when the organisation abandons the old system at the end of the day and starts using the new system the next day. This strategy is risky but avoids the cost of duplicating work by operating two systems concurrently.
- Pilot Conversion means applying the technology to a small area first and expanding its use once it has been found to operate properly. A pilot conversion is the best way to verify the feasibility of e-applications and how they will impact on business. It will also allow for teething problems to be solved without disturbing other business processes.

- Parallel Conversion, when e-business is introduced while traditional business is still operational. A parallel conversion will build the users' confidence, lower everyone's stress level and increase their chance of finding bugs that were missed in pilot conversion. This is a safe strategy because the company can continue to use the old system while the on-line business applications interface into the local environment.
- Phased Conversion means introducing e-business in stages, one component or module at a time. Although this approach can take a long time to automate the whole business, it is the most common approach adopted by many organisations around the world.

Performance Evaluation

Once e-business is implemented it is unwise to assume that it is operating successfully. Any technology is viewed as yielding a payoff if it provides value (Devaraj & Kohli, 2002). An evaluation method that will monitor and control the impact and implications of e-business should be put in place for monitoring of e-business applications. Formal evaluation will identify problems for which solutions can be developed to minimise any negative repercussions. The evaluation method put in place should be one that will document the apparent financial and non-financial costs and benefits associated with the new business system. Without performance evaluation of the innovation it will take a long time to identify any shortcomings and any unfavorable deviations from the plan leading to corrective action. Based on the size of the organisation, the business strategy, and e-business model adopted, a suitable evaluation model will capture the value of e-business for the organisation.

Continuous Improvement

If the performance evaluation of technology indicate that the hoped-for e-business objectives have not been achieved, and for continuous improvements based on evolving new models and technologies, it is important to addressing the issues discussed in the following section to keep realising value from e-business.

Redefine the Strategic Objective

Attempts should be made to communicate the company's mission with an emphasis on the role of e-business in achieving the strategic objectives such as a new channel of business, market expansion, customer satisfaction, reduced inventory, automated processes, acquisition of new business partners and customers, and other business efficiencies. Redefining the strategic objectives will identify the role of e-business and increase its acceptance rate.

Evaluate the Compatibility of Technologies

Characteristics of technology such as complexity and suitability for the task for which it was adopted should be reviewed and appropriate measures for any changes put in place. If any technology is incompatible with any of the existing technologies, an upgrade should be recommended for integration. Impact of newly developed technology platforms and their applications to the web should be reviewed for achieving business competitiveness. Re-engineering requirements of business processes to satisfy e-business and its technology platform should be revisited for achieving improved business efficiencies.

Revise Organisational Structure and Culture

An appropriate organisational structure and culture for e-business is essential for successful implementation and seamless operations. Organisational culture includes shared values, unwritten rules and assumptions within the organisation as well as the practices that all groups share (Chaffey, 2002). E-business led change has the capacity to alter corporate culture and relationships within different functional areas, which requires proper management.

The most appropriate organisation structure and culture for e-business will be one that promotes innovation and originality. Therefore, as suggested earlier, if the employees believe that e-business is important in achieving the goals of the company they will all work towards its strategic effectiveness. If e-business is implemented in a structure that is too rigid and mechanistic, the strategic potential available through empowering employees and integrated and automated business processes will be compromised.

Human Resource Strategy

The impact of e-business on the employees should be assessed to establish whether they have realised beneficial effects of this innovation. If they are not motivated enough, incentives and rewards should be increased to retain skilled staff, overcome resistance and reduce staff turnover. If employees have not become proficient users of new technologies, more education and training is recommended. Educational programs may need to be redesigned, more ongoing training put in place and method of delivery altered. Training to multi-skill employees should be reinforced to increase productivity, teamwork, morale and efficiency among workers and a larger sense of participation.

Risk Management

As suggested by Chaffey (2002), risk management is intended to identify potential risks in a range of situations, and then take actions to minimise the risks. With e-business technologies, communication-related risks can pose a significant threat to a trading partnership, customers and existing relationships. Electronic communication and transmission of documents, data and payments are essential in e-business and require security systems and protocols to address problems of authentication, integrity, non-repudiation, privacy and confidentiality.

Knowledge Management

Knowledge management in e-business has an important role due to its dependence on staff knowledge on all aspects of the business environment, which includes all internal and external functions, stakeholders and business processes. Chaffey (2002) supports this thought by emphasising knowledge transfer and knowledge management to be key competitive issues, with evolving business needs, technological developments and globalisation being fundamental characteristics of e-business. Knowledge management turns tacit knowledge to explicit knowledge which is shared between employees and used to train new employees. Explicit knowledge may include details of processes and procedures which can be detailed in manuals and databases. Tacit knowledge is less tangible and may include experience on how to react to a situation when many different variables are involved. Knowing how to respond to information in management reports depends on tacit knowledge (Chaffey, 2002). For e-business, although it is important to retain skilled and knowledge-able employees, it is more important for organisations to manage knowledge with technologies such as Intranets, electronic document management systems, expert systems and by encouraging communication, both formal and informal. Tools that support communication are usually part of e-business technologies, such as Intranets, chat, on-line discussions, video conferencing, emails, bulletin boards, which can be easily applied to knowledge management.

CONCLUSION

E-business is an innovation that modern day organisations cannot do without. It is based on technology, evolves with technological developments, digitises and automates business processes, is global and leads to improved competitiveness, efficiencies, increased market share, and business expansion. E-businesses models include business-to-business, business-to-consumer, government-to-government, government-to-business, government-to-consumer and numerous other models. Technological developments applied to e-business results in new issues in the organisation, in dealing with business partners and customers, and in dealing with new laws and regulations as well as automated processes. Conducting business electronically is a change from traditional ways of doing things, resulting in large-scale transformation to existing business. To attain business efficiencies from e-business, it is imperative that organisations effectively manage the e-business environment, and all associated changes. E-business applications have resulted in new ways of dealing with customers and business partners, automated business process application of new regulations and technologies, round-the-clock business hours, reduced number of employees, continuous monitoring of technology and information, electronic payment and data processing, an elevated need for security and privacy of information, and totally new ways of doing things. The change from traditional business to electronic business is not one of degree but of a kind that requires powerful and effective management. The issues discussed above are important for all organisations for successful management of change.

REFERENCES

Abdul-Gader, A., & Kozar, K. (1995). The impact of computer alienation on Information Technology investment decisions: An exploratory cross-national Analysis. *MIS Quarterly*, December, 535–559.

Alter, S. (1992). *Information systems: A management perspective*. USA: Addison Wesley Publishing Company.

Beatty, C., & Gordon, R. M. (1988). Barriers to the implementation of CAD/CAM systems. *Sloan Management Review*, Summer, 25–33.

Carter, J. (1991). Implementing supplier bar codes. *Production and Inventory Management Journal*, Fourth Quarter, 42–47.

Chaffey, D. (2002). *E-business and e-commerce management*. Great Britain: Prentice Hall.

Dayton, D. (1987). *Computer solutions for business*. Washington: Microsoft Press.

De, P. K., & Huefner, B. (1995). Technological competitiveness of Germany: A post-Second World War review. *Technology Management*, 2 (6), 265–274.

Devaraj, S., & Kohli, R. (2002). *The IT payoff*. New Jersey: Prentice Hall.

Diese, M., Nowickov, C., King, P., & Wright, A. (2000). *Executives' guide to e-business: From tactics to strategy*. New York: John Wiley and Sons.

Erickson, T. J., Magee, J. F., Rousel, P. A., & Saad, K. (1990). Managing technology as a business strategy. *Sloan Management Review*, Spring, 73–77.

Ettkin, L. P., Helms, M. M., & Heynes, P. J. (1990). People: A critical element of new technology implementation. *Information Management*, September/October, 27–29.

Farhoomand, A., & Lovelock, P. (2001). *Global e-commerce: Text and cases*. Singapore: Prentice Hall.

Gerwin, D., & Kolodny, H. (1992). *Management of advanced manufacturing technology - Strategy, organisation and innovation*. USA: John Wiley & Sons.

Gold, B. (1992). Senior managements' critical role in strengthening technological competitiveness. *International Journal of Technology Management*, Special Issue on Strengthening Corporate and National Competitiveness Through Technology, Vol 7, Nos 1,2,3, pp. 5–15.

Hackbarth, G., & Kettinger, W. (2000). Building and e-business strategy. *Information systems Management*, Summer, 78–93.

Hershfield, D. (1992). Proceed one step at a time to implement automation effectively. *Industrial Engineering*, June, 22–26.

Institute of Directors. (2000). E-business – Helping directors to understand and embrace the Digital Age. London: Director Publications.

Kramer, T. J., Chibnall, J. T., & Pederson, B. D. (1992). Managing Computer Integrated Manufacturing (CIM): Review of themes, issues, and practices. *Journal of Business and Psychology*, 6 (4) Summer, 415–442.

Kumar, A., & Motwani, J. (1995). A methodology for assessing time-based competitive advantage of manufacturing firms. *International Journal of Operations & Production Management*, 15 (2), 36–53.

Laudon, K. C., & Laudon, J. P. (1993) *Business Information Systems: A problem-solving approach*. USA: The Dryden Press.

Martin, E. W., Daniel, W., Jeffrey, H. A., & Williams, P. (1994). *Managing Information Technology*, (2nd Ed.). New York: Macmillan.

Meredith, J. R. (1986). Strategic planning for factory automation by the championing process. *IEEE Transactions on Engineering Management, 33* (4), 229–232.

Mikulski, F. (1993). *Managing your vendors*. New Jersey: Prentice Hall Inc.

Noori, H. (1990). *Managing the dynamics of new technology - Issues in manufacturing management*. New Jersey: Prentice Hall.

Patel, K. & McCarthy, M. P. (2000). The Essentials of eBusiness Leadership DIGITAL Transformation, McGraw Hill, USA

Rao, K. V. S., & Deshmukh, S. G. (1994). Strategic framework for implementing flexible manufacturing systems in India. *International Journal of Production Management, 14* (4), 50–63.

Saraph, J., & Sebastian, R. (1992). Human resource strategies for effective introduction of advanced manufacturing technologies. *Production and Inventory Management Journal*, First Quarter, 64–70.

Singh, M. (1997). *Effective implementation of new technologies in the Australian manufacturing industries*. PhD Thesis, Monash University, Melbourne, Australia.

Singh, M. (1998). An implementation model for new technologies. *Proceedings of the World Innovation & Strategy Conference, Sydney, Australia, August 2-5,* 649–654.

Singh, M. (2000). Electronic commerce in Australia: Opportunities and factors critical for success. *Proceedings of the 1st World Congress on the Management of Electronic Commerce (CD-ROM), Hamilton, Ontario, Canada, January 19–21.*

Venkataraman, N. (2000). Five steps to a dot-com strategy: How to find your footing on the web. *Sloan Management Review, Spring,* 15–28.

Whinston, A., Stahl, D., & Choi, S. (1998). *The economics of electronic commerce*. Indianapolis, Indiana: Macmillan Technical Publishing.

Zairi, M. (1992). Management of advanced manufacturing technology. Wimslow, UK: Sigma Press.

Zhuang, Y., & Lederer, A. (2003). An instrument for measuring the business benefits of e-commerce retailing. *International Journal of Electronic Commerce, 7 (3),* Spring.

Chapter II

Leadership in
E-Business

Owen Cope
Accenture, Australia

Dianne Waddell
Edith Cowan University, Australia

ABSTRACT

Inevitably, the adoption of any new technology brings about change, but e-business is significantly different in that it completely shifts global business into a fast-paced electronic environment. The old notions of management are totally ineffective and a new style, focused on 'leadership', is required—but what style of leadership? To determine the most appropriate leadership style, senior managers from the top 250 e-commerce companies in Australia were selected and surveyed. Using a change management matrix, each manager was positioned within this framework. This model consists of a four-by-four matrix encompassing the scales of change and the styles of change management. The model covers the broad spectrum of levels of change that an organisation can go through. The authors found that within the most successful organisations, leaders had a distinctive style that facilitated the appropriate change and established a conducive e-business environment. The data highlights that qualities such as visionary, consultative, ability to listen to others opinions, inclusive, risk taking, approachable, forward thinking, open to change, committed, determined, and the ability to communicate are required in leaders to lead an e-business transition.

INTRODUCTION

The management of change has always been a challenge. Historically, change occurred and people adapted. Often this was a relatively slow adaptation, as the pace of change was slow. Then there were times when general stability was punctuated by periods of chaotic change, most often when advances in IT were the catalyst. As such, those periods of change were managed as isolated events. Increasingly, the time between each change is reduced, requiring the change to be planned and managed—now the time between changes has gone! The result is that chaotic change is a constant factor in today's organisations. Even more so, the speed of change facilitated by e-business necessitates a unique style of leadership. It is obvious that organisations that are in constant transition need to be led—not managed.

Inevitably the adoption of any new technology brings about change, but e-business is significantly different in that it completely shifts global business into a fast paced electronic environment. The old notions of management are totally ineffective and a new style, focused on 'leadership', is required—but what style of leadership? The findings of this research indicate that organisations that have successfully integrated e-business have exhibited a particular style of leadership.

To determine the most appropriate leadership style, senior managers from 250 e-commerce manufacturing companies in Australia were selected and surveyed. Using a change management matrix, each manager was positioned within this framework. This model consists of a four by four matrix encompassing the scales of change and the styles of change management. The model covers the broad spectrum of levels of change that an organisation can go through. It was found that within the most successful organisations, leaders had a distinctive style that facilitated the appropriate change and established a conducive e-business environment. The particular characteristics are detailed later in the chapter.

Although a wealth of information can be obtained on e-business, most of the literature points towards e-business and the Internet being integral parts of business well into the future (Marchetti, 2000; Parry, 2000). Whilst there has been much written on the subject there has been little substantive research into how to deal with the new environment. This research presents a framework whereby organisations can identify 'under-performing' incumbent managers and then develop personal and professional training programs to assist with modifying their skills to facilitate the successful implementation of e-business in their organisation.

E-BUSINESS AND CHANGE MANAGEMENT

Radical changes have been taking place in the commercial industry with the advent of the Internet and e-business, which have swiftly changed traditional business practices, and are creating numerous avenues for the development of business-to-business and business-to-consumer initiatives. Fuelled initially by rapid business-to-consumer growth, e-business is now being seen as a tremendous engine for business-to-business (B2B) growth (Stewart, 2000). B2B commerce is growing rapidly. In the US market alone, Forrester Research expects B2B revenues to reach $1.3 trillion by 2003 (from a figure of $43 billion in 1998) (Marchetti, 2000; Smith, 2000). In a few years from now, companies will expect e-business to bring in an average of 41% of their total revenue, and they will be dedicating an average of $83 million per year to their e-business efforts (Caruso, 2000).

In traditional organisations, managers had time to craft and implement their business strategies knowing what actions competitors might take. In the next millennium, intellectual or knowledge resources will redefine managers' roles and erode traditional boundaries that separate people and organisations. The principal role of the management of the future will be to link competencies and resources that the organisation possesses to create a sustainable competitive advantage (Oetgen, 1999; Parry, 2000). The Internet and e-business have created a global market for ideas and exchange of information.

In relation to corporate views, company goals have had to change over the past few years to align with e-business initiatives. In the past, company goals have always focused on profitability and the bottom line. This decade the focus has shifted to competitiveness, staff and customer satisfaction with a view to long-term success (Schein, 1992). Traditional methods of evaluating corporate success are changing. Striving for profit at the outset is often seen as detrimental to survival (Smith, 2000). IT and business executives from all industries surveyed in the Information and Business Week survey agree that generating new sources of revenue is not the main goal of deploying e-business applications (Caruso, 2000). In fact, this factor ranked well behind creating or maintaining a competitive edge, improving customer satisfaction, and keeping pace with the competition (Dalton, 1999).

Another change that is developing is that of management versus the importance of leadership. In the past the manager's role was to organise, delegate and generally get the job done. Now those put in managerial positions are there because of the leadership qualities they display (Burnes, 1996; Handy, 1994). The previous role of managers is now a given. The extra skill sought after is leadership. Executives in these organisations are desperately searching for leaders who can develop cultures and teams that can capitalise on this new channel (Gray, 1995). According to the study these leaders possess three key traits: quick thinking, communication (selling the vision of the Internet internally), and flexibility (coping with constant change) (Marchetti, 2000).

The Dunphy and Stace (1990) model provides the most comprehensive method of evaluating all the various different levels and degrees of change and leadership styles. There is increasing pressure for some certainty to be brought back into such a volatile environment (Marchetti, 2000). As such, the simplistic nature of the Dunphy and Stace model would appear to aid in this process. The fact that e-business will dramatically change the way business operates is undeniable and one thing is clear: large-scale change requires large-scale leadership. But what's the right leadership model for thriving in today's technocentric world? And tomorrow's?

INNOVATIVE LEADERSHIP FOR E-BUSINESS

The e-business revolution is changing the face of today's and tomorrow's organisations. One of the most critical challenges emerging in the e-business domain is the issue of leadership. The transformation to an information economy necessitates new ways of working, and hence, new ways of leading. Innovative leadership strategies are required in the B2C domain most importantly if organisations are to succeed in an increasingly dynamic and volatile e-business environment (Keen, 1999).

Such visionary leadership is often identified as a salient characteristic of successful e-business (Roots, 2000). But what does visionary leadership mean in the e-business domain? Keen (1999) suggests that innovation in IT requires a middle-driven leadership approach, rather than a top-down approach that was common in the past. It is at the middle level of management where the real strategists and visionaries are found, since business is a process game and it is the people in the middle who understand the process (Keen, 1999: 1). Reliance on a middle-driven leadership approach will mean tangible changes in the workplace: there will be more non-technical leaders and colleagues who have greater knowledge of business processes where collaboration is the currency of innovation and diversity its enabler (Keen, 1999). A new style of middle-driven leadership will establish a sustainable competitive advantage for organisations (Keen, 1999).

A cross-industry study of managers at more than 55 well-known US companies at varying stages of leveraging the Internet by recruiting firm Spencer Stuart indicates that executives in these organisations are searching for leaders who can develop cultures and teams that can capitalize on new channels, are comfortable with ambiguity and possess an entrepreneurial spirit (Marchetti, 2000). According to this study, such leaders possess three key traits: quick thinking, communication and flexibility (Marchetti, 2000). Two of the top five critical functions of these leaders include marketing and business development (Marchetti, 2000).

The issue of innovative leadership is also addressed in studies that have examined the attributes of successful B2C e-business organisations. Willcocks and Plant (2001: 9), for example, examined 58 major B2C corporations from three continents in a wide range of industries. They found that B2C leaders share five key attributes. Firstly, leaders regard the Internet as the cornerstone of a network-centric business era. Secondly, leaders distinguish the contributions of information from those of technology, since they realize that enduring advantage comes not only from technology itself, but also from how information is collected, stored, analysed and applied. It is not enough for organisations to use technology strategically; organisations must also deploy technology in an appropriate organisational and managerial context. It is when technology is treated as an asset and afforded a key role in the transformation process that there is greater likelihood of technology leadership, business success and the establishment of a competitive advantage (Willcocks & Plant, 2001).

Thirdly, leaders recognize that competition, opportunities and customer expectations evolve rapidly. Related to this, leaders also learn quickly and have the capacity to shift focus, since leaders concentrate on building an integrated technology, information and marketing platform. For example, the practice of differentiation is a key to e-business success. The challenge for organisations in the domain of differentiation is to continually differentiate the product or service over time, to make it less price sensitive, yet in ways that remain attractive to the targeted market segment (Willcocks & Plant, 2001). Finally, leaders follow a top-down or outside-in route to business innovation, focusing on business plans and goals and the subsequent integration of technology into these business initiatives.

In a more specific study of leaders in B2C commerce in the retail area, Blumberg and Parker (2000) found retail leaders have four attributes: they know the strategic purpose behind their web sites; they build an organisational structure to suit that purpose; they install benchmark processes and practices to meet customer preferences; and they employ the technology necessary to execute their plan and decisions.

The issue of leadership in e-commerce has also arisen in the context of business strategy: which strategies are required to be formulated and implemented by leaders in order to succeed. Marchetti (2000) suggests that organisations must embrace sophisticated strategies: using the web, partnering with customers and building new brands as a means to get ahead.

Venkatraman (2000) suggests five different strategies serve as stepping stones to a successful web strategy: vision, governance, resources, infrastructure and alignment.

- It is necessary to approach the issue of strategic vision in e-business as a continuous cycle that involves both building on current business models and creating future business models through selective experimentation (Venkatraman, 2000). The aim is one of balance: refining current business rules while creating new business rules for the e-business domain (Venkatraman, 2000). Venkatraman (2000, p.5) suggests that the strategic challenge is to spearhead experiments to assess future states and migrate operations to the desired state. Establishing the vision and rationale for these experiments, including the mandate to proactively cannibalize the current business models, is a critical hallmark of leadership.
- The challenge of managing an e-commerce organisation is daunting since they differ markedly from traditional business operations. Essentially, the issue of governance entails two fundamental decisions: operational decisions and financial decisions. The governance of e-commerce organisations is best seen as trade-off between these two decisions: how organisations

differentiate and integrate operational and financial issues (Venkatraman, 2000, p.6).

- Interlinked with the issue of governance is the issue of resources: how do organisations best assemble and deploy resources in order to succeed in the e-commerce domain? Four different but interrelated approaches are required in order to assemble and deploy the required resources: placing strategic bets; learning how to leverage your alliances; outsourcing of operations and maintaining operational parity. Effective strategies for organisations in the e-commerce domain are based on the pattern and timing of resource deployment, since such decisions are different from traditional business models. Resources must be assembled from multiple sources and managed on a dynamic basis (Venkatraman, 2000, p.10).

- The establishment of operating infrastructure is the fourth critical strategy for organisations establishing a web strategy. The four characteristics of operational infrastructure that are the building blocks of an integrated physical-digital platform include: attaining superior functionality; offering personalized interactions; streamlining transactions and ensuring privacy.

- Venkatraman's (2000) main consideration of innovative leadership is reflected in the fifth strategy: the alignment of a management team. Articulating the roles of key members in the management team is critical in shaping the strategy of e-commerce organisations. Such organisations require a pattern of leadership that differs greatly from other transformational business activities. Value creation is at the heart of e-commerce. Hence, leadership in such organisations involves strategic challenges of business creation; issues of the governance of organisational structures; new avenues of financing; changes in operational infrastructure, external relationships and patterns of resource deployment (Venkatraman, 2000, p.13).

These models of leadership in an e-business environment give a diverse overview of what is required of an individual to be a leader in an e-business environment. But the question then arises as to which is more accurate.

LEADERSHIP STYLE IN E-BUSINESS

As technology develops, e-business will become more prevalent, forcing organisations to change more rapidly than ever before. Therefore it is of interest to explore how this change is led and managed. There is little empirical evidence about managing or leading change in this new context and what there is, is of limited use because they measure using the past frameworks or notions of leadership. Because of this, Cope and Waddell (2001) adapted an Australian developed change management model and applied it to an e-business environment, specifically looking at the manufacturing sector.

The objective of this study was to bring together leadership and change management in an e-business environment, then to explore if a relationship between the scale of change and the style of change management leadership exists in the new environment. This was achieved by looking at four specific relationships that covered the continuum of the scale of change and the style of leadership.

The secondary objective was to identify personal views of leadership and change management in an e-business environment. This was achieved by inviting personal comments in the survey of IT/e-business managers in the manufacturing industry.

RESEARCH FRAMEWORK

Australian researchers Dunphy and Stace (1990, 1994) argue that change management should be approached from a situational perspective. They have effectively combined leadership and change management into one model. This model covers the broad spectrum of levels of change that an organisation can go through and would include consideration of an e-business environment. The model consists of a four by four matrix encompassing the scales of change (Fine Tuning; Incremental Adjustment; Modular Transformation and Corporate Transformation) and the styles of leadership (Collaborative; Consultative; Directive and Coercive) (Figure 1). By the determination of the position of a particular organisation in that matrix, appropriate change strategies could be identified (Participative Evolution; Forced Evolution; Charismatic Transformation or Dictatorial Transformation).

Therefore in order to address the question, a total of sixteen separate hypotheses would need to be tested (refer to Figure 2). However, due to various constraints imposed on this study, it was necessary to restrict the investigation to one general hypothesis and four specific hypotheses. This decision was based on the recommendation that "the total number of hypotheses should not exceed four or five; if there are more, sufficient analysis may not be done on each within the space constraints of a thesis" (Perry, 1993, p.76).

Figure 1: Dunphy and Stace Matrix

	Fine Tuning	*Incremental Adjustment*	*Modular Transformation*	*Corporate Transformation*
Collaborative	Participative Evolution		Charismatic Transformation	
Consultative				
Directive	Forced Evolution		Dictatorial Transformation	
Coercive				

Figure 2: Testable relationships between the research constructs

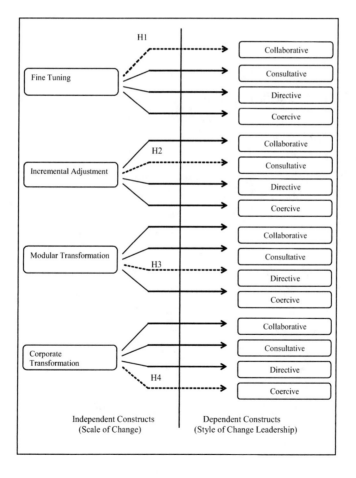

METHODOLOGY

One hundred and eighty-two participants were gathered from organisations within the Manufacturing Industry. Specific organisations were chosen from the *Business Review Weekly* magazine's Top 1000 list, as these were deemed as being the most successful organisations within the industry in Australia. E-business Managers, IT Managers or persons responsible for the IT department were targeted as being the appropriate staff to respond to the questionnaire. Descriptive statistics were applied to ascertain general trends in the data. Usage Proxy Variables were also created to establish more detailed results and to identify the most strongly answered question.

RESULTS AND GENERAL DESCRIPTIVE STATISTICS

The findings discussed in this section are from a 30% response rate.

Personal Profiles

It would appear that the positions of IT Manager, E-business Manager and those responsible for e-business are predominantly held by males (88.9%). However, given many companies are from the manufacturing industry this is not unexpected. Other details include:

- The age range of respondents was 20 – 58. The average age of respondents was 43 ($X = 42.98$, $SD = 8.28$). The majority of respondents (64.4%) were aged 45 or less.
- The majority of respondents (62.2%) were in positions of middle management. Interestingly, only 1 respondent regarded their position as lower management. As the questionnaire was targeted at IT or similar level managers it is therefore not surprising that 97.8% of respondents were from middle or senior level management positions.
- The average number of years the respondents had been with their respective organisation was 8 years ($X = 8.09$, $SD = 6.22$). The majority of respondents (73.3%) had been with the organisation 10 years or less. Overall, results indicate a large spread in the number of years the respondents had been with their respective organisation (minimum of 1 year to a maximum of 27).

- The majority (55.6%) of respondents had undergraduate degree or TAFE as their highest qualification. This was higher than expected, as only 20% of managers in Australia have tertiary education (Karpin Report, 1995). Only 5 respondents had Year 12 or lower as their highest level of education achieved. Surprisingly, more respondents (15) had post-graduate qualifications. Given the industry and the job position this result is unusually high.

Synopsis of Each Question

The following results provide a breakdown of responses given for each question in the questionnaire.

There were 8 constructs in total; 4 dependent constructs and 4 independent constructs. Each construct consisted of three questions that were randomly spread throughout the questionnaire. The four dependent constructs included the style leadership styles of Collaborative (Questions 1, 12 and 21), Consultative (Questions 2, 13 and 15), Directive (Questions 4, 16 and 22), and Coercive (Questions 3, 5 and 14). The four independent constructs were the scales of change including Fine Tuning (Questions 7, 8 and 20), Incremental Adjustment (Questions 6, 17 and 23), Modular Transformation (Questions 10, 19 and 24), and Corporate Transformation (Questions 9, 11 and 18).

Results in Table 1 indicate that the majority of the 45 organisations were not utilising a collaborative style of management as illustrated by the average response being 2.82. Similar results were found for both directive and coercive management styles, i.e., 2.96 and 2.99, respectively. It would therefore appear that the majority of organisations were utilising the consultative management style for leading change in e-business, with an overall average score of 3.56.

The results in Table 2 indicate that the majority of respondents agreed that their organisations were involved in fine-tuning stages of change, illustrated by the average score being 3.53. The majority of respondents felt their organisations have not reached the other scales of change in a large way as yet. This result is illustrated by the average scores for the remaining scales of change of incremental adjustment, modular transformation and corporate transformation as being 3.07, 2.59 and 2.40, respectively.

Looking at the raw scores, Table 3 confirms that fine-tuning is the most predominant level of change, as indicated by a score of 476. Likewise, the consultative style of change leadership predominates, indicated by a score of 481. In addition, when only the predominant score is used the degree to which these are the leading scale of change and style of leadership is clearly emphasised, i.e, scores of 385 and 367, respectively.

Table 1: Mean and overall scores for dependent variable constructs

Construct	Variable	Mean Score	Overall Score
Collaborative	Employees are involved in widespread participation to consult on important decisions about the organisation's future (Q1)	2.82	
	The power that employees have in establishing the goals and means of change in the organisation is significant (Q21)	2.80	
	The final decision on organisational change is determined in collaboration with other employees, not just those in management (Q12)	2.84	2.82
Consultative	Management makes the final decision about changes and goals for the company, only after gaining some feedback from employees (Q15)	3.42	
	Employees with relevant expertise or responsibility are called upon to assist with the decision making process and implementation of any change required (Q2)	3.82	
	The employee's opinion on what the change should involve is relatively important to the management team (Q13)	3.44	3.56
Directive	The management team is well respected and trusted to make appropriate decisions regarding change (Q22)	3.42	
	Issues of organisational change are determined by management and are generally well accepted (Q4)	2.93	
	Change is well received among employees even though they are not consulted about the change (Q16)	2.53	2.96
Coercive	Decisions on change strategies are made based solely on the key stakeholders' interests (Q5)	2.78	
	Employees are made to accept the changes regardless of their opinions on the issue (Q14)	3.20	
	It is best for management to decide on change strategies as they are the most skilled to secure the survival and effectiveness of the organisation (Q3)	2.98	2.99

Table 2: Mean and overall scores for independent variable constructs

Construct	Variable	Mean Score	Overall Score
Fine-Tuning	In this organisation change is usually an ongoing process with constant 'fine-tuning' occurring in various departments to prepare for e-commerce strategies (Q7)	3.89	
	Personnel are being developed and trained to suit the organisation's development into an e-commerce business (Q20)	3.00	
	Specialist units or groups are being formed within the organisation to focus on e-commerce strategies (Q8)	3.69	3.53
Incremental Adjustment	There have been some distinct modifications (not radical change) occurring in preparation for e-commerce initiatives (Q6)	3.27	
	The emphasis has shifted (or is shifting) from traditional business to a new technologically defined way of doing business (Q23)	3.11	
	Minor restructuring has occurred across divisions to allow for a more efficient internal business accommodating e-commerce (Q17)	2.84	3.07
Modular Transformation	One or more departments have been re-aligned to accommodate e-commerce strategies (Q24)	2.78	
	Significant managerial changes have occurred as more emphasis is being placed on those employees best positioned to manage e-commerce initiatives for the department (Q10)	2.49	
	Staffing members in particular departments have either increased and/or decreased due to e-commerce changes and demands (Q19)	2.49	2.59
Corporate Transformation	The whole organisation has undergone a radical shift in business strategy to include e-commerce in its operation (Q11)	2.22	
	Many processes and procedures have changed to accommodate the changing focus on e-commerce (Q18)	2.69	
	People outside the organisation have been employed and appointed key managerial positions due to their knowledge and experience in e-commerce (Q9)	2.29	2.40

Table 3: Overall construct synopsis

	Construct	Raw Score	Predominant Construct Score
Independent Variables	Fine Tuning	476	385
	Incremental Adjustment	415	154
	Modular Transformation	349	33
	Corporate Transformation	324	35
Dependent Variables	Collaborative	381	73
	Consultative	481	367
	Directive	400	87
	Coercive	403	135

LEADERSHIP AND
SCALE OF CHANGE MATRIX

The results from the questionnaire were applied to the Dunphy and Stace matrix. This gives a visual 'picture' of the relationships observed in the data. It also acts as a comparison to the expected results from the model.

The above matrix highlights the relationships between the independent and dependent constructs. It is clear to see that whilst there was some relationship between fine-tuning and collaborative as hypothesised, there is a very strong relationship between fine-tuning and consultative. The hypothesised relationship between incremental adjustment and consultative was partially confirmed. However, the hypothesised relationships between modular transformation and directive, and corporate transformation and coercive were not confirmed. Modular transformation did not appear to relate with any style of change leadership, whereas corporate transformation appeared to relate with coercive. It is also interesting to note that the results appear in the left side of the matrix; popular media hype would have predicted the results to appear in the lower right hand section of the matrix.

Figure 3: Leadership in e-business and scale of change matrix

	Fine Tuning	*Incremental Adjustment*	*Modular Transformation*	*Corporate Transformation*	
Collaborative	5	1			6
Consultative	27	10	1	2	40
Directive	5	4		1	10
Coercive	9	4	2	1	16
	46	19	3	4	*Total* 72

GENERAL DISCUSSION

Scale of Change with E-Business

It was expected that the majority of organisations would have exhibited modular transformation or corporate transformation scales of change based on research by Verkatraman (2000). However, the majority of organisations indicated that they were in the fine-tuning level of change with the next highest being incremental adjustment. Very few organisations exhibit modular transformation or corporate transformation scales of change.

The expected results would have been to find the scale of change in the modular transformation or corporate transformation area. This is because Dunphy and Stace (1990, 1994) predict that where there is a rapidly moving environment and the systems have become out of date, large-scale is required. However, this is not the case. The fact that the research found fine-tuning, and to a smaller extent, incremental adjustment, to be predominant indicates that the level of change in the manufacturing industry towards e-business is smaller than anticipated. This, however, could be explained when looking at the OD theorists who suggest small incremental changes are preferred to large-scale changes (Burnes, 1996).

This small level of change is confirmed by the responses given to the open-ended questions in the questionnaire. Very few organisations indicate that they are currently going through a large level of change. Furthermore, few organisations indicate that large-scale change has previously occurred and as such are now just tidying up the edges, whereas the majority of the responses indicate small changes or "a gradual shift" in preparation for e-business. The fact that organisations are predominantly experiencing fine-tuning may indicate that the industry is not as dynamic and unstable as predicted by the literature on e-business (Marhcetti, 2000). This is also supported, as one of the respondents noted the industry to be "slow moving". It may also indicate that the industry in general has not moved into an e-business environment, therefore not requiring the large-scale change to restructure for e-business. Perhaps e-business is only just starting to have an impact on the industry; therefore there is no need or demand to become e-business proficient. Only a few respondents indicated the reasons for change to be e-business related.

It is apparent that in the manufacturing industry in Australia, there are currently small incremental changes being made in relation to e-business. This could be because that is all that is required and that e-business does not require the big changes as indicated by literature (Parry, 2000) or that the industry has not moved into an e-business environment and as such a large scale change is still to come.

Style of Change Leadership in E-Business

By far the majority was consultative with very little collaborative and directive but surprisingly more coercive. Research by Dunphy and Stace (1990, 1994) indicates the more predominant style of management is coercive or top-down, which is more aligned to the hard approach to change management. Dunphy and Stace's observations regarding a coercive style of change leadership were made early last decade. The economy was in recession and many organisations were undergoing large-scale restructuring in order to survive (Ashkensas, Hsaffer & Associates, 1994). Therefore a coercive leadership style would have appeared to be necessary, whereas currently, organisations appear to be looking for ways to stay competitive. One possible way has been to focus on the human resources (Ashkenas et al., 1994). As job security has slightly increased and technology has advanced, more options are available to employees. The employees appear to be in a position to somewhat demand certain conditions from their employer such as flexible work hours and ability to work from home rather than having to work from a central location. The uncertainty appears to have changed from focusing on job security to having staff spread over numerous locations. In this uncertainty people need someone to follow or look to for direction and there is an increased emphasis on communication, as it is becoming more commonplace for staff to be spread over numerous locations (Dalton, 1999). Due to this apparent change, one may assume that the leadership style would also have to adapt to these changing conditions from a coercive, 'Do as I say' type attitude to a more open style of consultative change leadership. This appears to be the trend across the majority of industries (Oetgen, 1999); however, whether or not this is apparent in the manufacturing industry can not be clearly determined as it would appear that they are not fully engaged in e-business at present.

Therefore it is interesting to observe results that indicate that employees are being consulted on the change. There are two possible explanations, the first being the fact that most organisations are only going through a small level of change; therefore it gives the leadership time to consult on the small changes and to accommodate the employees. Secondly, it could be as a result of a shift in organisations to include their staff more in the change process. As more and more people are concerned about what the future holds and how technology is going to impact their jobs, they want to be involved to give them some kind of security (McClenahen, 1999).

CONCLUSION

The qualitative information highlights that qualities such as visionary, consultative, ability to listen to others' opinions, inclusive, risk taking, approachable, forward thinking, open to change, committed, determined, and the ability to communicate are required in leaders to lead an e-business transition. It is also clear from the qualitative data that obtaining employee opinions is important. Comments such as "a supportive and delegating leadership style that emphasises communication" and, "a persistent and patient business person focused on the individual with good people skills" highlight this trend.

This style of change leadership is important, as this is what effects the successful integration of e-business. A consultative style of change leadership is the most utilised in the manufacturing industry. As identified, two possible reasons for this are the scale of change that allows the leadership the time to involve employees in the change process. The other reason that is not exclusive to the aforementioned reason is the shift in organisations to focus more on the human element given the changing nature of the work environment and in particular, e-business.

REFERENCES

Ashkenas, R. N., Hsaffer, R. H., & Associates. (1994). Beyond the fads: how leaders drive change with results. *Human Resource Planning, 17* (2), 25–44.

Blumberg, W., & Parker, L. (2000). How the retail leaders are making B2C work. *Stores,* www.stores.org

Burnes, B. (1996). *Managing change.* London: Pitman.

Caruso, J. (2000). Revving the e-commerce engine. *Network World 17*(5), 1,80.

Coakes, S. J., & Steed, L. G. (1999). *SPSS: Analysis without anguish, Versions 7.0, 7.5, 8.0 for Windows.* Brisbane: John Wiley & Sons.

Cope, O., & Waddell, D. (2001). An audit of leadership styles in e-commerce. *Managerial Auditing Journal.* UK: MCB University Press.

Dalton, G. (1999). E-business evolution. *Informationweek Manhasset, 737,* 50–66.

Dunphy, D. & Stace, D. (1990). *Under new management.* Sydney: McGraw Hill.

Dunphy, D., & Stace, D. (1994). *Beyond the boundaries.* Sydney: McGraw Hill.

Gray, S. (1995). Fostering leadership for the new millennium. *Association Management 47* (1), 78–82.

Handy, C. (1994). *The age of paradox.* Massachusetts: Harvard Business School.

Keen, P. (1999). Middle-out ideas. *Computerworld,* Framingham, April 12.

Marchetti, M. (2000). Your survival guide for the new economy. *Sales and Marketing Management, 152* (3), 44–52.

McClenahen, J. (1999). Future profile. Industry Week, Cleveland. Vol 248, Issue 17, September, 24.

Oetgen, B. (1999). Cultivating communication skills. *HR Monthly,* March.

Parry, K. (2000). Futureshock. *Management Today,* May.

Perry, C. (1993). A structured approach to presenting a thesis. *Australasian Marketing Journal, 6* (1), 63–85.

Roots, J. (2000). Measuring success: Top line over bottom line. *Electronic Commerce News,* Potomac, January 24.

Schein, E. (1992). The role of the CEO in the management of change. In Kochan, T. & Useem, M. (Eds.), *Transforming the organisation.* New York: Oxford University Press.

Smith, K. (2000). E-commerce: Lead, follow or get out of the way. *Euromoney*, London. January, 6–9.

Stewart, P. B. (2000). A template for e-commerce. *Informationweek Manhasset, 777*, March 13, 170.

Venkatraman, N. (2000). Five steps to a dot.com strategy: How to find your footing on the Web. *Sloan Management Review,* Cambridge, Spring.

Willcocks, L., & Plant, R. (2001). Pathways to e-business leadership: Getting from bricks to clicks, *Mit Sloan Management Review,* Cambridge, Spring.

Chapter III

Executive Judgment and the e-Business Advantage

Valerie Baker
University of Wollongong, Australia

Tim Coltman
University of Wollongong, Australia

Joan Cooper
University of Wollongong, Australia

ABSTRACT

Although several leading corporations have reported sizeable gains from their decisions to invest in the Internet and related e-business technology, many other similarly situated firms have failed to realize any real advantage. This inconsistency has long been a source of frustration for corporate executives, as benefits appear to exist, but the best way to get there, remains unknown. One possible cause for this inconsistency is that scholars have largely ignored the messy process of strategic judgment and instead chosen to presume that strategic outcomes are due to strategic choice. We argue that this omission is problematic and set out a research agenda that offers two main benefits. Firstly, we begin to open up the 'black box' of strategic choice by deliberately measuring the impact of strategic judgment. Secondly, we outline a methodological approach that is capable of more accurately measuring the impact of mediating factors like strategic judgment.

INTRODUCTION

The realization of advantage from the Internet and related e-business technology investment has long been a source of frustration for corporate executives. Impressive performance returns by companies such as Dell Computers, Cisco Systems and General Electric illustrate that returns can be achieved by linking the Internet and related e-business technologies to firm strategy. These companies have shown that successful management of their IT investments can generate returns as much as 40 percent higher than those of their competitors (Ross & Weill, 2002). However, many executives view the Internet and related e-business technologies with intense frustration. They recollect investment in the great speculative bubble of the 1990s and excessive expenditure on year 2000 compliant systems (Keen, 2002). They recall high profile examples of botched enterprise resource planning (ERP) systems that have consistently run over time and budget and report that customer-relationship management (CRM) initiatives were largely a flop (Reinartz & Chugh, 2002).

Unfortunately, it is not yet clear how firms should go about capturing the potential that exists in e-business, as few normative frameworks exist to guide practitioner investment. One area where consistent advances have been made is in structural contingency theory, where the contingency factor (i.e., environment-structure) has enabled predictions to be made in a relatively unambiguous manner (Donaldson, 1995). Applied to an e-business setting, contingency theory argues that performance increases can be expected whenever information technology is applied in an appropriate and timely way, and in harmony with business, environmental and organizational conditions. Consider a typical scenario where an executive wants to make a strategic investment in information systems. The executive has two choices: (1) a system to support backend operations using ERP technology, and (2) a CRM support system. How does he/she prioritise between these competing investments? Contingency literature would argue that it depends upon the organization's strategy and decision-making information requirements (Chandler, 1962; Child, 1972; Galbraith & Kazanjian, 1986). Manufacturing excellence strategies associated with companies like Carrefour or Ford Motor Company would get greater value from ERP systems. Customer intimacy strategies at companies like CitiBank or IBM Global Services would benefit most by customer feedback systems.

As simple as this observation may appear, the application of alignment has proven elusive. Despite twenty years of effort and investment in consulting advice, CIOs are still struggling with the same set of alignment problems. A recent survey by *CIO Insight* (Patterson, 2001) highlights the point that only 34 percent of organizations considered the link between their IT priorities and their enterprise strategy to be "strong." While these statistics reflect the difficulties of coordinating complex organizations, they provide evidence that most managers are not using the basic tools of alignment that have been developed over several decades of research.

Priem and Cycyota (2000) equate the process of alignment between IT strategies and business goals with *executive judgment*. The literature regarding judgment theory argues that firm success can be explained by the judgments executives make concerning the current state of the environment and the vision of the organization. In uncertain times, where market pressures and time constraints dominate the business landscape, senior managers' perceptions, skill and vision often form the basis on which strategic choices regarding IT investments are made. For example, *Industry Week* recently named Lou Gerstner of IBM their "CEO of the Year". This award was based on "business skills, judgement and tough-minded leadership" (Stevens, 1997). In a similar vein, Steve Jobs of Apple has been widely praised for his skill in judging the commercial potential of convergent Internet technologies. The corollary here is that judgement is an essential skill for setting the overall direction of the organization and perhaps explains to some degree executive remuneration packages.[1]

While judgment appears to be important to organizational success, scholars have largely ignored executive intentions and no empirical link between executive choices and firm outcomes has been established. Instead, strategic outcomes are *presumed* to be due to strategic choice (Preim & Harrison, 1994). This omission may account in some part for why practitioners continue to pay little attention to the large amount of published work concerning the antecedents of strategy and IT performance. This is particularly problematic given the size of business and community investment in scholarly activity.

Clearly we need greater understanding of exactly what executives are basing their judgments on if we are to develop research that has an impact on practitioners. Are executives basing decisions on contingency type arguments or are there other factors at play? The remaining sections set about defining strategic judgment and its relationship with decision-making, discuss the relevant theory and then outline two approaches that can be used to measure the importance of contingency-based judgment to the successful application of e-business strategic change.

DECISION-MAKING AND JUDGMENT

Judgment and decision-making are important activities that continually engage the attention of academics and practitioners alike. The ability to form good judgments and make wise decisions is considered a successful attribute in almost every society (Arkes & Hammond, 1986). However, trying to understand and explain decisions made in organizations by both individuals and groups is a complex problem. Part of this problem is due to the unobservable or intangible nature of decision antecedents. The exact nature of these decision determinants varies but evidence suggests that the decision problem is based on the decision-makers' goal and their understanding of the decision problem (Brehmer, 1986). Neither of these can be easily observed. What can be observed, however, is the relation between a description of the decision problem and the actual decision or consequences from a decision. These observable actions are based on assumptions about the decision-makers' goal or their understanding of the decision problem (Hammond et al., 1980).

The assumption that is most often made is that of rationality. The rational view assumes that the decision-maker has a perfect understanding of the decision problem, which allows her to 'select the course of action which leads to [her] goal' (Brehmer, 1986). However, the rational assumptions that have underpinned mechanistic approaches to firm strategy and strategic choice have increasingly been questioned for their simplistic assumptions that the world is stable and predictable. Although rational thinking is commonplace, this paradigm is suitable only when asked to explain very simple decision problems. The paradigm, more often than not, is at odds with observed behavior that is characterized by constantly changing firms and markets. Figure 1 illustrates this contextual difference.

Figure 1: Context of judgment and decision-making theory

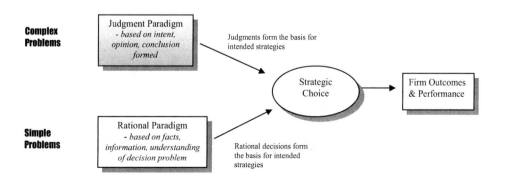

Decisions that need to be made in dynamic and turbulent environments—as is often the case with IT/IS strategic decisions—cannot be understood under the premise of rationality. When an executive makes a decision about his or her IT strategies it is unlikely that he or she has a 'perfect' understanding of the decision problem or what the consequences of that decision will be. Decisions are often based on projections of the future and this causes problems, as many unforeseen events can and do occur between the time a decision is made and the future state when the decision is put into practice. The path-dependent nature of technology adoption also means that firms must often make investments based on incomplete information. Investment decisions are made not based on rational returns, but to ensure the firm has in place the strategic options to more fully utilize technology in the future.

A major flaw with the rational paradigm is that it assumes that the decision maker's motives can be simply inferred from the consequences of the decisions that are made. But as Mintzberg's (1994) critique of rational planning points out, the 'design school' in strategic management is more fallacy than fact. Not all intended strategies are realized and not all realized strategies are intended. Much anecdotal evidence also indicates that there are good reasons for doubting the usefulness of the rational paradigm in explaining the actual behaviour of people. This means that we need to look for alternative perspectives that may also shed new light on the way managers deal with complex organizational problems.

One alternative is the judgment paradigm, an important feature of which is that this approach sees decisions as based on judgment rather than fact (Arkes & Hammond, 1986; Brehmer, 1986; Kaplan & Schwartz, 1975; Priem & Cycyota, 2000). It considers the analysis of these judgments as the key to understanding decision-making. In complex, real-world problems, the decision-maker often has to rely on something other than facts and a full understanding of the decision problem. Instead, the decision-maker bases his or her decisions on what Hammond (1974) describes as the "cognitive process of last resort: human judgment."

Defining Strategic Judgment

Judgment plays a central role in decision-making, particularly when making complex strategic decisions akin to IT strategic management. Yet what exactly is meant when we speak of an executive having good or bad judgment? The New Oxford Dictionary (1998) defines judging as a *process* involving "the ability to make considered decisions or come to sensible conclusions". Judgment as an *outcome* is simply "the opinion or conclusion formed" based on refined experience, training and maturity (op. cit.).

An analogy may help to clarify what we mean by "strategic judgment". When a paramedic is presented with an emergency incident, for example, a judgment process ensues. The paramedic first makes a judgment concerning the dangers to herself and crew by entering into any potentially hazardous environment. Having determined that the environment is safe, she then must make a judgment about what symptoms to look for on the patient, and then determine the presence or absence of these symptoms, or estimate their levels. Next she processes the particular combination of symptoms and their levels, reaches a diagnosis, and then commences emergency treatment. The paramedic's skill in making diagnoses based on training, experience, and personal qualities such as maturity and "common sense" represents her personal capacity for sound emergency diagnostic judgment.

Judgment, as we have defined it, can then encompass the ability to assess the environment, identify, perceive and attend to salient variables, to form objective opinions regarding relationships between these variables and to estimate the effect these relationships will have on performance. This definition is similar to that proposed by Vickers (1995), who described strategic judgment as the skill of managers along three dimensions: 1) determining the current situation, 2) determining how things should be, and 3) determining the best way to reduce the gap between 1 and 2. This comparison of a particular situation against the top manager's vision for the organization is, according to Mintzberg, Ahlstrand and Lampel (1998), central to strategic decisions. Furthermore, scholars have recently reinforced the link between judgement and decision-making, highlighting the primacy of strategic judgement as an essential ingredient of effective decisions.

IT Strategic Decisions

So far we have suggested that judgment is central towards developing a greater understanding of strategic choice. Therefore it is important to understand the judgments being made in complex decisions about IT/IS investments if we want to gain knowledge into how IT strategic choices influence firm outcomes. Before we continue, the term strategy needs to be defined in order to have a clear understanding of what is meant by *strategic* judgments and decisions.

Executives and academics often use the word strategy, but what does it actually mean? The standard definition of strategy is usually something along the lines of "top management's plan to attain outcomes consistent with the organization's missions and goals" (Wright et al., 1992, p.3). Mintzberg, Ahlstrand and Lampel (1998) argue, however, that strategy requires a number of definitions. The focus of this chapter is the definition by Mintzberg (1985) of intended and realized strategies, as this parallels the separation of executive judgment from organization outcomes (Priem, 1994).

Most people, as the definition above suggests, define strategy as a plan or course of action for the future. If you asked a person to then define the strategy that his or her firm actually implemented the answer would more often than not be different. Hence strategy is a term that is often defined in one way and used in another (Mintzberg et al., 1998). That is, a distinction exists between the strategies that are intended by decision-makers based on their judgments and the realized strategies, which are the tangible firm outcomes. The intentions of a decision-maker may or may not be realized, which makes it important to separate judgment from achieved firm outcomes (Priem & Harrison, 1994). The failure by organizational research to explicitly capture this link means that most models of performance are under-specified (Hambrick & Mason, 1984). Including judgment as a key variable is a necessary step towards improving our understanding of mental processes in strategy development and how these strategies and processes affect firm performance.

E-BUSINESS AND IT STRATEGIC CHANGE AND JUDGMENT

As we have suggested, existing research into the change process and the implementation of e-business related technology is limited because it fails to measure the link between judgment and firm outcomes. As we have suggested, the judgments that executives make provide important insight into how IT strategic change or e-business change is approached given different situations and organization contexts.

Peterson (2002) suggests that it is the processing of information and the judgments that are made by top management that leads to critical decisions being made about how firms deal with IT-related strategic change. As the business environment rapidly changes, the variance in possible outcomes ranges from failure to unparalleled success. These differences can largely be explained by the "mythical relationship between technology, ecology, human nature, decision cycles, IT and the speed and veracity of their interactions" (Peterson, 2002: p. 485). Executives process information about these relationships and form critical strategic judgments regarding the future direction of their organization through its e-business strategy.

We can liken the situation faced by most organizations, when making strategic decisions about e-business and, more broadly, IT, to that of a battlefield, where despite much intelligence planning, a military campaign is subject to change once the battle has begun. Similarly, managers face conditions such as dynamic markets, casual ambiguity and path dependence that make it extremely difficult to predict the outcomes of their IT strategic investments. As this illustration suggests, it is imperative that managers have in place strategies to cope with changes as they occur. Faced with external environmental changes (e.g., new rates of Internet adoption, killer mobile commerce applications, etc.), managers need to be able to adjust their strategic choices accordingly "just as water shapes itself according to the ground, an army should manage its victory in accordance with the enemy. Just as water has no constant shape, so in warfare there are no fixed rules and regulations" (Sun Tzu in Hussey, 1996, p.208)

What Sun Tzu highlights is the requirement that strategies be flexible in order to manage strategic change. Mintzberg, Ahlstrand and Lampel (1998) describe this as an emergent strategy, where rather than pursuing a strategy, an organization makes decisions based on the situation, effectively testing the market as they go.

Thus strategic decisions regarding IT management need to be a mixture of both deliberate and emergent strategies. "Real-world strategies need to mix these in some way: to exercise control while fostering learning" (Mintzberg et al., 1998, p.11). The importance of strategic alignment between the organization and its environment becomes even more critical given recent environmental turbulence and the evolving importance of technology and e-business to competitive advantage.

EXECUTIVE JUDGMENT AND STRATEGIC ALIGNMENT

Priem and Cycyota (2000) state that understanding judgements by strategic leaders is essential to determine the role of mental processes in strategy development and how these strategies and processes affect firm performance. They suggest that a number of theoretical platforms commonly found in the strategy literature provide a solid platform from which we can examine strategic judgement. The 'fit' or 'alignment' paradigm is perhaps one of the most pervasive in strategy. Good strategy requires, at a minimum, alignment with changing external conditions. In simple terms, the proposition is that there is an organizational structure that fits the level of contingency factor whether it is environmental uncertainty, organizational characteristics, technological characteristics or strategy design interdependence so that an organization in fit creates significant and positive implications for performance. This idea that fit between organization structure and contingency factor leads to superior performance has been empirically supported in both qualitative and quantitative studies (Donaldson, 1995).

The concept of alignment is not only central to strategic management, but is basic to disciplines such as economics, organization theory and marketing, on which strategic management draws. It underpins the thinking of contingency theorists; and it is also a normative concept used by consultants. Given this distinguished history it might reasonably be expected that executives would frequently make decisions based on the principles of organization congruence (Priem, 1994).

Most early theories of structural contingency focused on how the fit between bivariate variables (i.e., structure-environment alignment, strategy-structure alignment or strategy-environment alignment) are associated with increased firm performance. More recently the focus has shifted to multivariate approaches, which examine strategy-structure-environment alignment. Both theories are consistent, however, and relatively unambiguously purport that high fit is associated with high performance (Priem, 1994).

Despite this extensive empirical investigation there are few solid insights into the link between senior management choices, processes or skills and firm performance. Additionally, as Henderson and Venkatraman (1999) show, an important aspect of contingency theory is that the path to fit is not always externally driven but can arise from internal pressures as well. This school of thought complements the popular resource-based view (RBV) of the firm, where emphasis is placed on the importance of resources and distinctive capabilities (Teece, Pissano, & Sheun, 1997). If an empirical relationship exists between superior IT resources and performance then it is apparent from the above discussion that capabilities of this form warrant investigation. Preliminary results in this area indicate that firms with high IT capability (i.e., physical IT infrastructure components, human IT resources and IT-enabled capabilities) tend to outperform a control sample of firms on a variety of profit and cost-based performance measures (Bharadwaj, 2000).

An important 'offshoot' to the RBV that may be valuable in advancing the study of strategic judgment is the knowledge-based view of the firm (KBV). The KBV provides a new perspective through which to view strategic judgement because it directs attention specifically towards the extensive knowledge required for strategic decision-making and how that knowledge is built and retained. The theory essentially argues that the firm's "existence and boundaries can be explained by its unique ability to obtain, build, combine and retain knowledge" (Eisenhardt & Santos, 2000 in Priem & Cycyota, 2000, p. 9), and is directly applicable to e-business and CRM systems that manage interactions and knowledge exchange between the firm and its customers. However, the KBV is not as yet a new theory of strategy, but rather an important extension to the RBV whenever knowledge is a highly valuable resource. While operational difficulties regarding the completeness and primacy of knowledge have restricted the theoretical reach of this view, it nevertheless provides much insight if we restrict our focus to the way executives build and utilize knowledge in the judgment process. Clearly the KBV provides a fresh position in which we can empirically examine strategic judgement.

EMPIRICAL INVESTIGATION OF STRATEGIC JUDGMENT

The "integrative framework" developed by Lee (1989, 1991) in a series of papers regarding the management of information systems provides a suitable approach to the study of judgment. Lee's integrative framework formally presented in his 1994 paper combines three levels of "understandings": the subjective, the interpretive and the positivist. According to Lee, the three understandings are "far from being mutually exclusive and irreconcilable"; in fact, "they may be utilised as mutually supportive and reinforcing steps in organisational research". Priem and Cycyota (2000) also support this view by claiming that both qualitative and quantitative studies are necessary to increase our understanding of strategic judgement.

In the case of e-business, qualitative work can be useful in exploratory investigation that may highlight issues more formal approaches may miss. For example, case studies of the most spectacular strategic information systems initiatives Baxter Healthcare and American Airline's SABRE indicate that these

IT/e-business systems were largely accidental success stories (Clemons, 1986). However, these subjective and interpretive studies cannot test hypotheses adequately because of the close contact needed with research subjects and the resulting small sample size. Quantitative studies provide the crucial positivist link that complements exploratory work in a way that can generate more widely generalizable insights. Notable examples include the study of IT's contribution to performance in the retail industry (Powell & Dent-Micallef, 1997), and the investigation of organizational antecedents to e-business adoption (Srinivasan et al., 2002).

The following sections focus on measurement techniques, which can be used to examine individual judgment. These techniques can be grouped into two categories: 1) composition methods, and 2) decomposition methods (Priem & Harrison, 1994).

Composition Methods

Composition methods focus on the processes that underlie individual judgments. Composition involves methods such as verbal protocol analysis, information searches and cause mapping to gather interpretive information from executives about the processes that lead them to make certain judgments. These types of techniques would be useful in identifying the variables that executives use in their strategic decision-making, but which are not included in current management theory (Priem & Harrison, 1994).

Decomposition Methods

Decomposition techniques focus on the interactions that take place surrounding the judgment itself. The technique requires that the variables or judgment attributes be known *a priori*. The substantive nature of those variables must come from existing strategy theory (Priem & Harrison, 1994), and contingency theory provides an excellent starting point.

In this case decomposition methods are required to focus on executive choices in response to a series of decision scenarios (i.e., behavioural simulations regarding the environment, firm structure and the strategy-making process). The variance in executive choice is evaluated against these factors of interest, which can be manipulated across scenarios, using conjoint or choice analysis techniques.[2] Figure 2 shows the way we can manipulate the important choices outlined in structural contingency theory. Paired comparisons (or

Figure 2: Judgment evaluation survey

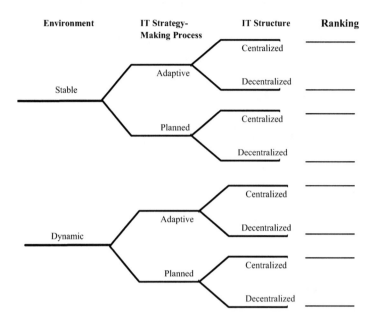

stated preferences) are collected and then used to evaluate direct and interaction effects. In this way we reveal the direction and strength of the three factors considered central to contingency theory. For example, an executive faced with a stable environment would lean towards a planned strategy and decentralized structure according to contingency prescriptions. Respondent rankings on each path reflect the perceived utility respondents have for each combination of variables.

This combination of composition and decomposition techniques enables one to test whether the prescriptions of at least one well-known theory (i.e., contingency theory) influence executive judgment. The extent to which these prescriptions are already 'obvious' to, or widely known by, practicing executives will shed new light on the role of judgment in IT strategy and change.

CONCLUSION

This chapter has outlined the importance of executive judgment to the strategic choice process and is particularly relevant to the study of e-business, where environmental turbulence increases the relevance of managerial discretion. By separating the outcomes from the actual decision choice we can begin to more fully understand how these strategic choices influence firm performance. Until now the process of strategic choice has largely been treated as a 'black box' where it is assumed that measured outcomes are the result of deliberate choices.

One of the reasons contingency theory has become so popular is that it provides managers with prescriptive advice regarding which configurations lead to higher performance. Further examination of executive judgments to ascertain whether executives are making decisions based on the idea of alignment or fit is required. This will help in our understanding of whether material taught by academics in business schools is actually being used by students in industry. Are executives using the ideas of alignment or fit as prescribed in theory or are they making judgments based on other factors? The answer to this question has important implications for relevance and improving the linkage between theory and practice.

Understanding the processes that occur in strategy development will lead to greater knowledge of the decisions that executives make in uncertain environments and hyper-turbulent contexts. This understanding is important if we want to develop e-business-related research that is applicable to practitioners. It is this type of research that will guide executives in the strategic management of change and allow them to gain advantage from leveraging their investments in e-business technology.

ENDNOTES

1   The seemingly excessive salary for the CEO of IBM Sam Palmisano was US $12.3 in 2001; Terry Semel, Chairman and CEO of Yahoo Inc., raked in $61 million; Paul Anderson, the departing boss of BHP Billiton, was on a package of nearly $8 million are perhaps justified by the skill they bring in terms of strategic judgment.

2   There are a number of conjoint analysis methods which can be used to test executive judgments. Each of the methods uses a variation of regression to decompose an executive's judgment. The most appropriate for evaluating executive judgments is metric conjoint analysis. For example, Priem (1994) used metric conjoint analysis to examine the judgments of CEOs in manufacturing firms. The outcome of this research was that the

executives in manufacturing firms often make contingent judgments, regarding key strategy variables.

REFERENCES

Arkes, H., & Hammond, K. (Eds.). (1986). *Judgment and decision making: an interdisciplinary reader*. Cambridge: Cambridge University Press.

Bharadwaj, A. (2000). A resource based perspective on Information Technology capability and firm performance: An empirical investigation. *MIS Quarterly, 24*(1), 169–196.

Brehmer, B. (1986). The role of judgment in small group conflict and decision making. In H. Arkes & K. Hammond (Eds.), *Judgment and decision making: an interdisciplinary reader*. Cambridge: Cambridge University Press.

Burn, J. M. (1997). A professional balancing act. In C. Sauer & P. Yetton (Eds.), *Steps to the future: Fresh thinking on the management of IT-based organizational transformation*. San Fransisco: Jossey-Bass.

Chan, Y. E. (2002). Why haven't we mastered alignment? The importance of the informal organization structure. *MIS Quarterly Executive, 1*(2), 97–106.

Chandler, A. (1962). *Strategy and structure*. Cambridge: MIT Press.

Child, J. (1972). Organisation structure, environment and performance. *Sociology, 6*, 1–21.

Clemons, E. K. (1986). Information systems for sustainable competitive advantage. *Information & Management, 11*(3),131–137.

Donaldson, L. (1995). *Contingency theory*. Aldershot, UK: Dartmouth Publishing Company.

Eisenhardt, K. M., & Santos, F. M. (2000). Knowledge-based view: A new theory of strategy? In Pettigrew, A., Thomas, H., & Whittington, R. (Eds.), *Handbook of strategy and management*. Thousand Oaks, CA.

Foss, N. (1999). Research in the strategic theory of the firm: Isolationism and integrationism. *Journal of Management Studies, 36*(6), 725–755.

Galbraith, J. R., & Kazanjian, R. K. (1986). Organizing to implement strategies of diversity and globalization: the role of matrix designs. *Human Resource Management, 25*(1), 37.

Hambrick, D. C., & Mason, P. A. (1984). Upper echelons: The organisation as a reflection of its top managers. *Academy of Management Review, 9*, 193–206.

Hammond, K. (1974). *Human judgment and social policy* (No. 170). Boulder: University of Colorado, Center for Research on Judgment and Policy.

Hammond, K., McClelland, G., & Mumpower, J. (1980). *Human judgment and decision making.* New York: Prager Publishers

Henderson, C., & Venkatraman, N. (1999). Strategic alignment: Leveraging Information Technology for transforming organizations. *IBM Systems Journal, 38*(2&3), 472–482.

Hussey, D. (1996). A framework for implementation. *The Implementation Challenge,* New York: John Wiley & Sons.

Kaplan, M., & Schwartz, S. (Eds.). (1975). *Human judgment and decision processes.* London: Academic Press.

Keen, P. (2002). Getting value from IT. *Sydney University*, 19 August.

Lee, A. S. (1989). A scientific methodology for MIS case studies. *MIS Quarterly 13*(1), 33–50.

Lee, A. S. (1991). Integrating positivist and interpretative approaches to organisational research. *Organization Science, 2*(4), 342–365.

Luftman, J. (2000). Assessing business-IT alignment maturity. *Communications of AIS, 4*(14).

Mintzberg, H. (1994). *The rise and fall of strategic planning.* Prentice Hall.

Mintzberg, H., & Walters, J. A. (1985). Of strategies, deliberate and emergent. *Strategic Management Journal, 6*, 257-272.

Mintzberg, H., Ahlstrand, B., & Lampel, J. (1998). *Strategy safari: a guided tour through the wilds of strategic management.* New York: The Free Press.

Patterson, S. (2001). The truth about CRM. *CIO Magazine*, May 1st http://www.cio.com/archive/050101/truth.content.html

Peterson, J. W. (2002). Leveraging technology foresight to create temporal advantage. *Technological Forecasting and Social Change, 69*, 485-494.

Plant, S. (2000). *eCommerce formulation of strategy.* New Jersey: Prentice Hall.

Porter, M. (2001). Strategy and the Internet. *Harvard Business Review*.

Powell, T. C., & Dent-Micallef, A. (1997). Information Technology as competitive advantage: the role of human, business, and technology resources. *Strategic Management Journal, 18*(5), 375–405.

Priem, R., & Cycyota, C. (2000). On strategic judgement. In M. Hitt, R. Freeman, & J. Harrison (Eds.), *Handbook of strategic management.* Blackwell.

Priem, R. L. (1994). Executive judgment, organizational congruence, and firm performance. *Organization Science, 5*(3), 421–437.

Priem, R. L., & Harrison, D. A. (1994). Exploring strategic judgment: Methods for testing the assumptions of prescriptive contingency theories. *Strategic Management Journal, 15*(4), 311–324.

Reinartz W. J., & Chugh, P. (2002). Learning from experience: Making CRM a success at last. *Int. Journal of Call Centre Management*, April, 207–219.

Ross, J. W., & Weill, P. (2002). Six decisions your IT people shouldn't make. *Harvard Business Review, 80*(11), 84.

Srinivasan, R., Lilien, G. L., & Rangaswamy, A. (2002). Technological opportunism and radical technology adoption: An application to eBusiness. *Journal of Marketing 66*(3), 47–61.

Stevens, A. (1997). Deja blue. *Industry Week, 246*(21), 82–88.

Teece, D. J., Pissano, G., & Sheun, A. (1997). Capabilities and strategic management. *Strategic Management Journal, 18*(7), 509–533.

Vickers, S. G. (1995). *The art of judgement* (Centenary Edition ed.). UK: Sage.

Weill, P., & Woodham, W. (2002). Don't just lead, govern: Implementing effective IT governance. *MIT Sloan*. Working paper, (April), 17.

Wright, P., Pringle, C., & Kroll, M. (1992). *Strategic Management Text and Cases*. Needham Heights, MA: Allyn and Bacon.

Chapter IV

A Change Management Framework for E-Business Solutions

Sushil K. Sharma
Ball State University, USA

ABSTRACT

Over the last decade, a significant number of companies have implemented e-business solutions because an investment in e-business technologies provides the promise of a competitive advantage through lower transaction costs and the integration of processes. Many of these companies have experienced failures, a few have closed down, and only a few have succeeded in achieving the objectives. Studies undertaken to examine the reasons for these failures have highlighted that most of these companies could not handle change. One of the major challenges with the implementation of e-business solutions is managing change. A successful e-transformation represents the greatest value-creation potential for any company. In this chapter, I present a change management framework that suggests how firms can manage their transition to e-business and prepare them for e-transformation. The change management framework may provide managers or change agents with structured and measurable implementation tools, techniques and approaches for managing and evaluating the change process.

INTRODUCTION

The harbingers of the new economy are: new digital marketplaces, the emerging role of alliances and hyper-partnering, new market indices, the emergence of Internet protocol-based enterprise software providers, and new cultural management and organizational expectations (McGarvey, 2001; Sharma, 2000). The new players such as dot-coms, net-markets, e-business infrastructure, and service providers have emerged as part of e-business revolution (Boulton, Libert, & Samek, 2000). The past few years have seen a significant shift in the way companies are managed, organized, and, most importantly, valued (McCrimmon, 1997; Sharma, 2000). Speed, new partners, real-time customer feedback, and supplier data shared on-line are all different aspects of a new way of doing business. E-business is bringing empowerment to customers, enhancement of trade, increased business agility, extension of enterprises in a virtual manner, evolution and invention of products and services, and the development of new markets and audiences. The pressures of e-business, mergers, globalization and tough competition are accelerating the pace of business change. Organizational responses to this have often included customer relationship management technologies, web-based solutions and Business-to-Consumer and Business-to-Business e-commerce initiatives (Stewart, 2000). However, none of these have a hope of working without having an effective change management for transition.

A significant portion of the e-business solutions has emerged over the last few years and many lessons have been learned from the challenges associated with implementing e-business solutions. One of the major challenges with the implementation of e-business solutions is managing change (Stuart, 1995). The e-business change management area is defined as a multi-disciplinary field of expertise that provides a systematic approach to orchestrate all components of business transformation (people, organization, technology, and processes). One of the most challenging responsibilities for any e-business solution lies in dealing effectively with the alignment of people, processes, and systems. This can be achieved through a solid change management framework. At each step, the e-business change management framework provides an integrated set of predefined and measurable implementation tools, techniques, and approaches. These are designed to help organizations and people understand why change is necessary, how the change will impact them, and how to take responsibility for a successful implementation. This chapter presents a change management framework that will suggest how firms can prepare themselves for e-transformation and can help organizations to successfully manage e-business solutions.

The chapter is divided into three parts. Firstly, it describes e-business and change management process. Secondly, there is the focus on e-transformation. The e-transformation model describes what kind of transformational changes are required when a company shifts from traditional business model to e-business. Thirdly, it also describes the change management framework that could be helpful for managing e-transformation.

E-BUSINESS AND CHANGE

E-business not only helps organizations to conduct business on-line, but also helps to connect the organization with all its internal and external value chain components; value chain-suppliers, logistics providers, wholesalers, distributors, service providers, and end customers for many different purposes (Fahey, Srivastava, Sharon, & Smith, 2001). E-business, in spite of its pervasiveness, visibility, and impact, often remains a poorly understood phenomenon. It has been stated that e-business embodies the most pervasive, disruptive, and disconcerting form of change (Fahey et al., 2001). E-business creates integrated networks of relationships with channels, end customers, suppliers, providers, and even rivals that were not possible before. E-business is transforming the solutions available to customers in almost every industry. Customers can shop on a 24/7 time schedule and companies can offer many self-service applications and deliver products and services on the request of customers when they want it and where they want it. These new solutions open up possibilities for customer value creation and delivery that were simply unimaginable a mere three years ago. E-business, due to its ability to target customers 1-to-1, offers the platform for new forms of marketplace that have been changing the competitive rules of the game. E-business is dramatically reshaping every traditional business process: from developing new products and managing customer relationships to acquiring human resources and procuring raw materials and components (Sharma, 2001, 2003). It places an especially heavy premium on new forms of integrated and intensive relationships with external entities, new sets of perceptions held by customers, channels, suppliers, and, of course, significant new knowledge (Ginige, Murugesan, & Kazanis, 2001).

'Change management' is the process of managing the effective implementation of organizational strategies, ensuring that permanent changes in goals, behaviors, relationships, processes and systems are achieved for business advantage (Bridges, 1991). Successful organizational change requires sophisticated planning, design, communications and implementation management, with continuous stakeholder involvement (Bryson & Anderson, 2000), and it needs proactive planning and implementation. A failed change can create poor morale, lack of credibility, customer irritation, competitors' advantage, and resistance to further change. Change management requires an understanding of all the points of impact, a system view; meticulous planning and scheduling, and excellent communications, and HR management (Buchanan & Badham, 1999; Carnell, 1995). The new e-business technologies necessitate not just the re-engineering of existing processes but also mandate design, development, and deployment of fundamentally new ways of conceiving and executing business processes (Fahey et al., 2001). Senior executives in every organization thus confront a central challenge: how to transition from traditional business methodologies into e-business transformation and how to manage the change successfully. According to Gartner Group, 80% of all e-business downtime incidents are caused by problems not due to failure of IT processes but to poorly executed changes (Liebmann, 2001). It is important to understand just how challenging change has become for technology teams. E-business applications now rely on an incredibly complex chain of elements, each of which must be in good working order and well-behaved in relation to every other element in the end-to-end chain for the whole thing to work. These elements include network hardware, servers running various operating systems, highly "componentized" software across multiple tiers, diverse types of web content, security systems, storage devices, processes, people, applications and more (Wargin & Dobiey, 2001).

E-TRANSFORMATION

Several trends in the marketplace are already pointing to the signs of e-transformation, all of which are focused on allowing businesses to get to the customer faster, with more velocity and more value. E-transformation involves changes in how a company does business, how it enters new markets, how it communicates across the enterprise, and how it deals with suppliers (Budhwani, 2001). Above all, transformation is about customers—changing the means by which companies find, sell to, service, and communicate with them (Wilder, 1999). In a recent Information Week Research survey of 300 IT executives, the most common "transformational" initiative under way at their companies was interaction with customers (Wilder, 1999). An e-transformed company is a company that has implemented a combination of aggressive deployment of e-business enablers to change business and supply-chain components. Examples of e-transformation are everywhere. Auto manufacturers are bringing on-line processes to a sales culture that has never been before. Many companies are offering on-line access to their products and services and offering self-service applications. Airline industry is bringing IT to bear on virtually every aspect of its customer experience.

E-transformation not only helps companies to hack away at the intermediaries between them and their customers, but also to reward and reinforce the links that are delivering new and different types of values to customers. Companies undertaking e-transformation are concurrently applying value management principles, reengineering their core business processes, and implementing enabling e-technologies—all with the intent of developing and implementing innovative business models. E-technologies provide the opportunities to build new business models but do not assure their success. To stay ahead, the e-transformed company will need to continue to implement innovation. The e-transformation strategic direction will provide the high-level description of new business concepts and the required modifications to the existing business model, organizational capabilities and infrastructure, and method of interaction with customers and external partners (Schuh, Mueller, & Tockenbuerger, 2002). At its core, e-transformation is about breaking down walls—internal walls between business and IT and between other company functions—but even more radically, walls between what is inside and outside the company. The Internet, of course, offers an unprecedented vehicle to do that for customers, suppliers, and business partners. But it is not just about opening doors with extranets and customer self-service web sites. It is about a new mind-set—opening the company to new partnerships and new ideas from unexpected sources. The Process-Technology-People (P-T-P) approach describes the operational behavior of organizations, in how an organization's business processes interact with each other, with the processes of its customers and suppliers, and with other external business processes. This simple, yet powerful framework is based on the fact that the processes are performed by people using relevant information systems applications and technologies. The interaction between business processes occurs, in fact, via the interconnection of applications and technologies, and via the cooperation of people. Thus the change management framework is divided into five different dimensions. The e-transformation model based on Process-Technology-People (P-T-P) Model (Sharpe, 1989) is presented in Figure 1.

Figure 1: E-transformation model

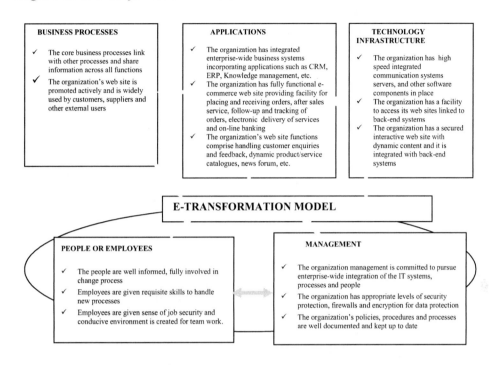

THREE-PHASE CHANGE MANAGEMENT FRAMEWORK FOR E-BUSINESS TRANSFORMATION

Theories concerning the nature of change include description of the main components of the change process and methods of introducing change (Carnell, 1995; Carney, 2001). There has been much debate on the factors that contribute to the successful implementation of change, but views differ on how this might be achieved. The change management framework could be highly effective in understanding how the change process is managed (Clarke & Garside, 1997). The components identified for e-transformation model in the previous section are a very useful guide in developing change management framework constructs. Initial lists of change management framework constructs are thus developed using e-transformation model (as shown in Figure 1). To derive a comprehensive change management framework, such constructs are adapted from ideas generated in a matrix related to change presented by Clarke and Garside (1997) and Process-Technology-People (P-T-P) Model

(Sharpe, 1989). The framework could be tested for validity and reliability. It attempts to make sense of the building blocks or components identified as being critical to the successful management of change. The principal components of the framework are: the people, processes, and technology, and customers and value chain partners. Ultimately, research constructs for the framework include qualitative and quantitative, internal and external factors (Stewart, 2000).

The proposed three-phase change management framework starts with preparing organizations for change, re-engineering efforts and building on new infrastructure and capabilities to enhance and extend the original business models, and then focuses on outward relationships to create new businesses (Davidson, 1999). The first phase of the change process is focused on people, which includes identifying champions for the change process, setting up a vision, communicating with all the constituents and preparing employees for a change. The second phase focuses on re-engineering processes and automation of existing activities to reduce cost and raise capacity, and expands to encompass a broader range of applications to optimize operations. Third phase begins shifting the focus from optimizing internal operations to enhancing transactions and relations with customers, suppliers and other value chain partners. Enhancements typically appear first in the form of value-added activities in areas such as order entry and tracking, delivery, and customer

Figure 2: Change management framework for e-business transformation

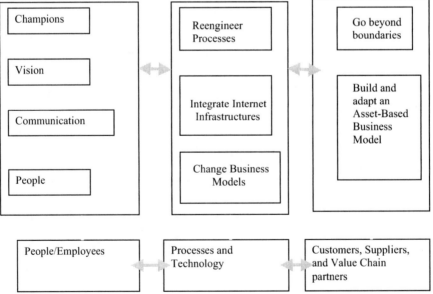

service functions. While these applications simply enhance existing activities, new services may appear in the form of augmented flows of information to the customer, new customer service functions, and new features and options (Schuh, Mueller, & Tockenbuerger, 2002). Such developments are central in the third phase of the transformation process. The details of change management framework and the various parameters that should be addressed in each phase are shown in Figure 2 and are described in the following sections.

Phase I - People
Identify Champions

It is very important to have a few champions who can spearhead the change process (Carney, 2001). If a company finds that there are no existing employee members who can own the e-transformation process, then the company needs to recruit from outside (Hartley, Benington, & Binns, 1997). These champions are not only visionaries but also knowledgeable on the subject, use energy, and are passionate about the transformation of the business (Doyle, 2002). Many companies could not handle change due to a lack of champions who could have otherwise led the transformational process successfully (Hambrick, Nadler, & Tushman, 1998).

A Vision

Vision is perhaps the most critical component. A clear vision of the task ahead can be imparted to a company directly by the champion, but it can also be developed by the senior management team with active participation by the champion (Hambrick, Nadler, & Tushman, 1998; Hartley, Benington, & Binns, 1997). What is most important, though, is that the vision is simple enough for everyone to understand. All constituents should associate a business' e-transformation process with a clear view of the end goal. The organization should clarify their current reality and change drivers, shape a vision for the desirable organization, develop action plans that move them toward that future and address information, processes, structures and relationship issues. The vision must be converted into a plan and the plan needs to exist in a document form. It must include milestones and metrics that describe and bind the e-transformation journey, and it should be reviewed by the champion and senior management at regular intervals (Thornhill, Lewis, Millmore, & Saunders, 2000).

Communication

Organizations need to open the lines of communication and explore new opportunities for bringing employees and other stakeholders to work together. A significant impact of the process is its ability to enhance the level of organizational awareness. There is opportunity in this new type of culture for open and honest communications, vertically and horizontally, across the company. It is important to have a vertical and horizontal communication strategy as well as a mechanism to elicit feedback from constituents (Carney, 2001). The communication should be such that everyone in the organization understands the need for change. All should agree on the methods to achieve the desired change and understand the consequences. The key variables in the communication process are the importance of consultation, education, and participation during the process (Swanson, 2001; Thornhill et al., 2000).

People

Engagement is the total number of employees actively involved in the planning phase of a change, which increases the level of commitment. Commitment is generated through the process of participation and involvement (Doyle, 2002). Engagement enhances the level of enthusiasm for a given change initiative so that people become committed to the cause. As with any e-transformation, technology is not the only stumbling block; user attitudes create significant problems as well. Employees have to be prepared to use the technology, and they have to learn to become comfortable with it. The success factors identified as being of critical importance in the management of change are: commitment levels amongst managers and staff involved in the change process, and the level of motivation present (Carney, 2001). The key variables are: the involvement and understanding of the need for change, and the likely impact of the proposed change on the social and cultural lives of the individuals concerned (Levasseur, 2001). Most of the staff affected by the change must be involved from the beginning. They must see the desirability for the change and understand the likely impact, and teams must be formed for carrying out the change.

Phase II – Processes and Technology

Reengineer Processes - Integrate Across Units and Businesses

Companies have a myriad of hardware, software, and application systems that are not working together. Companies cannot continue to compete in today's frenetic environment with disparate, disconnected IT infrastructures and disintegrated processes or applications. There is increasing pressure on companies to innovate, reconfigure, and customize their offerings. This demands that the existing processes are reengineered to integrate across units and businesses. This may necessitate not only the reengineering of processes, but also the Enterprise Application Integration (EAI) should have an emphasis on application-to-application integration. Here, the connections between applications, as well as the overall application or "business logic" must be taken care of to create Enterprise Business Integration (EBI) solutions. By focusing on business processes and leveraging workflow technology, the major components of EBI, organizations can tie together independent systems and processes to create a cohesive, integrated IT infrastructure. EBI solutions add the "business logic" that enables companies to incorporate their particular business processes while integrating multiple applications, ensuring a continuous flow of information between departments and throughout the enterprise.

Create a Flexible Technology Infrastructure

E-business infrastructure consists of the products and services needed to build or run e-business applications. E-business infrastructure should be flexible, reliable, scalable and quickly deployed to keep up with the ever-changing, unpredictable advances in technology. Enterprises' e-business infrastructures are growing larger and more complex all the time. Corporate mergers introduce unfamiliar software into the enterprise, and newly hired and distributed workers make it difficult for IT managers to keep track of which employees need which applications (Lee, 2001). New technologies, particularly the Internet, have rapidly been changing business models, relationships with customers and partners, processes and overall increased pace of business. Organizations face unique obstacles to these changes and need to deploy a flexible Internet-based technological infrastructure that can respond to dynamic business environments, and better manage rapid changes in business processes and relationships. New technology architecture should ensure that every business could collaborate successfully with virtually any business partner (Budhwani, 2001). Customers of tomorrow would expect businesses to serve them via the Internet, anytime, anywhere in the world, on any device, at any time. Therefore, it becomes mandatory to create a web-based infrastructure that can integrate back-office management systems, customers and business partners to respond to any situation. Such an infrastructure can also help to create self-service capabilities. Properly designed web portals can provide trusted business partners with a secure, flexible environment for activities ranging from self-service to collaborative commerce (Budhwani, 2001).

End-to-end integration of e-business solutions represents a significant challenge to today's corporations. Internet technologies and the business data that they present and act upon are deployed in a variety of application, database, platform, and network components. In addition, not all technologies have to be robust and predictable, but they must incorporate: adherence to documented requirements and expectations, "ease" of deployment, "ease" of "use", the vendor's adherence to industry and de facto standards, and customer preferences, (vendors, platforms, etc.). When considering new web infrastructure components, support functions will have to be created and developed from "scratch"; however, the more common and challenging practice of integration into an existing environment adds a significant amount of complexity to design, development, deployment, and support.

Change Business Processes and Business Models

The organization's management must understand that their business is going to be changed due to new technologies and business models that change industry dynamics and redefine what both shareholders value and customers desire. To prepare for that, the organization should work on an operating philosophy to change business processes and business models. Shifts in technology are causing a number of changes regarding customers. Customers are no longer just viewers or listeners, but are active users of interactive services and information. Many companies are offering opportunities for customers to produce their own products and services by providing interactive mode (Stewart, 2000). The easy access that buyers have to competitive information is placing pressure on prices and is encouraging customers to search for substitutes. New business models are emerging in every industry of the New Economy. In these emerging models, intangible assets such as relationships, knowledge, people, brands, and systems are taking center stage (Boulton et al., 2000; McGarvey, 2001). The relationship and interaction of various stakeholders such as customers, suppliers, strategic partners, agents, or distributors is entirely changed. Moving into e-commerce may require a major change in the commerce models that businesses use. Because companies are creating value in new ways, they need new business models that accurately reflect 21st century business realities. The key to survival in the new e-business environment depends upon organizations' ability to adapt to a new, more collaborative, corporate-competition model. Organizations have to shift from being product-centric to customer-centric, making customers a part of the organization. New marketing approaches of organizations must focus on long-term relationships and customization. Since most organizations are organized around product lines, one of the greatest organizational challenges is the art of being customer-centric.

Phase III – Customers, Suppliers and Other Value Chain Partners
Go Beyond Boundaries - Focus on External Value-Chain

Focusing on external value-chain partners is a major aspect of transformation. Internal sign-offs are being replaced by external relationships, and more of what was done internally is now done externally. The drastic fall in Dow, Nasdaq, and MSDW Internet indexes indicates that even careful examination of value creation is not enough. Companies would need a successful e-transformation for their survival and growth, and in most of the cases, companies are not able to e-transform due to their old-model organizational structures, operations, and business mindsets. Not only does the organization need to implement and utilize new technologies, it needs to make significant changes to the way it manages its relationships with external stakeholders, customers, suppliers, and service providers (Paton & McCalman, 2000). It also needs to develop a culture that embraces cross-functional teamwork. The company will need to develop sophisticated organizational capabilities that allow it to quickly take advantage of external changes and even drive external changes through the development of innovative business models (Schuh et al., 2002).

Traditional businesses are having trouble competing today because their organizational structures are based on a business environment that no longer exists. As a result, they cannot move quickly enough for the e-business economy. To overcome this, businesses must begin assigning initiatives outside traditional organizational boundaries. This has always been a best practice to drive innovation, but now it needs to be implemented more broadly. Successful e-transformation is all about relying on new leaders, forcing executives outside their comfort zone, and requiring them to rely on other people in the organization (Stuart, 1995).

Build and Adapt an Asset-Based Business Model

Every business uses a particular combination of assets to build a business model unique to its needs and goals. The e-transformation demands organizations to adopt new business models. In these emerging models, intangible assets such as relationships, knowledge, people, brands, and systems are taking center stage. For example, though not reflected in the balance sheet, employees and supplier assets are an important world of intangible value. Each component in the employee and supplier asset category, including all members of the supply chain, is considered a partner in producing products and services. Outsourcing, mergers, and alliances are the steps in acquiring asset base of customers, expertise, and brands to gain new efficiencies in the value chain (Rosenfeld & Wilson, 1999). An organization's new business model must consider these assets, both tangible and intangible, for value creation. They should not consider employees as expenses and customers as targets but both should be treated as partners. The organization can expand into new product or service markets, and change or develop new products to achieve value-creating synergies (Boulton et al., 2000).

CONCLUSION

The competitive environment is becoming increasingly more challenging, while at the same time, the complexity of doing business continues to increase at a parallel pace. The turbulence that has resulted from all this has forced organizations to become more fluid and agile than ever before. Unfortunately, traditional change approaches are incapable of accommodating all of these dimensions (Arena, 2002). As companies race to transform their businesses into e-businesses, they are discovering that the transformation process is not always straightforward. An e-business connects critical business systems directly to customers, employees, suppliers, and distributors via the web to improve time to market, access a broader base of customers and suppliers, improve efficiency, and reduce costs. To achieve these benefits, existing businesses must transform their traditional business processes with e-business applications. The proposed framework will support increasingly sophisticated e-business applications. A change management framework described in this chapter should assist in the management of change for e-business transformation. The framework is an objective framework that demonstrates how change management can be managed for successful e-business transformation. The goal of the framework is to help and enable businesses to quickly and easily build and deploy robust, secure, scalable, manageable, interoperable, and portable e-business applications. The proposed framework should bring the requisite people, methodologies, and solutions to make e-business initiatives successful. The framework should help to bring "seamless" integration and implementation of e-business solutions.

REFERENCES

Arena, M .J. (2002). Changing the way we change. *Organization Development Journal*, 20 (2), 33–47.

Bott, K., & Hill, J. (1994). Change agents lead the way. *Personnel Management,* 26(8), 24–27.

Boulton, R. E. S., Libert, B. D., & Samek, S. M. (2000). A business model for the new economy. *The Journal of Business Strategy,* 21(4), 29–35.

Bridges, W. (1991). Managing transitions—Making the most of change. *Addison-Wesley Publishing Company Inc*, Massachusetts, 2–35.

Broussine, M., Gray, M., Kirk, P, Paumier, K., Tichelar, M., & Young, S. (1998). The best and worst time for management development. *Journal of Management Development*, 17(1), 56–67.

Bryson, J., & Anderson, S. (2000). Applying large-group interaction methods in the planning and implementation of major change efforts. *Public Administration Review*, 60(2), 143–163.

Buchanan, D., & Badham, R. (1999). *Power, politics and organizational change: Winning the turf game.* London: Sage Publications.

Budhwani, K. (2001). Becoming part of the e-generation. *CMA Management*, 75(4), 24–27.

Carnell, C. (1995). *Managing Change in Organizations.* Prentice Hall International Ltd: UK.

Carney, M. (2001). The development of a model to manage change: Reflection on a critical incident in a focus group setting. An innovative approach. *Journal of Nursing Management*, 8(5), 265–273.

Clarke, A., & Garside, J. (1997). The development of a best practice model for change management. *European Management Journal, 15*(5), 537–545.

Damanpour, F. (1987). The adoption of technological, administrative and ancillary innovations: Impact of organizational factors. *Journal of Management, 13*, 675–688.

Davidson, W. (1999). Beyond re-engineering: the three phases of business transformation. *IBM Systems Journal, 38*(2/3), 485–499.

Doyle, M. (2002). Selecting managers for transformational change. *Human Resource Management Journal, 12*(1), 3–16.

Fahey, L., Srivastava, R., Sharon, J. S., & Smith, D. E. (2001). Linking e-business and operating processes: the role of knowledge management. *IBM Systems Journal, 40*(4), 889–908.

Ginige, A. Murugesan, & Kazanis, P. (2001). A road map for successfully transforming SMEs into e-business. *Cutter IT Journal, 14*(5), 39–51.

Hambrick, D., Nadler, D., & Tushman, M. (1998). *Navigating change: How CEOs, top teams and boards steer transformation.* Boston, MA: Harvard Business School Press.

Hartley, J., Benington, J., & Binns, P. (1997). Researching the role of internal change agents in the management of change. *British Journal of Management, 8*(1), 61–73.

Lee, S. (2001). Change management at the desktop. *InfoWorld,* 23(30), 35.

Levasseur, R. E. (2001). People skills: Change management tools – Lewin's change model. *Interfaces, 31*(4), 71–73.

Liebmann, L. (2001). Change management gets critical. *Communications News, 38*(10), 76.

McCrimmon, M. (1997). *The change masters: Managing and adapting to organizational change.* London: Institute of Management/Pitman Publishing.

McGarvey, R. (2001). New corporate ethics for the new economy. *World Trade,* 14(3), 43.

Michael, J. A. (2002). Changing the way we change. *Organization Development Journal, 20*(2), 33–47.

Paton, R., & McCalman, J. (2000). *Change management: a guide to effective implementation* (2nd Ed.). London: Paul Chapman Publishing.

Rosenfeld, R., & Wilson, D. (1999). *Managing organizations: Texts, readings and cases* (2nd Ed.). London: McGraw-Hill.

Schuh, G., Mueller, M., & Tockenbuerger, L. W. (2002). Successful change management from strategy to transformation: Results of an EC project. *International Journal of Manufacturing Technology and Management, 4*(1, 2), 90–95.

Sharma, P. (2000). E-transformation basics: Key to the new economy. *Strategy & Leadership, 28*(4), 27–31.

Sharma, S. K., & Gupta, J. N. D. (2001). E-commerce opportunities and challenges. In Singh, M., & Teo, T. (Eds.), *E-commerce diffusion: Strategies and challenges* (pp. 21–42). Heidelberg Press.

Sharma, S. K., & Gupta, J. N. D. (2003). Creating business value through e-commerce, edited by *Namchul Shin, Idea Group Publishing,* pp. 166–186.

Sharpe, J. (1989). *Building and communicating the executive vision, IBM Australia.* Working paper 89-001, Melbourne.

Stewart, T. A. (2000). Three rules for managing in the real-time economy. *Fortune,* 141(9), 332–334.

Stuart, R. (1995). Experiencing organizational change: Triggers, processes and outcomes of change journeys. *Personnel Review, 24*(2), 5–53.

Swanson, S. (2001). More than technology: User attitudes make a difference. *Informationweek, 826,* p.48.

Thornhill, A., Lewis, P., Millmore, M., & Saunders, M. (2000). *Managing change: a human resource strategy approach.* London: Financial Times/Prentice-Hall.

Wargin, J., & Dobiey, D. (2001). E-business and change: Managing the change in the digital economy. *Journal of Change Management, 2*(1), 72–82.

Wilder, C. (1999). E-transformation. *Information week, 752,* pp. 44–62.

Chapter V

Resistance: A Medium for the Successful Implementation of Technological Innovation

Dianne Waddell
Edith Cowan University, Australia

ABSTRACT

Resistance to change has long been recognised as a critically important factor that can influence the success or otherwise of implementing any technological innovation. Information technology (IT) focused interventions, for example, business process re-engineering (BPR) and enterprise resource planning (ERP), are often quoted as examples of costly failures, with reported levels of dissatisfaction with strategic IT investments ranging from 20-70 percent and that employee resistance was to blame. The intention of this chapter is to rethink resistance. The author suggests that resistance remains to this day a complex, multi-faceted phenomenon that continues to affect the outcomes of change, both negatively and positively. Although research has procured a solid understanding of resistance and the benefits that can accrue to an organisation through its proper utilisation, it appears that the classical adversarial approach remains the dominant means of managing resistance because such learning is not reflected in modern management techniques. The author concludes that as companies in every industry are now translating the power and possibilities of e-business into strategic and operational realities, new approaches in change management are required to help organisations to understand the complex dynamics of technological innovation and especially the multifaceted nature of resistance.

INTRODUCTION

While the explosion of Internet-centered business has produced an unrelenting focus on e-commerce strategies, new business models, and processes, surprisingly little attention has been paid to how e-business is changing the competencies needed to manage effectively in this new business environment (Harris, DeLong, & Donnellon, 2001).

Resistance to change has long been recognised as a critically important factor that can influence the success or otherwise of implementing any technological innovation. Research undertaken by Maurer (1996) indicated that one-half to two-thirds of all major corporate change efforts fail and resistance is the "little-recognised but critically important contributor" to that failure (p. 56). The 1990s witnessed the failure of many planned change interventions to achieve their original objectives or realise significant 'hard' or 'soft' business benefits.

Gardner and Ash (2003) argue that the relatively low level of organisational benefits realized by strategic Information Technology over the past decades is often a product of poor adoption and implementation practices on the part of senior managers and IT practitioners, who have failed to understand the complex and sensitive nature of change in complex organisations. Scott's study (2002) on insurance companies in particular discovered that they spent hundreds of millions of dollars on the software and hardware of Information Technologies to effect cost controls and operating efficiencies, gain market share, and improve customer service, yet many complain that not enough of these investments show up as return of investment (ROI). Whereas research undertaken by Parker (2002) identifies disappointment with current e-procurement technology, and resistance to change, which are hindering e-business take-up in the manufacturing sector in the UK. Manufacturers have attributed low customers demand, a "wait and see" attitude among management and the desire to wait for improved technology as the main impediments.

Information Technology (IT) focused interventions, for example, business process re-engineering (BPR) and enterprise resource planning (ERP), are often quoted as examples of costly failures, with reported levels of dissatisfaction with strategic IT investments ranging from 20-70 percent, and employee resistance reportedly was to blame (Gardner & Ash, 2003; Marjanovic, 2000; Wells, 2000).

Not that resistance is solely to blame for these statistics. Kotter, Schlesinger and Sathe (1986) comment that there is a tendency amongst managers to approach change with a simple set of beliefs that end up exacerbating the problems that arise because they fail to understand them in any systematic manner. One such "simple belief" is that a change process that occurs with only minimal resistance must have been a good change that was managed well. This assumption is somewhat naïve and belies a common perspective that casts resistance in a negative light. Resistance is often viewed by managers as the enemy of change, the foe which must be overcome if a change effort is to be successful (Schein, 1988, p. 243).

However, careful examination of the literature surrounding resistance indicates that this adversarial approach has little theoretical support. Rather, a great deal of work undertaken during the 1990s found that there is in fact utility to be gained from resistance, and therefore it should not be avoided or quashed as suggested by classical management theory.

The comments presented in this chapter find that this notion of utility in resistance has been largely disregarded by present day prescriptions for the management of technology, and perhaps this is contributing to the lack of success organisations have in securing a successful transition.

DEFINITIONS OF RESISTANCE

Schein (1988) believes resistance to change to be one of the most ubiquitous of organisational phenomena. A number of authors have defined resistance. For example, Ansoff (1988, p. 207) defines resistance as a multifaceted phenomenon, which introduces unanticipated delays, costs and instabilities into the process of a strategic change, whilst Zaltman and Duncan (1977, p. 63) define resistance as any conduct that serves to maintain the status quo in the face of pressure to alter the status quo.

In Henry's article (1994, p. 21) on computer-based technology (CBT) he accepted the consensus that resistance is behaviour on the part of the end-user intended to prevent or circumvent the use of CBT or to prevent CBT designers (analysts) from performing their job. He further comments that past research on factors thought to cause resistance has focused on general factors such as innate resistance to change, lack of involvement in the implementation process, lack of management support, poor technical quality which makes the system appear 'unfriendly', and the interaction of the designers and users.

Thus, resistance, in an organisational setting, is an expression of reservation which normally arises as a response or reaction to change (Block, 1989, p. 199). This expression is normally witnessed by management as any employee actions perceived as attempting to stop, delay, or alter change (Bemmels & Reshef, 1991, p. 231). Thus resistance is most commonly linked with negative employee attitudes or with counter-productive behaviours.

UNDERSTANDING
RESISTANCE OVER TIME

The writers of classical organisation theory viewed conflict as undesirable, detrimental to the organisation. Ideally it should not exist. Their prescription was simple: Eliminate it (Rowe & Boise, 1973, p. 151).

Resistance has been classically understood as a foundation cause of conflict that is undesirable and detrimental to organisational health. During the 1940s theorists considered unity of purpose to be the hallmark of a technically efficient and superior organisation, whilst considering pluralism and divergent attitudes as greatly reducing the organisation's effectiveness and impeding its performance. Resistance was therefore understood as the emergence of divergent opinions that detract from the proficiency of the organisation and the resistant worker was painted as a subversive whose individual self-interest clashed with the general interest and well-being of the organisation. Resistance quickly became understood as the enemy of change, the foe which causes a change effort to be drawn out by factional dissent and in-fighting. The prescription of this viewpoint was to eliminate resistance, quash it early and sweep it aside in order to make way for the coming change (Rowe & Boise, 1973, p. 151).

Early human resource theory also cast resistance in a negative light by perceiving it as a form of conflict that was indicative of a breakdown in the normal and healthy interactions that can exist between individuals and groups.

Once again, the prescription was to avoid resistance in order to restore harmony to the organisation (Milton et al., 1984, p. 480).

In the years that followed, the conception of resistance to change benefited greatly from the application of psychological, sociological and anthropological disciplines to the study of management. As the understanding of resistance became increasingly sophisticated, it became clear that resistance is a far more complex phenomenon than once thought. Rather than being simply driven by the parochial self-interest of individual employees, this research concluded that resistance was a function of a variety of social factors, including:

- Rational factors: resistance can occur where the employees' own rational assessment of the outcomes of the proposed change differ from the outcomes envisaged by management. Such differences of opinion cast doubt in the employees' mind as to the merit or worth of the changes, and thus they may choose to stand in opposition or voice concern (Ansoff, 1988, p. 211; Kotter et al., 1986, p. 352).

- Non-rational factors: the reaction of an individual worker to a proposed change is also a function of predispositions and preferences which are not necessarily based on an economic-rational assessment of the change. These may include instances of resistance workers who simply do not wish to move offices, prefer working near a particular friend, or are uncertain of the outcomes of implementing new technology (Judson, 1966, p. 19; McNurry, 1973, p. 381).

- Political factors: resistance is also influenced by political factors such as favouritism or "point scoring" against those initiating the change effort (Ansoff, 1988, p. 212).

- Management factors: inappropriate or poor management styles also contribute to resistance (Judson, 1966, p. 32).

As organisational theory developed over time, it drew attention to the fact that resistance to change is also built into organisational factors. Systems, processes, sunk costs and so on all contribute to a kind of inertia that influences an organisation toward greater reliability and predictability which, in turn, acts against change (White & Bednar, 1991, p. 509). Planned change in its various forms had a fairly poor track record throughout the 1990s, with TQM, BPR and IT failures incurring massive financial and human resource deployment costs, with limited returns to the client organisation (Gardner & Ash, 2003).

Henry's research on CBT indicated that many professionals believe that end-users tend to blame specific features of the training program for problems they incur. He explains that this is more because of the difficulties that end-users encounter and this results in resistance to learning and adaptation - such "early perceptions of failure are extremely difficult to reverse" (Henry, 1994, p. 22). This is reinforced by the belief that a substantial number of people are "computer-anxious or have a 'negative attitude' towards computers" (p. 22). This perception is extrapolated to suggest that end-users are generally resistant to innovations or changes.

As a result of all of this research, resistance to change became recognised for what it truly is: a complex, multi-faceted phenomenon that is caused by a variety of factors. Furthermore, a consensus of opinion began to form that, contrary to classical theory, resistance (and the conflict that it can cause) may not be an enemy of change. Rather, there is a strong case that suggests that resistance should not be approached adversarially because it can play a useful role in the implementation of technology innovation.

THE UTILITY OF RESISTANCE

Industrial progress finds one of its greatest handicaps in the frequent resistance of both management and workers to change of any sort (McNurry, 1973, p. 380).

Hultman (1979, p. 54) writes, "Unfortunately, when the word resistance is mentioned, we tend to ascribe negative connotations to it. This is a misconception. There are many times when resistance is the most effective response available." Leigh (1988, p. 73) also writes that "resistance is a perfectly legitimate response of a worker" and Zaltman and Duncan (1977, p. 62) cite Rubin saying that resistance should be used constructively.

That resistance can play a useful role in technology innovation efforts certainly stands juxtaposed to a traditional mindset that would view it as an obstacle that is normally encountered on the way to a successful e-strategy. Nevertheless, it is a conclusion reached by a variety of authors who suggest that there are a number of advantages of resistance. When managed carefully, these advantages can in fact be utilised by the organisation to greatly assist in gaining a competitive advantage.

First of all, resistance points out that it is a fallacy to consider change itself to be inherently good. Change can only be evaluated by its consequences, and these cannot be known with any certainty until the change effort has been completed and sufficient time has passed (Hultman, 1979, p. 53).

To this end, resistance plays a crucial role in influencing the organisation toward greater stability, particularly in a time of environment uncertainty. While pressure from external and internal environments continues to encourage change, resistance is a factor that can balance these demands against the need for constancy and stability. Human systems remaining in a steady state encourage processes and specialisations to stabilise, consolidate, and improve, which allows the organisation a level of predictability and control. Thus, the system is able to gain a certain momentum or rhythm that is also critical for organisational survival (Hultman, 1979, p. 53). While these maintenance needs are widely recognised, the emphasis in the literature certainly remains on the requirements of change and dynamism. The challenge therefore is to find the right balance between change and stability; avoiding the dysfunctionality of too much change while ensuring stability does not become stagnation.

As our understanding of resistance has become increasingly clear, it has also become apparent that people do not resist change per se; rather they resist the uncertainties and potential outcomes that technology can cause.

Resistance to a change is not the fundamental problem to be solved. Rather, any resistance is usually a symptom of more basic problems underlying the particular situation. Resistance can therefore serve as a warning signal directing the timing of technological innovation (Judson, 1966, p. 69).

As such, resistance plays a crucial role in drawing attention to aspects of change that may be inappropriate, not well thought through, or perhaps plain wrong. Either way, it is the organisation's method of communication; therefore attempting to eliminate resistance as soon as it arises is akin to shooting the messenger who delivers bad news. Specifically, IT managers can use the nature of the resistance as an indicator of the cause of resistance. It will be most helpful as a symptom if IT managers diagnose the causes for it when it occurs rather than inhibiting it at once (Bartlett & Kayser, 1972, p. 407).

A further advantage that resistance contributes to the change process is an influx of energy. Psychologists have long understood the danger of apathy or acquiescence when there is a need for growth and development. We are all familiar with the classic adage 'you can not help the person who will not first help themselves'; rather, the individual requires a certain dissatisfaction with his or her current or future states in order to gain sufficient motivation to do something about it. In the same way, there is a certain level of motivation or energy required to adapt innovation in an organisation.

Where a workplace is marked by apathy or passivity, implementing change is a very difficult task (Litterer, 1973, p. 152). With resistance and conflict comes the energy or motivation to seriously address the problem at hand. Where energy is lacking, change is often uncreative, sparsely implemented, and inadequately utilised. Where resistance is at play, there is a need to examine more closely the problems that exist and consider more deeply the innovations proposed. Once again, though, a balance must be maintained. Where conflict becomes too great, it may assume the focus of the energy, causing the issues created to recede into the background. Consequently, authors speak of an "optimal level of motivation" (Thomas & Bennis, 1972, p. 383) that will serve the change process and possibly improve its outcome.

In addition to injecting energy into a change process, resistance also encourages the search for alternative methods and outcomes in order to synthesise the conflicting opinions that may exist. Thus resistance becomes a critical source of innovation in a technology imlementation as more possibilities are considered and evaluated.

Often a particular solution is known to be favoured by management and consequently does not benefit from a thorough discussion. Under such circumstances, acceptance is built in, and the organisation's growth and change is limited to the diagnostic and prescriptive capabilities of those who proposed the innovation.

This aspect of resistance cannot be understated in its importance. Herbert Simon's (1976) work into the rational decision, for example, drew attention to the fact that many management decisions are non-rational because they simply do not generate a sufficient number of alternative solutions to a problem, nor are these alternatives adequately evaluated. Furthermore, Janis's (1982) notion of group-think highlights the danger of conformity in group decision making and the importance of vigorous debate; thus resistance similarly plays a crucial role. As Maurer points out: "Resistance is what keeps us from attaching ourselves to every boneheaded idea that comes along" (Maurer, 1996).

In combination, these aspects of resistance make a persuasive case for re-evaluating the classical understanding of resistance. Equally, they call into question the assumption that a change effort that is met with little resistance should be automatically deemed a "good" change. The legislative process, for example, is predicated upon resistance playing a crucial role in ensuring the best possible laws are produced. Resistance, in the form of rivalry between (at least) two parties, injects energy into the process and sparks debate where opinions differ. Resistance encourages greater scrutiny of legislation. It prompts the search for a variety of alternatives and evaluates these with greater rigour. It also means that the implementation process will be considered carefully, thereby improving the adoption of these changes by the general public.

Imagine then, a situation where new legislation that considerably alters an established law is enacted by parliament via a process that is marked by little resistance. It would certainly raise concerns that the new law has not been adequately scrutinised, nor had the benefit of vigorous debate. If the process of implementation is not well thought out, it may only be sparsely adopted by the general public, rendering the law ineffective.

THE MANAGEMENT OF RESISTANCE

The suggestions and prescriptions of correct resistance management contain a curious dualism; while they appear to embrace much of the understanding of resistance gained from the 1990s they simultaneously ignore the suggestion that, in certain instances, there is utility to be gained. There is a need for shared understanding of the role of technology, especially innovative technology, within the change management and strategic development process as this will be a unifying theme (Garner & Ash, 2003).

Scott (2002) refers to an e-culture, a culture that enables and propels the organisation's e-business strategy and goals. In the past organisations have proceeded directly to operational issues affecting the bottom line. But Scott (2002) suggests that this is where problems have occurred because of the lack of consideration of the human factor. By not addressing the basic concerns of the people who will be using those systems, organisations create the potential for self-defeating, project-prolonging change resistance.

The technological turbulence that is transforming business can only increase employee resistance, and e-managing requires a whole new set of competencies with the effect of rendering traditionally competent managers ineffective (Harris et al., 2001). The demand for technological innovation that drives e-business also creates an overpowering sense of urgency. This not only requires organisations to sustain the intense pace but also creates a work environment where employees are energized and valued.

The overwhelming suggestion in the management literature is that participative techniques are the best method of handling resistance. Employee participation in management as a means of resolving resistance has been investigated since the mid-1940s. The now classic studies by Lewin (1991) concluded that involvement in the learning, planning and implementation stages of a change process significantly influences commitment to change and apparently lowers resistance. This theme has been taken up widely in management literature and forms the backbone of significant management schools of thought, such as organisation development theory and human resource management (Milton et al., 1984, pp. 481-482).

Essentially, the argument behind participative management techniques is that, through a carefully managed process of two-way communication, information sharing and consultation, employees tend to become more committed to the technological innovative effort, rather than simply remaining compliant with it (Kotter et al., 1986; White & Bednar, 1991; Burn & Robins, 2002; Kuruppuarachchi, Mandal & Smith, 2002). Henry's (1994) simple solution to resistance is to determine the actual cause and adapt the training or job at hand. This then identifies specific features of the program associated with an end-user's resistance and assesses whether or not they are appropriate. It also facilitates a process of re-examination of new and existing procedures. This then has two benefits: it provides a method of evaluating existing and planned programs; and, it demands collaborative interaction between end-users and designer.

Without entering the debate with regard to the pros and cons of participative management styles, it is apparent that such techniques are strongly advocated where resistance is expected to be high; the goal being to simply reduce the level of resistance actually encountered. The latent assumption apparently is that the less resistance encountered by a change effort, the better. Very rarely is it suggested that resistance should be utilised.

It appears, then, that the learning of the 1990s has been ignored in the narrowly focused race to be innovative. There is a notable absence of change management models and theories that actually incorporate the possibility of utility in resistance. While it is commonly suggested that managers prepare for the implementation of technology process by estimating the degree of resistance they expect to encounter, rarely is it suggested that the nature of this resistance be diagnosed to see if there is any benefit to be gained from its utilisation.

The fact that management theory has apparently not embraced the notion of utility in resistance suggests that an adversarial approach to resistance, reminiscent of that found in classical management theory, is still the prevalent mindset of managers. Resistance continues to be viewed as the enemy of innovation that must be "overcome" and participative techniques are the techniques advocated to achieve this end.

Research conducted by Maurer (1996) supports this point. He found that the predominant way implementors of change responded to employees' reactions was to resist their resistance—that is, meet force with force. Most often this occurred through the force of reason. Information "sharing" often amounted to little more than information "battering" where the recipients of change are confronted with a barrage of slide shows, data analysis and hefty reports. Though these techniques may be categorised as participative in form, they are far from participative in nature. They amount to little more than an exercise in salesmanship and clearly illustrate an adversarial management mindset.

As Harris et al. (2001) comment, intense information overload and the revolution of e-business at e-speed require that effective managers stay focused on their strategic objectives and help their employees do the same. Unless e-managers develop techniques to handle the load, there is tremendous potential for distraction.

CONCLUSION:
RETHINKING RESISTANCE

The intention of this chapter is not to provide neat answers to the complicated problems associated with resistance. Rather, it is to point out that, although the theoretical understanding of resistance is well advanced, it is apparent that this knowledge has not impacted common perceptions of management and therefore has not transferred into the development of solid resistance management technique when implementing innovation.

The chapter has found that resistance remains to this day a complex, multi-faceted phenomenon that continues to affect the outcomes of change, both negatively and positively. Although research has procured a solid understanding of resistance and the benefits that can accrue to an organisation through its proper utilisation, it appears that the classical adversarial approach remains the dominant means of managing resistance because such learning is not reflected in modern management techniques.

It would be drawing a long bow to say that the answer to the problem of resistance management is to simply begin to employ techniques that hold the possibility of utility in resistance. This is not the conclusion of this chapter. Rather it is to point out that modern management has only applied certain aspects of earlier research (for example using participative techniques) while apparently ignoring others. The suggestion is that resistance management may improve significantly if the adversarial approach is replaced with one that retains the possibility of benefiting through the utilisation of resistance.

As has already been mentioned before, people do not resist change per se; rather, they resist the uncertainties and the potential outcomes that change can cause. Managers must keep this in mind at all times. Resistance can play a crucial role in drawing everyone's attention to aspects of change that may be inappropriate, not well thought through or perhaps plain wrong. In this case managers should be encouraged to search for alternative methods of introducing the innovation. They must communicate and consult regularly with their employees. This is perhaps one of the most critical success factors in implementing technology in an organisation. Employees must be given the opportunity to be involved in all aspects of the change project and they must be given the opportunity to provide feedback. Teamwork involving management and employees can overcome many of the difficulties experienced by organisations in the past. Managers should facilitate teamwork, they should empower their workers to be involved and they should provide the right environment and the necessary resources for employees to take part.

As companies in every industry are now translating the power and possibilities of e-business into strategic and operational realities, new approaches in change management are required to help organisations to understand the complex dynamics of technological innovation and especially the multifaceted nature of resistance.

REFERENCES

Ansoff, I. (1988). *The new corporate strategy*. New York: John Wiley & Sons.

Bartlett, A., & Kayser, T. (1973). *Changing organisational behaviour*. Englewood Cliffs, NJ: Prentice Hall.

Bemmels, B., & Reshef, Y. (1991). Manufacturing employees and technological change. *Journal of Labour Research, 12*(3), 231–246.

Block, P. (1989). Flawless consulting. In McLennan, R. (Ed.), *Managing organisational change.* Englewood Cliffs, NJ: Prentice Hall.

Burn, J., & Robins, G. (2003). Moving towards e-government: a case study of organizational change processes. *Logistics Information Management, 16*(1), MCB University Press.

Gardner, S., & Ash, C. (2003). ICT-enabled organizations: a model for change management. *Logistics Information Management, 16*(1), 18–24.

Harris, J., DeLong, D., & Donnellon, A. (2001). Do you have what it takes to be an e-manager? *Strategy & Leadership, 29*(4). MCB University Press.

Henry, J. (1994). Resistance to computer-based technology in the workplace. *Executive Development, 7*(1). MCB University Press.

Hultman, K. (1979). *The path of least resistance*. Denton, TX: Learning Concepts.

Janis, I. (1982). *Groupthink: Psychological studies of policy decisions and fiascos* (2nd ed.). Boston, MA: Houghton Mifflin.

Judson, A. (1966). *A managers guide to making changes*. London: John Wiley & Sons.

Kotter, J., Schlesinger, L., & Sathe, V. (1986). *Organisation* (2nd ed.). Homewood, IL: Irwin.

Kuruppuarachchi, P., Mandal, P., & Smith, R. (2002). IT project implementation strategies for effective changes: a critical review. *Logistics Information Management, 15*(2). MCB University Press.

Leigh, A. (1988). *Effective change*. London: Institute of Personnel Management.

Lewin, K., White, D., & Bednard, D. (1991). *Organisational behaviour*. Boston, MA: Allyn & Bacon, p. 510.

Litterer, J. (1973). Conflict in organisation: a re-examination. In Rowe, L., & Boise, B. (Eds.), *Organisational & managerial innovation*. Santa Monica, CA: Goodyear.

Marjanovic, O. (2000). Supporting the 'soft' side of business process reengineering. *Journal of Business Process Management, 6*(1). MCB University Press.

Maurer, R. (1996). Using resistance to build support for change. *Journal for Quality & Participation*, 56-63.

McNurry, R. (1973). The problem of resistance to change in industry. In Bartlett, A., & Kayser, T. (Eds.), *Changing organisational behaviour*. Englewood Cliffs, NJ: Prentice Hall.

Milton, C., Entrekin, L., & Stening, B. (1984). *Organisational behaviour in Australia*. Sydney: Prentice Hall.

Parker, R. (2002). *Manufacturer shun e-procurement*. London: Supply Management.

Rowe, L., & Boise, B. (1973). *Organisational & managerial innovation*. Santa Monica, CA: Goodyear.

Schein, E. (1988). *Organisational psychology* (3rd ed.). Englewood Cliffs, NJ: Prentice Hall.

Scott, S. (2002). E-business transformation in insurance companies: Three critical needs. *LIMRA's MarketFacts Quarterly*, Spring, Hartford.

Simon, H. (1976). *Administrative behaviour*. New York: The Free Press.

Thomas, J., & Bennis, W. (1972). *The management of change and conflict*. Harmondsworth, UK: Penguin.

Wells, M. (2000). Business process reengineering implementations using Internet technology. *Journal of Business Process Management, 6*(2), MCB University Press.

White, D., & Bednar, D. (1991). *Organisational behaviour*. Boston, MA: Allyn & Bacon.

Zaltman, G., & Duncan, R. (1977). *Strategies for planned change*. Toronto: John Wiley & Sons.

Chapter VI

Building Effective Online Relationships

Byron Keating
University of Newcastle, Australia

Robert Rugimbana
University of Newcastle, Australia

Ali Quazi
University of Newcastle, Australia

ABSTRACT

The application of relationship management strategies to the online environment has been met with great enthusiasm. However, research indicates that many of the traditional drivers of effective relationships may need to be re-interpreted when applied in Cyberspace. This chapter proposes an enhanced model for the management of customer relationships (CRM) in an online context. It builds on the traditional strengths of CRM, namely processual efficiency and profitability, to ensure that a greater emphasis is given to the interpersonal nature of relationship development.

INTRODUCTION

To succeed in business, it is imperative that firms identify the threats and opportunities that exist, and meet these with appropriate competitive methods (Olsen, 1996). Daly (2001) asserts that in the online arena to date, competitive advantage has been derived mainly through aggressive customer acquisition strategies with little attention placed on building long and loyal customer relationships. Mackey (2001) adds that "an appreciation of customer loyalty will represent the next frontier in e-business" (p. 1). The impact of this new outlook will present new challenges for managers, as they manage the emerging technologies to draw closer to their customers. Successful firms will be those that can identify what drives their customers to value their service, and ultimately, to become loyal in the face of growing competition.

However, knowing what needs to be done and knowing how best to go about achieving it are very different things. Recent research has revealed that online loyalty is very low. A study by Digital Idea (Mackey, 2001) indicated that less than 15% of online consumers exhibit any real commitment to a nominated e-business. Another study by Georgidis, Singer, Harding and Lane (2000) has also found that while firms are managing to attract eyeballs and turn the occasional online transaction, they have a hard time getting people to come back. They add that this situation is further complicated by the finding that most firms spend more on customer acquisition than they are likely to make in profit during the buying life of a typical customer.

De Kare-Silver (2000) states that achieving loyalty gains is hard, and requires extraordinary effort, motivation and commitment. He adds that in order to develop lasting and satisfying customer relationships, e-businesses need to develop a better understanding of what drives customer loyalty. Payne (1995) argues that most firms do not realize that customer retention and customer loyalty are not the same. He asserts that being able to achieve and measure customer retention is only the first step in the loyalty creation process.

This situation is further complicated by the increased interest in the use of customer relationship management (CRM) tools that use sophisticated profiling as a means of identifying the characteristics of profitable customers, while seemingly ignoring the attitudinal factors that impact so heavily on the creation of customer loyalty. Wong and Sohal (2001) contend that while loyalty is the product of effective relationship marketing, it is *only* achieved when customers purchase repeatedly and hold a favourable attitude towards the exchange. It is this recognition of the importance of the interpersonal nature of relationships that will enable practitioners to achieve the espoused benefits of a CRM investment—loyal and profitable customers (Keating, Rugimbana, & Quazi, 2003).

Therefore, given the importance of achieving customer loyalty in Cyberspace and the need to understand how it can be improved, this chapter will endeavour to clarify the role of CRM in the development of effective online relationships. In particular, the chapter will discuss the benefits and limitations of traditional CRM, before moving onto a detailed discussion of the importance of relationship marketing in the development of an effective CRM strategy. By focusing on relationship marketing, practitioners and academics alike can identify those factors that contribute to the strength and longevity of a relationship, as well as the drivers of profitable relationships. The chapter will posit a conceptual model that will attempt to identify the key drivers of relationship marketing success, and its impact on attitudinal and behavioural loyalty.

LITERATURE REVIEW

Traditional CRM Perspective

With its origins in sales management systems, customer relationship management (CRM) has been espoused as the means of creating loyal and profitable customer relationships (Wyner, 1999). In particular, Gray and Byun (2001) state that the potential benefits of adopting CRM can be an improved ability to retain and acquire customers; a greater share of the customers' lifetime consumption value; and greater service quality without commensurate cost increases.

Peppers, Rogers and Dorf (1999) assert that there are four underlying principles to effective customer relationship management. First, firms must be able to identify customers individually and capture information on their consumption behaviours. Second, firms must be able to differentiate between good and bad customers on the basis of predictors such as lifetime customer value. They must then use the data that they capture on customers to identify the most attractive segments, and focus only on those customer segments that are able to deliver the greatest financial return. Third, firms must interact with customers. They need to establish a dialogue with their customers to ensure that they are kept abreast of changes in their preferences, using the information acquired to strengthen and increase customer loyalty. Lastly, firms must customize and cater service delivery to meet the customers' personal preferences.

Figure 1: Process for effective CRM (Adapted from Winer, 1999)

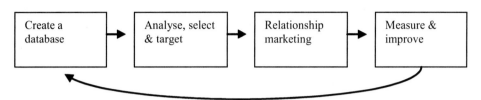

Winer (2001) suggested a simple 7-step process that firms could use to develop an effective CRM approach: 1) create a database of customer activity; 2) analyse this data; 3) based on the analysis, decide which customers to target; 4) acquire the tools for targeting; 5) use relationship marketing to build relationships with targeted customers; 6) provide protection and security for customer information; and 7) measure the outcomes of the CRM program. The essence of this process has been summarized in Figure 1.

From the figure above, it can be seen that CRM is essentially a quality-based process that is premised on using accurate information to facilitate effective interactions, and then using the feedback from these interactions to improve the quality of the information and facilitate better interactions, and so forth.

Assumptions and Limitations of CRM

Related to the application of CRM are a number of basic assumptions. These are presented below with their associated limitations.

1. *Habitual action*: a basic tenet of CRM is that the future behaviour of a customer can, at least in part, be determined by his or her past behaviours. The caveat of this assumption is that even though some behaviours exhibit robustness in the short term, they tend to change in the medium to long term. Furthermore, by focusing only on behavioural characteristics, firms are ignoring the attitudinal factors that have contributed to a customer's purchasing profile. Christian Gronröös, in a recent interview, asserted that most firms often adopt a myopic approach to CRM (Powell, 2001). He adds that by focusing energy on pleasing only their existing most profitable customers, firms run the risk of offending the next generation of future profitable customers.

2. *Accurate information*: conventional CRM relies on the accumulation of accurate data. The complexity of bringing together information from such

a wide variety of sources, and the challenge of ensuring that data is free from errors requires a significant ongoing commitment of financial and human resources. Gray and Byun (2001) suggest that information redundancy is one of the greatest single inhibitors to the success of CRM, and that while it can be minimized, it cannot be eradicated – people move, change jobs, marry, divorce and die.

3.   *Personalization preference*: the idea that customers prefer differentiated treatment, services and products lies at the very heart of CRM. However, *true* customization may not always be achievable or desirable. For instance, the cost of customizing some products may be prohibitively high. Likewise, the issue of customization runs counter to the notion of trends and fashion, where collectivism is preferable to individualism. Peppers et al. (1999) suggest that delivering the right product for the right occasion is the optimum example of personalization.

4.   *Customer trust*: there is an underlying assumption in CRM that customers are comfortable with the accumulation of detailed and sometimes sensitive information, and that they trust firms to act in a responsible and ethical manner. Winer (2001) suggests that many organisations seem unaware that CRM carries a level of implied customer trust. He adds that a failure by firms to recognize this ethical requirement has necessitated greater regulatory intervention by government.

5.   *Repeat visitation*: one of the key misgivings of the CRM approach to management is that it confuses repeat visitation with customer loyalty. While it is true that repeat visitation is an espoused outcome of loyalty, the reverse is not necessarily the case. Research has confirmed that customers will tolerate poor service in the absence of an alternative, but conversely, will only resist competitive offerings where *true* loyalty exists (Dick & Basu, 1994).

ONLINE CRM SUCCESS STRATEGIES

Relationship Marketing

Berry (1983, p. 25) has been credited with providing the first workable definition of relationship marketing, stating that it is the practice of "attracting, maintaining, and enhancing customer relationships". In addition to defining the construct, Berry (1983) also conceptualized the conditions that were required to facilitate effective relationship marketing, stating that the exchange needed to have a degree of continuity of demand, that the customer had to have a choice, and that the customer needed to be in control of this choice.

The importance of relationship marketing is often underestimated in the management of customer relationships online. While the concepts of relationship management and relationship marketing are often interchanged, current management practices have tended to ignore the interpersonal aspect of the relationships. By focusing on the drivers of effective relationship marketing, practitioners and theorists can identify and harness those aspects of a relationship that impact most significantly on the development of loyalty.

Gronröös (1991, p. 8) extended this definition to include the requirement for "mutual exchange and fulfillment of promises", arguing that commitment from both the supplier and customer was required in order to develop long and profitable exchanges. Gronröös (1994) added that transactional and relational exchanges occupy alternate ends of a continuum, and that all relationships begin with a transactional exchange. This process of moving from transaction to profitable relationship has been examined by a number of academics (Rust, Zahorik, & Keiningham, 1995; Liljander & Strandvik, 1993; Storbacka, 1993), and is illustrated in the relationship profitability model shown in Figure 2 (Storbacka, Strandvik, & Gronröös, 1994).

The model holds that service quality at a transactional level will result in customer satisfaction, which if repeated regularly will lead to trust, commitment and relationship strength. Relationship strength will in turn result in a reduced consideration of alternatives and greater relationship longevity. The associated benefit of increased relationship strength is also posited as increased profitability, where the authors assert that the cost of attracting new customers is higher than that of keeping existing customers.

Figure 2: Relationship profitability model (Storbacka et al., 1994)

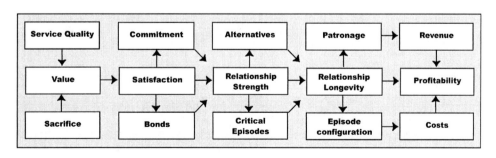

This view of a relationship developing over time through accumulated value from a number of discrete transactions is consistent with most definitions of relationship marketing (Wong & Sohal, 2001). It supports the idea that customer acquisition is only the first step in the relationship marketing process, where the ultimate aim of any exchange relationship is to move customers up the loyalty ladder from a prospective customer to a loyal partner (Payne, 1991). Given the scope of this chapter, this conceptualization of relationship marketing is particularly useful in that it highlights the importance of moving beyond CRM as a segmentation tool, and acknowledges the significance of measuring the interpersonal aspects of relationship management.

Service Quality

Gronröös (1984) was among the first academics to consider the issue of service quality, asserting that it resulted when a customer's service expectations were exceeded. Parasuraman, Zeithaml and Berry (1985) added that it is the outcome measure of effective service delivery, and is influenced by a number of factors, including: the degree of intangibility of a service; the heterogeneity of services; and the inseparability of service creation and consumption. First, most services are intangible and cannot be counted or measured in the same way as physical products. Second, while service delivery can adhere to a particular process or pattern, the outcome can vary significantly from producer to producer. Lastly, production and consumption of services are inseparable. In many cases, the consumer is actually part of the production process, and contributes to the quality of the service provision.

The work of Parasuraman, Zeithaml and Berry (1988) resulted in the development of the SERVQUAL instrument, a widely endorsed battery of questions that is used to assess service quality perceptions of consumers. It was the outcome of exploratory research involving executives and consumers from a variety of service industries, including retail banking, credit card, securities brokerage, and product repair and maintenance. It resulted in a measurement scale comprised of the dimensions of reliability, responsiveness, assurance, empathy and tangibility.

Berry and Parasuraman (1988) assert that the pursuit of service quality has become an effective competitive tool, and Zeithaml, Berry and Parasuraman (1996) add that it has the potential to lead to greater customer loyalty. However, Cronin and Taylor (1992) contend that the espoused benefits of adopting a service quality orientation has been hindered by the difficulty in measuring the construct. They cite the main challenge as the difficulty in quantifying expectations given the volatility and variability of attitudes. To resolve this quandary, they support a performance-only[1] measure of service quality (SERVPERF) over the computed-disconfirmation[2] model posited by Parasuraman et al. (1988).

The debate regarding the most appropriate measurement model dominated the services marketing literature during the 1990's (Cronin & Taylor, 1992, 1994; Parasuraman, Zeithaml, & Berry, 1994; Teas, 1993). More recently, the debate surfaced in the retail arena with evidence suggesting that the performance-only measurement model is superior to the disconfirmation model in the retail context (Dabholkar, Thorpe, & Rentz, 1996). However, irrespective of the preferred measurement model the outcome benefits of high service quality are not in dispute. They include: greater customer satisfaction; reduced customer defection; greater market share; and greater profitability (Zeithaml, 2000).

Relationship Quality

There has been considerable debate regarding what constitutes an effective relationship (Gale & Wood, 1994). Gummesson (1987) was one of the earliest to consider the issue of relationship quality, suggesting that it can be regarded as the quality of the interaction between a firm and its customers, and claiming that it could be interpreted in terms of accumulated value. This definition was to become a central theme in the Nordic School's work in relationship marketing, and has led to the fundamental hypothesis that repeated service quality at a transactional level will lead to increased satisfaction and value at a relational level.

Ravald and Gronröös (1996) add that the value experienced in relationships will also vary in nature, with the customers experiencing an episodal value at the early stages of a relationship and relational value as the duration increases. The different types of value are said to reflect how the customers' expectations change from a consideration of transactional factors such as product qualities and a comparison of alternatives to a greater emphasis on relational qualities such as security, trust and credibility. Gale and Wood (1994) also add that such a conceptualization of relationship quality will also consider intrinsically the impact of a customer's perceived sacrifice.

This idea of achieving an effective relationship by reducing or eliminating sacrifice is akin to Crosby, Evans and Cowles' (1990) seminal work on relationship quality in services selling. The authors held the view that relationship quality is achieved as a firm reduces the customers' perceived uncertainty, and that the construct was a higher order construct consisting of at least two dimensions—trust and satisfaction. Their work resulted in the development of a relationship quality model that confirmed the virtue of the trust and satisfaction as dimensions of relationship quality, and the link between a strong relationship and future purchase intentions.

However, while the work by Crosby et al. (1990) did much to establish the virtue of relationship quality as an indicator of long-term relationships, Mohr and Spekman (1994) argued that more work still needed to be done to understand the underlying characteristics of partnership success. Their study of business-to-business (B2B) manufacturer-distributor relationships revealed that the dimensions of commitment, coordination, communication, goal congruence and conflict resolution could also characterise relationship effectiveness. In contrast to earlier contributors, they also asserted that satisfaction was not an antecedent of relationship quality, but a consequence of an effective relationship.

Wilson and Jantrania (1996) saw relationship effectiveness in terms of a customer's commitment to a supplier, and asserted that strong commitment was positively associated to the degree of structural and social bonding. They interpreted structural bonding as the internal barriers that prevented customers from switching to a competitor's offering, and were based on endogenous variables such as technology; comparison to alternatives; adaptability of a firm; and the perceived importance of the partnership. Social bonding was derived from Crosby et al.'s dimensions of trust and satisfaction.

Another significant contribution in the defining of relationship quality was made by Storbacka et al. (1994). They provided an effective summary of the work of the earlier contributors when they proposed their relationship profitability model (see Figure 2). While their work was primarily conceptual, it did highlight some of the complexities encountered when considering the impact of relationship quality on the development of long-term relationships. It also introduced the idea that relationship quality was influenced by both transactional and relational variables.

Customer Loyalty

Pritchard, Havitz and Howard (1999) argue that understanding how or why a sense of loyalty develops in customers remains one of the most crucial management issues. Sharp, Rundle-Thiele and Dawes (1997) suggest that part of the difficulty with conceptualizing loyalty could be related to the many different definitions available for the construct. They add that loyalty has been defined as both an attitudinal construct and a behavioural construct.

However, Dick and Basu (1994) contended that the customer loyalty needed greater integration into the broader marketing theory, and posited a framework that combined both attitudinal and behavioural measures. They suggested that while loyalty was influenced by a customer's repeat purchase behaviours and intentions, it was determined by a "favorable attitude that is high compared to potential alternatives" (p. 100). They contended that true or premium loyalty only occurs when the customer has both attitudinal and behaviour commitment to a firm.

Day (1969) was the first to suggest using a composite index to measure loyalty, recognizing that a customer's decision to choose one firm over another was primarily a factor of attitudinal commitment. Day (1969) argued that pure behavioural loyalty was a spurious indicator of loyalty, and could be influenced by low prices and weak competition. He addressed this issue by proposing the following equation:

- $L = P[B]/A$

Using this equation, loyalty, 'L', could be estimated by dividing the ratio of probability of purchasing, 'P[B]', by an inverted mean attitude score, 'A'. This would result in a loyalty index of closer to 1, indicating that 'true loyalty' is obtained when a high probability of purchasing was divided by a strong attitudinal component. Further, a loyalty index of closer to 0 indicates that 'low loyalty' is obtained when a poor probability of purchase is divided by a weak attitudinal component.

The main benefit of assessing loyalty in this manner is that it allows investigation of the causal relationship between attitudes and behaviours. This in turn can assist in the resolution of underlying questions regarding how "underlying processes influence loyalty" (Dick & Basu, 1994:192). The next section of this chapter will focus on the role of relationship quality in the retention of customers, and the determinants of an effective relationship.

CONCEPTUAL FRAMEWORK FOR RELATIONSHIP MARKETING

Despite the popularity of customer relationship management, and the belief that effective relationship marketing leads to increased customer loyalty and greater profitability, this notion has not been afforded the necessary attention of previous researchers. Furthermore, the widespread adoption of customer relationship strategies by online businesses has been espoused as the key to the creation of long and lasting relationships with customers, business partners and other stakeholders (Reichheld, 1996). To assist with the examination of this phenomenon, we will now examine the central proposition of the relationship marketing theory—that service quality leads to relationship quality and consequently to customer loyalty.

Relationship Quality as an Indicator of Loyalty

Relationship quality is viewed as a significant and critical variable in customer retention (Crosby et al., 1990; Storbacka et al., 1994; Wilson & Jantrania, 1996). It is considered to be the key determinant in the development of long-term exchanges between a supplier and its customers, and is the focal variable of this chapter.

Interest in this variable stems from the idea that customer retention is a product of loyalty, and can only occur when a customer has formed a strong relationship with the supplier. This is not to say that customer retention does not occur in situations of low relationship strength, but that in such situations the likelihood of future purchase intentions is more dependent on external factors such as low level of alternatives or high switching barriers.

Crosby et al. (1990) asserted that relationship quality was the main driver of a customer's future purchase intentions. They contended that as customer trust in the firm's ability to deliver satisfying service increased, their intention to remain loyal also increased. Storbacka et al. (1994) add that a strong relationship will reduce the impact of critical incidents and lower the desire to experiment with substitute products or services. They suggested that relationship strength was the ultimate measure of whether a dyadic relationship would be enduring and profitable.

Wilson and Jantrania (1996) also contend that customer retention is positively related to commitment, which is an incremental benefit associated with attitudinal commitment. They add that unless a customer forms social bonds with his or her supplier, the probability of developing a long-term relationship was unlikely. However, they do make the point that an anomaly to this situation occurs when there are significant structural barriers that prevent a customer from switching.

Antecedent Nature of Service Quality

Crosby et al. (1990) were amongst the first to explore the service quality and relationship quality association, stating that service quality was necessary for the development of relationship quality and retaining customers. Storbacka et al. (1994) referred to this as the chain of impact where service quality affects satisfaction, which in turn affects customer loyalty, where their conceptualization of satisfaction is synonymous with that of relationship quality, and is defined as "customers' cognitive and affective evaluation based on the personal experience across all service episodes within the relationship" (p. 149). Page (2000) concurs with the proposition that service quality is antecedent to relationship quality, stating that there is a widespread belief in service industries that service quality leads to relationship quality.

However, there is also significant support for the direct relationship between service quality and customer loyalty (Cronin & Taylor, 1992; Parasuraman et al., 1988; Zeithaml et al., 1996; Dick & Basu, 1994). Zeithaml (2000), in a review of literature pertaining to service quality and profitability, identified eighteen articles that espouse a direct relationship between service quality and behavioural intentions or customer retention.

However, Zeithaml (2000) is also of the opinion that a lot is not known regarding the link between service quality and loyalty, citing that more research is needed to explore why the strength of the service quality-loyalty association varies across and within specific contexts.

Dimensions of Relationship Quality

Most research that has examined relationship effectiveness has concentrated on the impact of one or more variables, while failing to address the specific determinants of relationship quality (Naude & Buttle, 2000). Furthermore, there has been considerable confusion arising from the use of components that are not clearly defined or distinguished from each other. From the previous discussion of relationship quality, it can be seen that there are a number of hypothesized dimensions of relationship quality, including: trust and satisfaction (Crosby et al., 1990); commitment, coordination, communication, goal congruence and conflict resolution (Mohr & Spekman, 1994); and social and structural bonding (Wilson & Jantrania, 1996).

For the purpose of this chapter we will consider the dimensions explored in the work by the Marketing Science Center (MSC) associated with the University of South Australia (Page, 2000). Their work has attempted to clarify the elements of relationship quality through extensive empirical research and statistical analysis over a six (6) year period. The first stage of their work resulted in the identification of eleven (11) elements of relationship quality as well as items for the global construct of relationship quality (Page & Sharp, 1995).

Subsequent research has seen the number of relationship quality dimensions reduce from eleven (11) to seven (7), and the total number of items from fifty-three (53) to just sixteen (16). The dimensions included in the final

Figure 3: Relationship quality dimensions

Dimension	Definition and discussion
Trust	It is defined as reliance upon information received from another person about uncertain environmental states and their accompanying outcomes in a risky situation. In the web marketplace, trust has emerged as an issue of critical importance, where consumers perceive higher risks in performing on-line transactions, and the development of long-term relationships.
Effort/value	The amount of effort made by a firm and the value that they are perceived to place in their customers are viewed as being strong indicators of the firm's commitment to customers. In the on-line environment, firms can demonstrate their commitment to customers by increasing the level of security, depth and breadth of services, and customized nature of the interaction.
Understanding	The knowledge gained by the supplier regarding the customer and their particular needs. Special consideration in on-line environment regarding how this knowledge is compiled, shared and used.
Communication	The exchange of information is considered a valued and necessary requirement for the development of any lasting attachment. Effective communication is based on sharing of information in an open, two-way and flexible manner. The adoption of web-related technologies assists in the coordination of timely and relevant information sharing.
Cooperation	The need to work together to achieve mutually beneficial outcomes is well established in the extant literature. Cooperation is defined as a high degree of goal congruence between dyad partners, and an un-adversarial approach to the exchange. In the on-line context, the espoused shift in power from supplier to consumer is expected to impact on the relevance of this dimension.
Liking	Conceptualized in terms of social bonding, liking is seen as the critical variable in the formation of friendship, and is operationalised as the degree of socialization between the customer and a specific contact person. The lack of interpersonal exchanges in the on-line context raises questions regarding the relevance of this construct, and whether bonding of a social nature can occur between consumer and the web interface.

instrument are trust, value, effort, communication (info to/from), cooperation, liking and understanding.

Dimensions of Service Quality

While it is acknowledged that service quality has been the subject of many investigations over the past two decades, the application of the construct to the

Figure 4: Service quality dimensions

Dimension	Definition and discussion
Physical aspects	Reflecting the tangibility of the service encounter, it was broadened by Dabholkar et al. (1996) to reflect the importance of the physical aspects of retail stores. In addition to reflecting the physical appearance of the retail environment, it also considers the convenience of the store layout. In the on-line context the physical aspects are expanded to reflect how effectively the web site is designed, suggesting that poor design makes it difficult to locate information, in turn leading to frustration and perceptions of poor service quality.
Reliability	The need to perform reliably is an effective means of reducing some of the uncertainty associated with the intangible nature of services. Parasuraman et al. (1988) add that reliable service delivery is linked to the customer's desire for credible and dependable service, and is usually manifest in a retailers ability to 'do it right the first time' and 'keep promises'. In the on-line context, reliable service performance reduces perceived risk, and lowers the barrier to future purchase intentions.
Personal interaction	Similar to Parasuraman et al.'s (1985) 'empathy' dimension, personal interaction builds on the basic requirement for courteous and helpful service to include the need to inspire confidence at an interpersonal level. The dimension also reflects the ability of strong personal relationships to reduce post-purchase dissonance. While web interaction is not inter-personal, it is often more personalized, with firms claiming a higher degree of responsiveness and more individualized content.
Problem Solving	This dimension addresses the handling of returns, exchanges and complaints. Customer perceptions of service quality have been shown to be particularly sensitive to the way firms attend to problems and complaints. On-line businesses are no different in their need to identify, isolate and solve service problems. Failure to develop effective problem solving strategies will significantly reduce the attractiveness of moving shoppers on-line.
Policy	This dimension captures the aspects of service quality that are directly related to business operating policies, with perceptions of service quality directly influenced by the empathetic and responsive nature of a company's policies. In the on-line context, this consideration is particularly important for reducing perceived risk, where consumers often undertake an extended information search when shopping on-line in order to overcome the lack of tangibility and reduced interpersonal interaction. As such, effective policies relating to security, pricing, assortment (merchandising), and accessibility are necessary requirements for on-line businesses.

online context is still very much in its infancy (Wong & Sohal, 2001). Furthermore, our efforts will be directed towards investigating whether traditional conceptualisations of service quality are applicable in the online context. In particular, we will explore the relevance of the retail service quality conceptualisation to the online environment (Dabholkar et al., 1996; Dabholkar et al., 2000).

The work of Dabholkar and colleagues examined service quality in various retail contexts, and reaffirmed previous definitions of the construct (Parasuraman et al., 1988; Cronin & Taylor, 1992). Their work resulted in the identification of a hierarchical structure composed of a global service quality construct supported by five underlying dimensions: physical aspects, reliability, personal interaction,; problem solving and policy.

FUTURE TRENDS

Implications for Theory and Practice

The model proposed below could have several implications for marketing practice. For instance, while relationship marketing theory has recently received inspired attention through the prevalence and widespread adoption of customer relationship management (CRM) tools, the users of these tools have tended to focus only on the purchasing characteristics of customers whilst ignoring those factors that drive loyal relationships.

The enhanced model for CRM could assist marketing managers to identify these factors, and achieve the espoused financial benefits that flow from a loyal and dedicated customer base. In particular, the framework could assist marketers by identifying the key drivers of 'service quality' and 'relationship quality' in the online context, and in doing so, impact on the task of moving customers up the 'loyalty ladder' from a prospect, to a supporter, to a partner (Payne, 1991).

While this analysis took a macro view of relationship marketing in the online context, it also has implications for the development of effective relationships within industries, and within firms. By capturing data on attitudinal and behavioural drivers of superior relationships, marketers can also apply the model as a tool for investigating the implicit differences in customer perceptions across and within market segments and product categories. This could be

Figure 5: Enhanced model for CRM

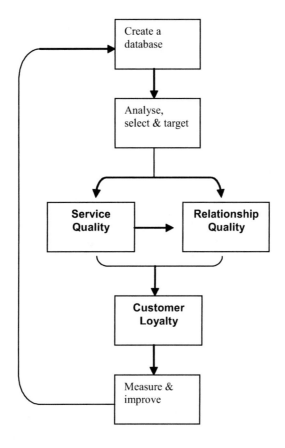

particularly valuable for marketers already acquainted with CRM, with segmentation possible on the basis of attitudes as well as behaviours.

In terms of theory, this model could contribute in two principle areas. First, it would clarify the interaction of the three critical variables in the relationship marketing conceptual space. Second, the model could also add to theory by clarifying the nature of customer loyalty. In examining customer loyalty, the model would address a recent call for a better understanding of how loyalty applies to different situations (Sharp et al., 1997). It would also confirm the importance of the dyadic conceptualization including both attitudes and behaviours, where attitudes are espoused to influence behaviours.

Future Research

In addition to the potential implications of the posited model, there are also several opportunities for future research that stem from the application of the model. For instance, future research could build on the model by considering the direct impact of loyalty on profitability, or the consideration of alternative internal and external variables. Internal factors such as psychographics and demographics could be examined as possible confounders. Likewise, external factors such as the defensive marketing tactics of competitors, and the activities of supply chain members, could also be explored to assess their effect on the structural relationships between service quality, relationship quality and customer loyalty.

Second, research could be undertaken into whether customers develop relationships according to some systematic process. For instance, capturing data on attitudinal and behavioural indicators over an extended period of time could reveal a direct link between different customer groups. In particular, this could provide support for a more holistic approach to relationship marketing, where potentially profitable customer groups are identified and nurtured along with currently desirable groups.

Lastly, research could be undertaken into how relationship marketing varies across different organisational networks. For example, research could be undertaken into the drivers of effective customer relationship management with internal stakeholders such as employees and shareholders. Likewise, research could also be undertaken into the quality of relationships with other external markets such as those with suppliers and influencers such as government.

CONCLUSION

Delivering on the promises of customer relationship management requires an appreciation of the importance of relationship marketing. The emergence of more powerful computers and more responsive and sophisticated profiling techniques are helping managers to identify the characteristics of potentially profitable customers, but such tools seem to concentrate exclusively on historic behaviours at the expense of seeking a better understanding of what drives 'true loyalty'. Drawing on the extant literature in the area of relationship marketing, this chapter espoused an enhanced model of CRM that incorporated a tripartite appreciation of effective service delivery, strong interpersonal relationships and attitudinal loyalty. In short, service quality was viewed as a key driver of relationship quality, which in turn was viewed as a key driver of customer loyalty.

The model highlighted the importance of capturing and integrating attitudinal preferences of customers in order to better facilitate CRM. In doing so, it highlighted the need to explore these constructs at their sub-dimension level, with careful consideration of how these dimensions translate to the electronic marketplace. For instance, while the physical environment would ordinarily provide cues regarding the quality of service that could be expected, in the online environment such cues are provided by the quality of the web site. Once understood, these dimensions and their associated measurement tools can play a vital role in improving the overall quality of an online firm's relationship management efforts, as well as providing valuable metrics for assessing the ongoing health of these relationships.

ENDNOTES

[1] Performance-only refers to the practice of measuring service quality outcomes or performance only, without reference to prior expectations.
[2] Computer-disconfirmation refers to the practice of measuring service quality by considering performance against pre-determined expectations.

REFERENCES

Berry, L. (1983). Relationship marketing. In *emerging perspectives on services marketing*. Chicago, IL: American Marketing Association.

Berry, L., & Parasuraman, A. (1988). The service quality puzzle. *Business Horizon, 31*(5), 35–43.

Cronin, J., & Taylor, S. (1992). Measuring service quality: A re-examination and extension. *Journal of Marketing, 56*(July), 55–66.

Cronin, J., & Taylor, S. (1994). SERVPERF versus SERVQUAL: Reconciling performance-based and perceptions-minus-expectations measurement of service quality. *Journal of Marketing, 58*(January), 125–131.

Crosby, L., Evans, K., & Cowles, D. (1990). Relationship quality in services selling: An interpersonal influence perspective. *Journal of Marketing, 54*(3), 68–82.

Dabholkar, P., Shepherd, D., & Thorpe, D. (2000). A comprehensive framework for service quality: An investigation of critical conceptual and measurement issues through a longitudinal study. *Journal of Retailing, 76*(2), 139–173.

Dabholkar, P., Thorpe, D., & Rentz, J. (1996). A measure of service quality for retail stores: Scale development and validation. *Journal of the Academy of Marketing Science, 24*(1), 3–16.

Daly, J. (2001). Measuring customer loyalty. *Business 2.0,* (January 8), 1–2.

Day, G. (1969). A two-dimensional concept of loyalty. *Journal of Advertising Research, 9*(September), 29–35.

De Kare-Silver, M, (2000). *E-shock: The new rules. Strategies for retailers and manufacturers.* Hampshire, UK: Palgrave.

Dick, A. S., & Basu, K. (1994). Customer loyalty: Toward an integrated conceptual framework. *Journal of the Academy of Marketing Science, 22,* 99–113.

Gale, B., & Wood, R. (1994). *Managing customer value: Creating quality and service that customers can see.* New York: Free Press.

Georgiadis, M., Singer, M., Harding, D., & Lane, K. *(2000). Online* customer management: Five killer actions to drive your e-Business (White Paper). Harvard: McKinsey Marketing Solutions, McKinsey and Company.

Gray, P., & Byun, J. (2001). Customer relationship management. California: Centre for Research on Information Technology and Organisations, University of California.

Gronröös, C. (1984). A service quality model and its implications. *European Journal of Marketing, 18*(4), 10–20.

Gronröös, C. (1991). *Service management and marketing.* Ontario, Canada: Lexington Books.

Gronröös, C. (1994). From marketing mix to relationship marketing: Towards a paradigm shift in marketing. *Asia-Australian Marketing Journal, 2*(1), 9–30.

Gummesson, E. (1987). The new marketing – Developing long-term interactive relationships. *Long Range Planning, 20*(4), 10–20.

Keating, B., Rugimbana, R., & Quazi, A. (2003). Differentiating between service quality and relationship quality in cyberspace. *International Journal of Managing Service Quality, 13*(3).

Liljander, V., & Strandvik, T. (1993). Different comparison standards as determinants of service quality. *Journal of Consumer Satisfaction, Dissatisfaction and Complaining Behaviour, 6,* 118–132.

Mackey, P. (2001). *Customer loyalty: The next online frontier.* Westport, USA: Digital Idea.

Mohr, J., & Spekman, R. (1994). Characteristics of partnership success: Partnership attributes, communication behaviour and conflict resolution techniques. *Strategic Management Journal, 15,* 132–152.

Naudé, P., & Buttle, F. (2000). Assessing relationship quality. *Industrial Marketing Management, 29,* 351–361.

Olsen, M. (1996). *Into the new millennium: A white paper on the global hospitality industry.* Paris: International Hotel Association.

Page, N. (2000). *Developing subjective and objective measures of relationship quality and investigation the discriminant validity between relationship quality and service quality.* Doctoral Thesis. Adelaide, Australia: Marketing Science Centre, University of South Australia.

Parasuraman, A., Zeithaml, V., & Berry, L. L. (1985). A conceptual model of service quality and its implications for future research. *Journal of Marketing, 49*(Autumn), 41–50.

Parasuraman, A., Zeithaml, V., & Berry, L. L. (1988). SERVQUAL: A multiple item scale for measuring consumer perceptions of service quality. *Journal of Retailing, 64*(Spring), 12–40.

Parasuraman, A., Zeithaml, V., & Berry, L. L. (1994). Reassessment of expectations as a comparison standard for measuring service quality: Implications for future research. *Journal of Marketing, 58*(January), 111–124.

Payne, A. (1991). *Relationship marketing: the six markets framework.* Working paper. Cranfield, UK: Cranfield School of Management.

Payne, A. (1995). *Advances in relationship marketing.* London, UK: Kogan Page/Cranfield University.

Peppers, D., Rogers, M., & Dorf, B. (1999). Is your company ready for one-to-one marketing? *Harvard Business Review,* January-February.

Powell, S. (2001). Spotlight on Christian Gronröös. Retrieved 14 June 2001, from *Management First,* Website: http://www.managementfirst.com/general_marketing

Pritchard, M., Havitz, M., & Howard, D. (1999). Analysing the commitment loyalty link in service contexts. *Journal of the Academy of Marketing Science, 27*(3), 333–348.

Ravald, A., & Grönroos, C. (1996). The value concept and relationship marketing. *European Journal of Marketing, 30*(2), 19–30.

Reichheld, F. (1996). *The loyalty effect: The hidden force behind growth, profits, and lasting value.* Boston, MA: Harvard Business Press.

Rust, R., Zahorik, A., & Keiningham, T. (1995). Return on quality: Making service quality financial accountable. *Journal of Marketing, 59*(April), 58–70.

Sharp, B., Rundle-Thiele, S., & Dawes, J. (1997). *Three conceptualisations of loyalty*. Proceedings of Australian and New Zealand Marketing Academy (ANZMAC) Conference. Melbourne, Australia.

Storbacka, K. (1993). Customer relationship profitability in retail banking. *Research Report No 29*. Helsinki: Finland, Swedish School of Economics and Business Administration.

Storbacka, K., Strandvik, T., & Grönroos, C. (1994). Managing customer relationships for profit. *International Journal of Service Industry Management, 5*(5), 21–28.

Teas, R. K. (1993). Expectations, performance evaluation and consumers' perceptions of quality. *Journal of Marketing, 57*(October), 18–34.

Wilson, D., & Jantrania, S. (1996). Understanding the value of a relationship. *Asia-Australia Marketing Journal, 2*(1), 55–66.

Winer, R. (2001). A framework for customer relationship management. *California Management Review, 34*(4), 89–106.

Wong, A., & Sohal, A. (2001). *On service quality, service quality dimensions and customer loyalty*. Working paper. Melbourne, Australia: Monash University.

Wyner, G. (1999). Customer relationship measurement. *Marketing Research, 11*(2), 39–41.

Zeithaml, V. (2000). Service quality, profitability, and the economic worth of customers: What we know and what we need to learn. *Journal of the Academy of Marketing Science, 28*(1), 67–85.

Zeithaml, V., Berry, L., & Parasuraman, A. (1996). The behavioural consequences of service quality. *Journal of Marketing, 60*(April), 31–46.

Chapter VII

E-Partnership and Virtual Organizations: Issues and Options

Fang Zhao
RMIT University, Australia

ABSTRACT

With the convergence of information technology and communication, the Internet has changed the way organizations communicate internally and externally, the way organizations are configured and the way organizations build partnerships. As a result, e-partnerships and virtual organizations become increasingly popular in today's corporate world. This chapter aims to address issues of change and innovation associated with e-partnerships and virtual organizations. The chapter (i) discusses the advantages of e-partnerships and virtual organizations and the driving forces behind them; (ii) identifies issues and problems relating to the emergence of e-partnerships and virtual organizations; (iii) explores key factors for achieving the best performance and best results of e-partnerships and virtual organizations; and (iv) speculates future trends of the development of e-commerce and e-business which affects directly the viability of e-partnerships and virtual organizations. This author maintains that a total quality partnership approach holds the key to success. The present study draws upon the current leading literature in the field and a case study of Amazon.com, one of the world largest on-line dealers and virtual enterprise with the most extensive e-networks and e-partnerships.

INTRODUCTION

With the convergence of information technology and communication, the Internet has changed the way organizations communicate internally and externally, the way organizations are configured and the way organizations build partnerships. The **virtual organization**, which is actually a network form of organization, is an innovation in organizational design and has changed the definitions, boundaries and forms of inter-organizational collaboration and partnerships. **E-partnerships** where business partners transact and communicate with each other mainly through electronic technologies are no longer a gimmick. Technology, particularly web-based resources and systems, are indispensable for the e-partnerships and virtual organizations.

Innovation and creativity are needed to construct new theories and knowledge base to help to sustain the innovative e-partnerships and virtual organizations. Today's complex and volatile business world calls for changes and alternatives to the old and conventional paradigm of organizational design and new ways of doing business with others. Those who are adept at adapting to changes are the only winners. This chapter aims to address the issues of changes and innovation associated with e-partnerships and virtual organizations. The specific objectives of this chapter are:

- To discuss the advantages of e-partnerships and virtual organizations and the driving forces behind them;
- To identify issues and problems relating to the emergence of e-partnerships and virtual organizations;
- To explore key factors for achieving the best performance and best results of e-partnerships and virtual organizations; and
- To speculate on future trends of the development of e-commerce and e-business which affect directly the viability of e-partnerships and virtual organizations.

This author maintains that a total quality partnership approach holds the key to success. The total quality approach is based upon the principal components of Total Quality Management (TQM), namely, continuous improvement, empowering, teamwork and collaboration, and achieving the ultimate goal of customer satisfaction (Aggarwal & Zairi, 1998, Rounthwaite & Shell, 1995). The study draws upon the current leading literature in the field and a case study of Amazon.com, one of the world largest on-line dealers and virtual enterprise with the most extensive e-networks and e-partnerships.

BACKGROUND

Information technology and globalization are shaking up the concept and boundaries of organizations. The word "virtual" associated with "cyber", Meta and the Internet become popular buzzwords today. Virtual commercial services such as virtual banks, virtual supermarket, virtual offices and the like are no longer a surprise to ordinary customers. Network organizations taking different names like virtual corporations, virtual companies, virtual teams and meta-enterprises become increasingly popular in the perception of managers and in business operations as we move from an industrial to a knowledge-based economy.

The Virtual Revolution is the defining business transformation of this generation (Malone & Davidow, 1994). Take Cisco system for example. Cisco is actually a network of suppliers, contract manufacturers, assemblers and other partners, which is connected through an intricate web of information technology. Seventy percent of Cisco's products are outsourced through Cisco's network. As soon as a client's order is placed (usually through the Internet), suppliers send the required materials to assemblers who ship the product directly to the client, usually on the same day (McShane & Glinow, 2000). Over the past several decades, Japanese managers have chosen network organizations to facilitate the cooperation between big, medium and small enterprises and in manufacturing industries (Jin, 1999).

Accompanied with the virtual organization, an informal and network-based e-partnership is an inevitable trend in this globalization and information era. Theoretically, e-partnership refers to a partnership relying on electronic (information) technologies to communicate and interact among partners. In practice, the term e-partnership is mostly associated with e-commerce or e-business partnerships. It may take different forms and involve various partners from or between virtual enterprises and brick-and-mortar companies, depending on the nature of e-business activities. It is suggested that "e-business can enhance the interchange of information between partners by breaking down communication, negotiation and co-ordination barriers" (Ratnasingham, 1998, cited in Cheng et al., 2001, p. 2). In the manufacturing industry, the e-partners may include raw materials providers, component manufacturers, final assembly manufacturers, wholesalers, distributors, retailers and customers. This supply chain may involve a number of, even hundreds or thousands of, suppliers and distributors. The use of the Internet and other electronic media and the introduction of inter-organizational information systems are constitutive to e-partnerships and help to extend the e-partnerships.

E-partnerships as "a new breed of on-line alliances, are fast emerging as the result of an incredible amount of Internet business in recent years" (Trask, 2000, p. 46) and are no longer a soft option but a vital need for gaining a competitive advantage and customer satisfaction in the trend of globalization of customers and suppliers and the economy. On the other hand, globalization is pushing companies to build informal network organizations, such as virtual organizations, that are able to work in a faster, cheaper and more flexible way. Obviously, e-partnerships and virtual organizations are products of the globalization and IT advancement over the past decade and they have fundamental synergy between them. They interrelate and interact with each other in this digital era.

ADVANTAGES OF E-PARTNERSHIPS AND VIRTUAL ORGANIZATIONS

The greatest advantage of e-partnership and virtual organization lies in the fact that it eliminates the physical boundaries of organizations, and that cross-functional teams and organizations are able to operate and collaborate across space and time by communicating with each other via electronic channels. The Internet becomes the most important interface between participating organizations, teams and individuals. The e-partnerships and virtual organizations allow businesses to sell and deliver products and services across the world in the most efficient way. Other perceived benefits of e-partnerships and virtual organizations may include greater business opportunities, better integration of suppliers and vendors, better management information, lower operational costs, better market understanding and expanded geographical coverage (Damanpour, 2001). The e-partnership and virtual organization also offer the opportunity of consolidating resources of all partners and organizational flexibility, as other forms of inter-organizational partnerships and alliances do.

In this rapidly changing competitive landscape, few organizations can rely on their internal strengths only to gain a competitive advantage in national and/ or international markets. Inter-organizational collaborations, alliances, joint ventures, partnering and the like are gaining unprecedented momentum, regardless of their organizational and management structures and styles and communication channels. An organization's resources are limited in one way or another. Forming a business e-partnership and taking a network form of organization is increasingly one of the most popular strategies available to an organization to take advantage of an Internet Highway on the one hand, and share risks, capabilities and revenue with partners on the other. The driving forces behind building an e-partnership and a virtual organization share a lot in common with those driving any other forms of inter-organizational collaborations. They include:

- To gain a competitive advantage or increase market share in national and/ or global markets;
- To share revenue and expand sales between merchants and partners;
- To prevent competition loss;
- To tackle complexities of integration of technologies involving an ever-wider range of expertise;
- To meet changing demands of customers and markets; and
- To gain core competencies from competitors (Sierra, 1994; Dussauge & Garette, 1999; Trask, 2000).

E-PARTNERSHIPS AND VIRTUAL ORGANIZATIONS: ISSUES AND PROBLEMS

However, like e-business and e-commerce, e-partnership is also facing a range of issues related to the use of the Internet as well as the reliance on inter-organizational interfaces. The key issues identified are:

- Challenges and risks of e-partnerships and virtual organizations;
- Productivity and revenue-sharing in e-partnerships and virtual organizations;
- Transferring and sharing core competencies between participating organizations;
- Sharing power and empowering among participating organizations; and
- Quality and effectiveness of communications.

Addressing each of these issues has posed a formidable task in front of e-managers of various kinds of inter-organizational collaboration through electronic technologies and e-network. The following discussion explores each of these issues in detail.

Challenges and Risks

On the technological side, e-partnership and virtual organization take the lead in the current Internet-driven business environment that assimilates the most advanced electronic technologies and the knowledge-based economy. Companies involved in e-partnerships must participate in external business relationships by using computer interactions (Damanpour, 2001). This is a great challenge confronting e-partners to re-engineer their IT strategies and resources and re-think their ways of communication and doing business with e-partners. The main issues to be considered are IT infrastructure and managers' and operatives' knowledge and skills associated with e-business and e-commerce.

On the human resource's side, while e-partnerships and virtual organizations in whatever form may entail optimization of organizational resources and attainment of competitive advantages of parties involved, e-managers are surely confronting management complexities of making cooperation work. The biggest challenges to management in this regard are conflict in different organizational and country cultures, taxation, financial and commercial risks, legal risks concerning on-line intellectual property, national and international on-line trade and law, etc.

Culture is about shared assumption, beliefs, values and norms. Each organization has its own culture developed from its own particular experience, its own role and the way its owners or managers get things done (Hellard, 1995). In addition to the cultural differences at the organizational level, multi-national e-partnerships inevitably encounter barriers caused by cultural differences between nations. Legal, political and economic differences among countries are also obvious. For instance, EU member states must enact legislation to ensure that transfers of data outside their boundaries are allowed only to jurisdictions that can offer adequate protection of the data. The US believes that minimal domestic regulation would foster cross-border Internet trade (Damanpour, 2001). Managing the cultural and system differences across organizations and across nations is one of the high agendas that challenge managers of e-partnerships and virtual organizations.

Compounded with the challenges are particular risks facing e-partnerships and virtual organizations such as information technology risks and financial and commercial risks. While the Internet and network organizations facilitate improved communication of data, information and knowledge, they give rise to issues and problems of privacy, data security and intellectual property protection in the Internet. The information database created through Internet transactions may lead to legal disputes among e-partnerships over ownership of the IP and possible loss of the potential profit generated from the IP (Greif, 2000). Moreover, electronic research projects usually involve new technologies and innovative development, which creates a high level of technological and commercial risk for every organization involved. However, it is the motivation of sharing and minimizing the risks that entails e-partnering and e-alliance.

Productivity and Revenue Sharing

Productivity, including volume of sales and services, and profit are no doubt central issues to tackle for all organizations, no matter whatever forms they take. The primary aim of building e-partnerships and virtual organizations is to generate more profit and achieve the best business results through taking advantage of on-line resources and extensive e-network. Trask (2000, p. 46) considered that "a well-designed revenue-sharing program may be the best and fastest way to generate on-line business". Revenue sharing becomes the most important issue in e-partnerships and virtual organizations when productivity increases and revenue goes up. The nature, timing, and amount of compensation (in the form of referral fees, royalty and commission) together with the financial stability and honesty of commission reporting are core considerations of e-partners and crucial factors of success in sustaining e-partnerships.

Transferring and Sharing Core Competencies

According to Lei, core competencies comprise a company's specific and special knowledge, skills and capabilities to stand out among competitors. They are intangible and an integrated part of a company's intellectual capital and un-tradable assets rather than legally protected intellectual property (Lei, 1997, p. 211). As shown in the previous section, one of the drivers for entering partnerships is to gain core competencies from competitors. Inter-organizational collaboration provides an opportunity for participating organizations to acquire and absorb the core competencies from each other (Couchman & Fulop, 2000). This opportunity is particularly valuable for innovative business such as e-business. However, transferring and sharing core competencies will not just happen—participants have to work, and work hard, to overcome barriers to transferring and sharing. The greatest barrier is competitive concerns over information leakage. This is an unavoidable dilemma facing e-partnerships, which makes it difficult for e-partners to achieve the potential that IT technology can offer.

Sharing Power and Empowering

It is normal that a decision-making body of inter-organizational collaboration is proportionately represented by participating organizations in terms of equity holdings in an on-line joint venture. It should be noted that due to differences in equity holdings, power disparity occurs and is likely to affect performance of inter-organizational collaboration, although division of power and responsibility has been clearly defined in legally binding agreements between e-partners. This author holds that a total quality partnership approach (see the Recommendations section of this chapter for a detailed discussion) helps to solve the problem through offering each individual and/or organization an opportunity to participate, contribute and develop a sense of ownership in the virtual organization.

Quality and Effectiveness of Communications

Networking and communications play a key role, particularly in coordinating and liaising inter-organizational collaboration. Expanding e-networks and achieving effective communications among e-partners are a top priority. Like culture and commitment, communications are soft outcomes of a total quality partnership approach and the foundation for inter-organizational collaboration. Effective networking and communications help to eliminate barriers to collaboration. Therefore, continuous improvement of the quality and medium of communications is another key issue in the agenda of e-partnerships and virtual organizations.

CASE STUDY OF AMAZON.COM

Amazon.com "opened its virtual door on the World Wide Web in 1995 and today offers Earth's Biggest Selection of product, including electronic greeting cards, on-line auctions, books, CDs, videos, DVDs, toys and games, electronics, kitchenware, computers and more", and, "Amazon.com is the place to find and discover anything you want to buy on-line" (Amazon.com, INC., 2002a). Amazon.com focuses on both customer relation management (CRM) and infrastructure management. It has been a successful and leading player in the e-commerce industry and has survived the worldwide disastrous waves of collapse of dot.com industries over the past two years.

The growth and success of Amazon.com are largely built on its syndication strategy through aggressively expanding its extensive networks and e-partnerships. Through its on-line affiliate program, Amazon.com has developed e-partnerships with hundreds of thousands of e-partners, ranging from tiny, personal home pages to big brothers like Yahoo and Excite. Over 600,000 web sites have joined Amazon.com and placed hyperlinks to Amazon.com for e-shoppers to make on-line purchases (Werbach, 2000; Hagel & Singer, 1999; Amazon.com, INC., 2002b). Amazon's e-alliances have extended to the UK, France, Germany and Japan. Amazon has also developed close alliances with other big book distributors and publishers to strengthen its e-commerce capacity. By doing so, Amazon is able to provide its customers with lower prices, a vast selection and speedy delivery. For example, as soon as an on-line order for a book is received, Amazon passes it immediately on to its partners if the book is not in Amazon's stock and makes sure the delivery is in its next daily shipment to Amazon's facility. As soon as the book arrives, Amazon repackages it and delivers it to the customer. In this regard, Amazon saves its costs of inventories through its e-partnerships (Hagel & Singer, 1999). Amazon was hailed "a model of a successful, efficient, constantly evolving Internet information broker" (LaPorte et al., 1997, p. 1694).

Amazon.com has expanded its e-partnership network even further through establishing on-line shops, called zShops, in which Amazon hosts hundreds of small e-commerce providers. Amazon's outstanding mission is to provide the biggest selection of goods possible through its warehouse and e-partnerships. According to Diego Piacentini, Amazon's senior vice president of world-wide retail, the only way to achieve the mission is to host as many products as possible through its web pages (Wingfield, 2002). Clearly, it is this syndication strategy that has placed Amazon in a competitive advantage and driven the increasing expansion of e-partnership. Amazon's supply chain networks and e-partnerships help to increase its sales and extend its infrastructure business. Its e-partners also benefit from selling Amazon's products in return for revenue sharing, namely, up to 15 percent in referral fees. This appears to be a win-win partnership.

However, Amazon has been beset with problems in the expansion of e-networks and e-partnerships. Firstly, it is seen that Amazon's customer information business is weakened due to the fact that its e-partners have fiercely competed with Amazon for customer information and loyalty through joining Amazon's e-networks. Secondly, Amazon's long-term profitability has been affected by its "poor management of logistics and supply processes in this e-business". "Losses have increased in line with a growth in turnover last year, and it has been stated that the growth of the company led to an increase in inventory, especially with product diversity increasing" (Hoek, 2001, p. 22). The annual report of Amazon.com in 2001 confirmed its heavy losses in financial results, although its financial situation is improving in 2002. Amazon's financial reports in 2002 revealed the problems and issues facing Amazon's current and future operation, such as risks of inventory management, significant amount of indebtedness, customer or third-party sellers' fraud, uncertainty of business combinations and strategic alliances, etc. (Amazon.com, INC., 2002c).

RECOMMENDATIONS

Dealing with the challenges and risks of e-partnerships and virtual organizations is a difficult and complicated task for e-business management, as shown in this chapter. While sufficient support of IT infrastructure and resources are definitely important to successful e-partnerships and virtual organizations, reducing potential financial, commercial and legal risks and effectively dealing with human and cultural factors exceed the complexities of technical setup and support in building e-partnerships and virtual organizations.

This section proposes solutions to the issues and problems discussed above, based upon a total quality partnership approach that helps to achieve the desired business operation and results. The total quality partnership approach is built upon the primary concept of TQM and is an actual extension of TQM into the context of inter-organizational collaboration (Zhao, 2000). Vital principles of the total quality partnership approach include:

- Customers include business partners, employees, investors and all the stakeholders.
- Meeting and exceeding customer needs is the ultimate goal of partnership and the highest priority among participating organizations.

- Teamwork and collaboration are the primary methodology for effective partnership.
- The highest levels of integrity, honesty, trust and openness between business partners are essential ingredients of a total quality partnership.
- Mutual respect, mutual trust and mutual benefit of all partners are important successful factors.
- Total quality partnership offers each individual and participating organization the opportunity to participate, contribute and develop a sense of ownership.
- Total quality partnership involves continuous and measurable improvement at all levels of a participating organization.
- Total quality partnership requires consistent and precise performance to high standards in all areas of the participating organization (Aggarwal & Zairi, 1998; Rounthwaite & Shell, 1995; Hellard, 1995).

Clearly, these total quality partnership principles provide a theoretical and practical guideline for the success of e-commerce and e-partnerships. Achieving the best collaboration among e-partners requires more than tangible resources like IT infrastructure and support. It needs a high level of intangible commitment and efforts to understand the needs and values of e-partners and customers. By resorting to a total quality partnership approach, it means that business ethics, integrity, honesty, trust and sharing are required of e-managers of inter-organizational entities at the top and of the individuals and teams throughout the entire virtual organization (Rounthwaite & Shell, 1995). Disputes and conflicts caused by culture and system differences could be reduced if e-partners could maintain a flexible and realistic attitude towards the differences.

The author considers that the critical success factors for e-partnerships and virtual organizations concern both IT and inter-organizational interfaces and include:

- Level of accessibility, security and compatibility of inter-organizational information systems;
- Level of traffic in collaborative e-commerce activities;
- Level of customer service and e-partner support service;
- Level of transferring and sharing information and knowledge between e-partners;
- Building and sustaining an effective virtual network structure among e-partners;
- Level of individual and organizational commitment to e-partnerships;

- Level of mutual trust, understanding, respect and openness;
- Level of corporate and business ethics and integrity;
- Level of credibility of e-partners in relation to financial situation and business experience;
- Level of mutual benefit through revenue sharing;
- Effectiveness and efficiency of real-time commission reporting system;
- Level of performance and productivity of e-partners;
- Actively pursuing and sharing core competencies;
- Willingness to share power and empower among e-partners; and
- Quality and effective networking and continuous improvement of communications.

FUTURE TRENDS

"The world has finally become a Global Village, not just in rhetoric, but in reality" (Hennessey, 2000, p. 34). In the new millennium, it will be more difficult for businesses to survive without joining an e-partnership and taking advantage of the Internet. The fast expansion of Amazon through e-partnerships and e-networks and its business success reinforce the importance of on-line strategic alliance in today's business world. Corporate e-partnerships and network-based organizations will be a crucial factor in the future success of on-line business activities. The author speculates on possible trends of the development of e-commerce and e-business in the near future. The speculation for the future direction is based upon the current development patterns of e-commerce and e-business which contribute directly to the viability of e-partnerships and virtual organizations. The future trends will be characterized by:

- More mature (rather than experimental) nature of e-commerce and e-business practices in terms of the scope, quality and credibility of on-line customer services and products;
- More needs for devising and popularizing e-supply chains due to the needs for integrating the flow of information with the flow of goods (Hoek, 2001);
- Greater monopoly of the flow of e-commerce and e-business by bigger on-line syndicates like Amazon.com through building extensive on-line alliances with on-line retailers and suppliers;
- Greater reliance on joint efforts across nations in on-line legislation to protect IP, security and privacy of e-commerce and e-business; and

• Greater challenge for dot.com industries to achieve sustainability, due to a more uncertain economic environment and the increasing complexities of new technologies and the more globalized economy.

Enhanced research in e-partnerships and virtual organization is needed to tackle the management and technology complexities in e-commerce and e-business and to help sustain the innovations.

CONCLUSION

Running inter-organizational partnerships implies multiplication of decision-making bodies from each participating organization and potential clash of interest and values among participants. As illustrated in this chapter, total quality partnership embodies the fundamental principles for managing collaborative partnerships, including e-partnerships, and can be developed and extended to help inter-organizational collaboration to achieve desired outcomes. However, managing e-partnership and virtual organization is more complex than managing intra-organizational collaboration and collaboration between brick-and-mortar companies due to the IT issues and inter-organizational issues as discussed in the chapter. Failure to consider the complexities of any of these issues will lead to a divorce of e-partnerships and collapse of virtual organizations.

REFERENCES

Aggarwal, A. K., & Zair, M. (1998). Total partnership for primary health care provision: A proposed model - part II. *International Journal of Health Care Quality Assurance, 11*(1), 7–13.

Amazon.com. INC. (2002a). *Company information.* [On-line]. Retrieved from the World Wide Web June 27, 2002: http://www.amazon.com/exec/obidos/ subst/misc/ company-info.html

Amazon.com. INC. (2002b). *Amazon.com Associates: Link up with the leader.* [On-line]. Retrieved from the World Wide Web June 27, 2002: http://associates. amazon.com

Amazon.com. INC. (2002c). *AMZN Q2, 2002 financial results.* [On-line]. Retrieved from the World Wide Web June 27, 2002: http://corporate-ir.net

Cheng, W. L. E., Li, H. Love, E. D. P., & Irani, Z. (2001). An e-business model to support supply chain activities in construction. *Logistic Information Management, 14* (1/2), 68–78.

Couchman, P., & Fulop, L. (2000). Transdisciplinary research bodies: the changing nature of organizational networks and R & D in Australia. *Journal of World Business, 8,* 213–226.

Damanpour, F. (2001). E-business e-commerce evolution: Perspectives and strategy. *Managerial Finance, 27*(7), 16–32.

Dussauge, P., & Garrette, B. (1999). *Cooperative strategy: Competing successfully through strategic alliances.* New York: John Wiley & Sons.

Greif, J. (2000). Risky e-business. *Association Management, 52* (i11), 55.

Hagel, J., & Singer, M. (2000). Unbundling the corporation. In N. G. Carr (Ed.), *The digital enterprise: How to reshape your business for a connected world.* (pp. 3–20). Boston: Harvard Business School.

Hellard, R. B. (1995). *Project partnering: Principle and practice.* London: Thomas Telford Publications.

Hennessey, A. (2000). Online bookselling. *Publishing Research Quarterly, 16* (i2), 34.

Hoek, V. R. (2001). E-supply chains–Virtually non-existing. *Supply Chain Management: An International Journal, 6* (1), 21–28.

Jin, Z. (1999). Organizational innovation and virtual institutes. *Journal of Knowledge Management, 3* (1), 75–83.

LaPorte, E. R., Sekikawa, A., Aaron, D., Nishimura, R., & Acosta, B. (1997). Looking to the future: Amazon.com and four trends. *British Medical Journal, 315* (7123), 1694.

Lei, D. T. (1997). Competence building, technology fusion and competitive advantage: The key roles of organizational learning and strategic alliances. *International Journal of Technology Management, 14,* 208–237.

Malone, M., & Davidow, B. (1994). Welcome to the age of virtual corporations. *Computer Currents, 12* (1), 12–24.

McShane, L. S., & Von Glinow, A. M. (2000). *Organizational behavior.* Sydney: Irwin McGraw Hill.

Rounthwaite, T., & Shell, I. (1995). Techniques: Designing quality partnerships. *The TQM Magazine, 7* (1), 54–58.

Sierra, M. C. D. L. (1994). *Managing global alliances: Key steps for successful collaboration.* Wokingham: Addison-Wesley.

Trask, R. (2000). Developing e-partnerships. *Association Management, 52*(i11), 46.

Werbach, K. (2000). Syndication: the emerging model for business in the Internet era. In N. G. Carr (Ed.), *The digital enterprise: How to reshape your business for a connected world.* (pp. 21–34). Boston, MA: Harvard Business School.

Wingfield, N. (2002, July 23). Could Amazon be another eBay? *The Asian Wall Street Journal.* p.A4.

Zhao, F. (2000). Inter-organizational excellence: a TQM approach. In R. L. Edgeman (Ed.), *Proceedings of the 1st Annual Conference of the Multinational Alliance for the Advancement of Organizational Excellence* (pp. 260–266). Estes Park, Colorado.

Chapter VIII

A B2E Solution: Change Management Perspectives

Paul Hawking
Victoria University, Australia

Susan Foster
Monash University, Australia

Andrew Stein
Victoria University, Australia

ABSTRACT

This chapter looks at the evolving nature of enterprise resource planning systems and how companies are using these systems to support the implementation of a business-to-employee (B2E) solution. In recent times there has been a plethora of research associated with the impact and implications of e-commerce/e-business. Much of this research has focused on the various business models such as business-to-business and business-to-consumer with the importance of developing customer and partner relationships being espoused. However, there has been little attention paid to the potential of business-to-employee systems, and the role the Internet can play in improving business-to-employee relationships. This chapter looks at the emerging B2E model and uses Australian case studies to look at the change management issues associated with employee self-service applications.

INTRODUCTION

An Enterprise Resource Planning (ERP) system can be defined as 'an accounting-oriented information system for identifying and planning the enterprise-wide resources needed to take, make, ship, and account for customer orders' (APICS, 1998). The ERP software infrastructure facilitates the flow of information between all business functions. This infrastructure is built upon a common database responsible for storing all data from processes that are essential for business operations and decision-making. ERP systems are enterprise-wide and they claim to incorporate best business practices. They replace separate functional legacy systems and impact significantly on the existing business processes.

The global market for ERP (Enterprise Resource Planning) software, which was $16.6 billion in 1998, is expected to have a compound annual growth rate of 32%, reaching more than $66 billion in sales by 2003 (Carlino, 1999), and is estimated to have had $300 billion spent over the last decade (Carlino, 2000). Initially, many companies implemented an ERP system as a technological solution to the Y2K issue, as the system replaced many of their existing legacy systems (Deliotte, 1999). Companies were forced to initiate business process engineering for the purpose of "gap analysis", to determine what had to change either in their company or in the ERP system to facilitate effective implementations. Companies initially struggled with their ERP implementation due to inexperience with projects of this scope, underestimating the impact the system would have on their organization, and lack of skilled resources. For some companies these barriers have been insurmountable (Calegero, 2000). However, even with these impediments many large companies considered the implementation of an ERP system as necessary infrastructure.

The leading ERP vendors: SAP, Oracle, Peoplesoft, JD Edwards, and Baan, account for 62% of the total ERP market revenue (Carlino, 1999). SAP is the largest client/server and mainframe ERP software vendor with approximately 52% market share. The company has approximately 28,900 employees, 19,300 customers, in 120 countries (SAP, 2002). Curran et al. (1999) sought to establish the extent that SAP's ERP software (SAP R/3) had been adopted by major US companies. They reported that SAP software had been implemented by:

- 6 out of the top 10 Fortune 500 companies;
- 7 out of the top 10 most profitable companies;
- 9 of the 10 companies with the highest market value;

- 7 of the top 10 pharmaceutical companies;
- 7 of the top 10 petroleum companies;
- 6 of the top 10 electronics companies;
- 8 of the top 10 chemical companies; and
- 8 of the top 10 food companies.

SAP has a similar penetration in large Australian companies. A recent report (BRW, 2002) identified the top 100 IT users in Australia, and using the SAP customer list it was determined that 9 out of the top 12 IT users were SAP customers. In Australia there are 506 implementations of SAP R/3 representing 374 customers.

Traditionally ERP systems were implemented by large companies due to their complexity and associated costs. ERP vendors soon realized that the large company market was limited in Australia and was quickly becoming saturated. This has resulted in a slowing in demand for core ERP systems with an increasing emphasis on upgrades and extended functionality "bolted on" systems (Bennett, 2001). There are several reasons for this diversification of ERP systems: integration of business processes, need for a common platform, better data visibility, lower operating costs, increased customer responsiveness and improved strategic decision making (Iggulden, 1999; Stein & Hawking 2002). The slowing in the market for core ERP systems has also resulted in added functionality installed to prepare organizations for e-business.

To generate new sales, SAP looked at the creation of new products and/or functionality to extend their ERP reach. The expansion of the existing core R/3 system through business process optimization or by the addition of either third party "bolt-on" products or SAP's new products are often referred to as "second wave" implementations. SAP's "second wave" products included Business Information Warehouse (BW), Knowledge Warehouse (KW), Strategic Enterprise Management (SEM), Customer Relationship Management (CRM), Employee Self-Service (ESS) and Advanced Planner and Optimization (APO). SAP recently has grouped its "*second wave*" products and R/3 with added e-commerce functionality (Workplace/Portal and Marketplace) and referred to it as mySAP.com. Even though SAP is attempting to develop new markets for its R/3 product, it would be expected that the sales of the "*second wave*" products will increase while sales of R/3 will decrease due to market saturation. Table 1 indicates the sales of these products per year in the Australasian region.

Table 1: Second wave implementations by year (Bennett, 2001)

Software	Pre 2001 Implementations	Post 2001 Implementations
CRM	19	51
eProc	25	31
BW	168	95
APO	32	41
ESS	20	13
Workplace	44	78

It could be argued that the implementation of *"second wave"* products is a measure of maturity of the ERP implementation. It would be expected that companies would not be implementing any of the *"second wave"* products until their ERP implementation has stabilized. Therefore there would be a relationship between a company's experience with SAP R/3, as defined by Nolan and Norton's (2000) maturity classification, and the implementation of the *"second wave"* products.

HUMAN RESOURCES

The function of Human Resource Management (HRM) has changed dramatically over time. It has evolved from an administrative function primarily responsible for payroll to a strategic role that can add value to an organization. Companies have now realized the importance of this function and are investing large sums of money into supporting HRM information systems. Many of the world's leading companies are using Enterprise Resource Planning (ERP) systems to support their HR information needs. This has partly been due to the realization of the integrative role HR has in numerous business processes such as work scheduling, travel management, production planning and occupational health and safety (Curran et al., 1999).

Business-to-Employee

Much attention in recent times has been applied to the various e-business models such as business-to-business (B2B) and business-to-consumer (B2C), but very little attention has been given to the business-to-employee (B2E) model. This model involves the provision of databases, knowledge management tools and employee-related processes on-line to enable greater accessibility for employees (Deimler & Hansen, 2001). They believe that there are large savings to be made from implementing such solutions. Killen and Associates (2000) believe that these solutions can provide as much as a 4% gross margin improvement. A recent study of UK top 500 firms revealed that the majority of B2E solutions was still at a basic level and have focussed on improved efficiency and electronic document delivery (Dunford, 2002).

Business-to-Employee (B2E)

With advances in network and browser technology, companies have been moving more and more of their corporate information resources to web-based applications, making them available to employees via the company intranet. Originally these applications only allowed employees to view and browse electronic versions of existing documents such as policy documents and on-line forms. Companies found that there was a savings in publication costs and an empowerment of employees through the increased availability of corporate procedures and knowledge to enable them to perform their day-to-day tasks.

Figure 1: The employee relationship management landscape (Hamerman, 2002)

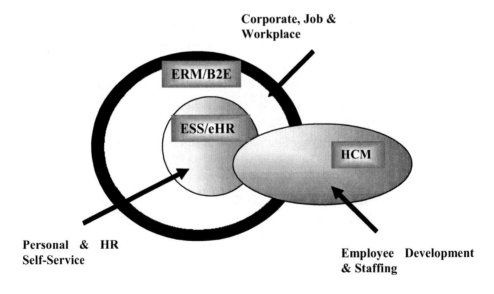

The increased familiarization of employees in the use of browser technology and the maturing of this technology within companies has resulted in these applications evolving to incorporate transactional interactions such as the booking of equipment and the enrolment in training courses. This has a number of benefits including the move towards paperless transactions, the implied reduction in administrative overheads and the provision of a better level of service to employees. One area in which this technological solution is being applied is in the area of human resources. Hamerman (2002) encapsulates the application of technology in his Employee Relationship Management (ERM) landscape with corporate, personnel and employee elements (see Figure 1). Hamerman (2002) sees ERM suites as being platforms for information delivery, process execution and collaboration in the organization. The advantages in empowering employees through an ERM suite include: multiple value propositions, consistent portal GUIs, all employee 24x7, real-time dynamic information delivery and a comprehensive collaborative work environment. Employees can now access a range of information pertinent to themselves without having to rely on others. They can compare pay slips for a number of given periods. They can view their superannuation and leave entitlements and then apply for leave on-line. SAP has developed a proprietary model outlining the role that human resources plays in the activities of employees. SAP views Employee Relationship Management (ERM), Employee Lifecycle Management (ELM) and Employee Transaction Management (ETM) as addressing three distinct functions of HR within an organization (see Figure 2) (Ordonez, 2002).

Figure 2: SAP employee (relationship, lifecycle, transaction) management (Ordonez, 2002)

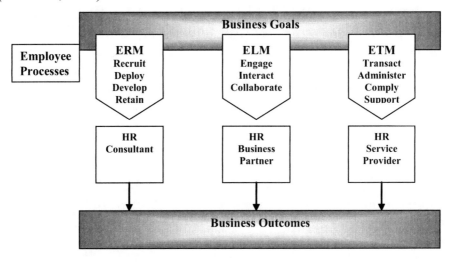

Human resources for many companies are evolving from the traditional payroll processing function to a more strategic direction of human capital management (Malis, 2002). As HR has evolved the level of associated administrative duties has increased proportionally, with some research estimating that as much as 70% of HR personnel time is spent on administrative duties (Barron, 2002). This has been estimated to represent a cost of up to US $1700 per employee per year (Khirallah, 2000). It has been estimated by Wagner (2002) that HR paper forms cost $20-$30 to process, telephone-based HR forms cost $2-$4 to process, but Internet-based HR forms cost only 5-10 cents. Obviously, in an attempt to reduce these high costs, companies are increasingly looking to the Internet-based solution.

Employee Self-Service (ESS)

Employee Self-Service (ESS) is an Internet-based solution that provides employees with a browser interface to relevant HR data and transactions. This enables employees' real-time access to their data without leaving their desktop. They can update their personal details, apply for leave, view their pay details and associated benefits, view internal job vacancies and book training and travel. The benefits of this type of technology have been well documented (Webster Buchanan, 2002; McKenna, 2002; Alexander, 2002; Wiscombe, 2001). They include reduced administrative overheads and the freeing of HR staff for more strategic activities, improved data integrity, and empowerment of employees. One report identified a major benefit as the provision of HR services to employees in a geographically decentralized company (NetKey, 2002). Tangible measures include reductions in administrative staff by 40%, a reduction in transaction costs of 50% (Wiscombe, 2001) and the reduction of processes from two to three days to a few hours (NetKey, 2002). Ordonez (2002) maintains the theme of information delivery in presenting ESS as allowing employees access to the right information at the right time to carry out process transactions, allowing the ability to create, view and maintain data through multiple access technologies. Companies such as Toyota are now extending this functionality beyond the desktop by providing access to electronic HR kiosks in common meeting areas. This caters for staff that do not have ready access to a PC. The above benefits have encouraged significant growth in companies implementing ESS solutions (Webster Buchanan, 2002). The return on investment of ESS applications has been substantial (Lehman, 2000). Transforming labour-intensive paper-based HR forms to digital enabled forms allows a 50% reduction of transaction costs, 40% reduction in administrative staffing, 80% reduction in management HR duties and a 10-fold speed-up of HR processes (Workforce, 2001). Many of Australia's larger companies and public sector organizations are implementing ESS functionality as an adjunct to their enterprise resource planning (ERP) systems. Approximately 320 of Australia's top companies have implemented SAP's ERP system (SAP R/3), and of these approximately 150 have implemented the HR module, with 33 implementing the ESS component. These companies include Toyota, Westpac, RMIT, National Australia Bank, Siemens, Telstra, and Linfox (Bennett, 2002).

Implementation Issues

Many of the world's largest companies have implemented enterprise-wide information systems, commonly referred to as an Enterprise Resource Planning (ERP) system, in an attempt to streamline and improve business processes, better manage information systems' expenditure, increase customer responsiveness and strategically position themselves for the move towards electronic business (Ross & Vitale, 1999). An increasing number of researchers believe that the adoption of Enterprise Resource Planning (ERP) systems by businesses may be the most important use of information technology (Davenport, 1998). However, implementing an ERP system and associated software can present considerable challenges to an organization, with many of these being non-technical in nature. In order for an implementation to be successful these challenges need to be identified and managed properly. Nah et al. (2001) documented eleven critical success factors (CSFs) that have proved to be vital to a successful ERP implementation. These are: ERP teamwork and composition, top management support, business plan and vision, effective communication, project management, project champion, appropriate business and legacy systems, change management program and culture, business process reengineering and minimum customization, software testing and trouble shooting, and monitoring and evaluation of performance. Other researchers have identified similar critical success factors and have also stressed the importance of change management (Somer & Nelson, 2001).

CHANGE MANAGEMENT

Change management implementation approaches vary from company to company (Hawking, Stein, & Foster, 2003). Two accepted definitions are:

Change management refers to:

> *"the effort to manage people through the emotional ups and down that inevitably occur when an organisation is undergoing massive change" (Nah & Sieber, 2002).*

In the context of the organization Goff (2000) defines change management as:

> *"a planned approach to integrating technological change. This includes formal processes for assessing the impact of the change on both the people it affects and the way they do their jobs. It also uses techniques to get users to accept a change caused by technology and to change their behaviour to take advantage of the new IT functionality."*

This statement implies that Information Technology projects require change management practices in order to fundamentally change the way people work and behave within an organization and across organizational boundaries. Other authors refer to the concept of resistance as an expression of reservation that invariably results as a response or reaction to change (Block, 1989, cited in Sohal & Waddell, 1998). Turbit (2002) goes further by describing change management in terms of setting expectations to alleviate the resistance to change by people within organizations. Current research points to the failure of most ERP implementations as being due to resistance to change by users in the organizations (Aladwani, 2001). A fairly simplistic framework that classifies the types of user resistance to innovations like ERP implementation by source of resistance is that of Sheth (1981) cited in Aladwani (2001). The framework demonstrates that there are two fundamental sources of resistance to innovations: perceived risk and habit. Perceived risk refers to one's perception of the risk associated with the decision to adopt the innovation; that is, the decision to accept the ERP system. Habit refers to current practices that one is routinely doing. Sheth (1981) argues that in order to reduce employees' resistance to ERP implementation, top management of the organization must analyse these sources of resistance and employ the appropriate set of strategies to counteract them. This argument implies that resistance is a negative influence on and in conflict with the organizational strategy. Therefore it is something to be managed and ultimately eliminated. Others argue that it should be recognized as something to be utilized to support a successful change management initiative (Mabin et al., 2001).

There are numerous prerequisites for change to be successful: the list includes a clear vision for change, communicating that vision articulately and clearly from a top-down perspective; preparing a culture for change, setting strong leadership and providing an environment for participation. Developing a vision, describing a picture of the future shape of an organization, gaining commitment to that vision and synchronization of purpose and effort are clearly seen as important leadership qualities. This development of vision and mission sets the scene for organizational change (Hamel & Prahalad, 1994; Senge & Roberts, 1994, cited in Mabin et al., 2001). Once the direction for organizational change has been established, the next important step in the change process is influencing the culture of the organization. Organizational culture is the shared understanding of how an organization works, and has a major impact and influence on successful change initiatives (Schein, 1988; Handy, 1996; McAdams, 1996). A culture that has shared values and common aims is conducive to success. Organizations should aim to have a strong corporate identity that is open and willing to change (Nah et al., 2001).

Communication and strong leadership play a vital role in preparing any organization for change and in guiding the organization through the upheavals that result from changes. The ability to create trust by developing an environment where the people who make up an organization feel change is required and then commit to that change process are two of leadership's most important qualities (Carlzon, 1989; Schermerhorn, 1989; Zand, 1997). Creating trust can be achieved through the sharing and discussion of issues and ideas.

RESEARCH FOCUS

In terms of ERP system implementations, change management is a planned approach to integrating technological change. Initially, formal processes are applied to assess the impact the new system will have on individuals within the organization and on the way they perform their roles. Then change techniques are adopted to prepare users to accept the change and modify their cognitive set. These processes and techniques provide the impetus for a positive behavioural change to take place and lay the groundwork for a successful implementation. The specific research questions addressed in this chapter are:

- What is the impact of Employee Self-Service (ESS) in large organizations?
- What are the change management issues associated with this B2E solution?

Research Methodology

The move to ESS functionality is detailed through the use of two mini-case studies. Case study research methodology was used as the chapter presents an exploratory look at implications of the implementation of a B2E solution (ESS). Yin (1994, p. 35) emphasises the importance of asking "what" when analysing information systems. Yin goes further and emphasises the need to study contemporary phenomena within real-life contexts. Walsham (2000, p. 204) supports case study methodology and sees the need for a move away from traditional information systems research methods such as surveys toward more interpretative case studies, ethnographies and action research projects. Several works have used case studies (Chan & Roseman, 2001; Lee, 1989; Benbasat et al., 1987) in presenting information systems research. Cavaye (1996) used case study research to analyse inter-organizational systems and the complexity of information systems. Two companies were chosen for case study research in an attempt to identify the impact an ESS implementation has and the associated change management issues. Both of the companies chosen attended a forum on ESS conducted by the SAP Australian User Group. They were large companies from both the private and public sectors from different industries. They had both implemented the same ESS solution using the same ERP platform (SAP R/3), and as such were selected to help validate the findings, as they came from different industry sectors but were using the same B2E. Initially, information was collected as a result of the companies' presentations at the ESS forum. Over the next month interviews were conducted with key managers on site in each company. Predetermined questions formed the basis of the interviews, supported by observations through access to the ESS systems. Project documentation and policy documents were also supplied. Interviews were transcribed and follow-up queries and clarification of points were conducted via email and telephone. Confidentiality guidelines were adhered to in the presentation of findings.

CASE STUDIES

Government Department (ABC)

The department employs approximately 5,000 staff at more than 200 diverse locations across Victoria. They first implemented SAP R/3 in 1999. Prior to that, they were using another HR system with a customised ESS solution. One of the major benefits they noticed with the implementation of SAP's ESS was the reduction in payroll processing, which was partly achieved through the introduction of on-line payslips. There was improved data integrity not just with the use of ESS but also with the integrative nature of the ERP system. Data only needed to be entered once and employees could then ensure the accuracy of their own data. Staff were also able to apply for leave and overtime electronically and apply and receive approval for training courses.

Change Management

One of the major problems associated with the implementation of the ESS solution was associated with change management; that is, staff that were inexperienced with personal computing technology and who were forced to adopt this technology. However, even staff who were experienced still took a while to accept the new functionality. Staff had to get used to the concept of not receiving a paper payslip each pay period and were partly compensated through union negotiations. Passwords became a significant issue, as the move towards increased security required passwords to change every 90 days, with a large number of employees forgetting their last password and needing it reset.

From a management perspective there were also change management issues. As managers were now required to approve a number of applications (leave, overtime, training) on-line through workflow technology, there was a tendency to leave the applications sitting in their inbox just as long as the paper applications. So even though the technology sped up the process of application and had the potential for the same gains for approvals this was not being realised. Related to this was that while managers were processing an employee's application the record was locked from that particular employee. If managers left this record open while they completed other tasks then an employee could not access his or her details. This was a frequent problem and attempts were made to educate management on procedures for application approval. The Department believes that the ESS solution has become an integral part of the workplace and it would very difficult to return to the previous procedures.

Bank (NBW)

The bank is one of Australia's largest, with more than 30,000 employees based in Australia, New Zealand, England and throughout the Pacific. Bank NBW first implemented SAP R/3 in 2000 and soon after implemented ESS in

Australia. They saw ESS as a solution to simplify many of their HR processes, that would increase manager accountability while at the same time empowering employees. They believed that is was an essential "building block" in their HR strategy. The ESS solution, other than handling the standard HR administrative tasks, would also be a medium for payroll-based transactions, training and event management and recruitment.

Change Management

The bank realised the importance of change management through the implementation process and assigned a "change champion" to each business area to assist with the process. In addition to this position, an ESS coach was assigned for every sixty employees. A just in time (JIT) methodology was employed to deliver appropriate training with an emphasis on change management; however, they still felt it was not enough. Initially staff had too much functionality delivered, and for future implementations the initial level of functionality would be reduced. Additional functionality would be added once staff became confident and competent with the available functionality. Also it was thought that too much emphasis was placed on telling employees what to do rather than selling the virtues of the solution. However, there is strong support for the solution and the next stage for the bank is to increase functionality and roll out the solution to New Zealand.

CONCLUSION

As with the evolution of traditional human resource information systems the initial focus of ESS was on efficiency in payroll processing and simple administrative tasks. This was due to the quick return on investment that can be calculated for administrative tasks. This is reinforced by a recent report from AMR Research (Carruso, 2002), which interviewed a number of companies who identified HR self-service applications as a way of increasing ROI on their ERP implementation. However, efficiency is believed by analysts to be only the starting point for these types of solutions. It is argued that solutions that improve efficiency together with employee development and loyalty is where the real success of these applications are (Dunford, 2002). Both the case studies could be considered early adopters of this technology as the ESS solution has only been available for approximately four years and these companies have installed this solution over the last two years. It would be expected that as the companies and their employees became more familiar with the ESS solution that more strategic functionality would be incorporated. This appears certainly the case for the bank.

It would have been easy for both companies to undervalue the role of change management for the implementation of the ESS solution. The solution was browser-based and therefore familiar to many employees and supposedly easy for the inexperienced to grasp the concepts. Also implied in the solution is that there are numerous reasons why employees would want to learn this technology. However, both companies emphasised the importance of change management in the implementation process. They still believed that their strategy could be improved as was evident by the number of issues they faced post-implementation.

ESS has proven to provide a number of quick wins in the business-to-employee e-business model. It provides a number of benefits to companies and streamlines many of the HR processes while at the same time empowering employees. Compared to other e-business solutions it has a relatively low impact on the organization, employees and processes. The risks are minimal as it provides a web interface to an existing system, and improves data integrity as employees are responsible for much of their own data. However, as with most IT projects, change management stills remains a major stumbling block. Many companies are now evolving their ESS solutions into employee portals where the HR functionality is just another tab that appears on their web page with their business transactions, corporate data, calendar and e-mail functionality. ESS will eventually disappear as a term as web interfaces become standard in HR software.

REFERENCES

Aladwani, A. M. (2001). Change management strategies for successful ERP implementation. *Business Process Management Journal*, 7(3), 266–275.

Alexander, S. (2002). *HR e-Power to the people.* Located at http://staging.infoworld.com/articles/ca/xml/01/02/010212cahr.xml. Accessed August.

APICS Dictionary Ninth Edition, (1998). *Defining Enterprise Resource Planning.* Falls Church, VA, USA.

Barron, M. (2002). Retail web-based self-serve isn't just for customers, it's for employees. Cited in *Internet Retailer*. Located at http://

www.internetretailer.com/dailynews.asp?id=6688. Accessed September 2002.

Benbasat, I., Goldstein, D. D., & Mead, M. (1987). The case research strategy in studies of information systems. *MIS Quarterly, 113*, 369–386.

Bennett, C. (2001). *SAP Update.* Delivered to ASUG Plenary, Sydney, Australia, December.

Bennett, C. (2002). *SAP expands mySAP.com user base with new contracts and additional licenses.* Retrieved July 2002 from http://www.sap.com/australia/company/press/2002/0508.asp

BRW2002. (2002). *Business Review Weekly*, The BRW1000. Retrieved October 2002 from http://www.brw.com.au/stories/19991113/intro.htm

Calegero, B. (2000). *Who is to blame for ERP failure?* Sunsaver, June.

Carlino, J. (1999). *AMR research unveils report on enterprise application spending and penetration.* Retrieved July 2001 from www.amrresearch.com/press/files/99823.asp

Carlino, J. (2000). *AMR research predicts enterprise alication market will reach $78 billion by 2004.* Retrieved August 2002 from www.amrresearch.com/press/files/

Carlzon, J. (1989). *Moments of truth.* New York: Harper & Row.

Carruso, D. (2002). Driving ROI through ERP implementation. *AMR Research Report.*

Cavaye, A. (1996). Case study research: A multi-faceted approach for IS. *Information Systems Journal, 6*(3), 227–242.

Chan, R., & Roseman, M. (2001). Integrating knowledge into process models — A case study. *Proceedings of the Twelfth Australasian Conference on Information Systems*, Southern Cross University, Australia.

Curran, T., Ladd, A., & Keller, G. (1999). *SAP R/3 business blueprint.* New Jersey: Prentice Hall.

Davenport, T. (1998). *Mission critical: Realizing the promise of enterprise systems.* Boston, MA: Harvard Business School Press.

Deimler, M., & Hansen, M. (2001). *The online employee.* Boston Consulting Group. Retrieved March 2003 from http://www.bcg.com/publications/files/Online_Employee_Aug_01_perpsective.pdf

Deloitte. (1999). *ERPs second wave.* Deloitte Consulting.

Dunford, I. (2002). *B2E: the future looks rosy.* Retrieved March 2003 from http://www.computing.co.uk/Analysis/1136393

Goff, L. J. (2000). *Change management.* Retrieved July 2001 from http://www.computerworld.com/news/2000/story/0,11280,41308,00.html

Hamerman, P. (2002). *Extending employee relationships with web applications*. Presentation to SAHIRE Lisbon Conference, July.

Handy, C. (1996). The gods of management. *Executive Book Summaries*, *18*(2), 1-8.

Hawking, P., Stein, A., & Foster, S. (2003). Change management: the real struggle for ERP Systems. *Industry Report commissioned by the SAP Australian Users Group.*

Iggulden, T. (Ed.). (1999). Looking for payback. *MIS*, June, 75–80.

Khirallah, D. (2000). *Picture this: Self-service HR at Sony.* Retrieved September 2002 from http://www.informationweek.com/811/sony.htm

Killen and Associates. (2000). *Communicating with employees via digital delivery systems.* Report 2000.

Lee, A. (1989). Case studies as natural experiments. *Human Relations*, *422*,117–137.

Lehman, J. (2000). HR Self-service strategies: Lessons learned. *Gartner Research Note*, September 26.

Mabin, V. J., Foreson, S., & Green, L. (2001). Harnessing resistance: Using the theory of constraints to assist change management. *Journal of European Industrial Training*, 168–191.

Malis, E. (2002).. Corporate intranets include automated time and attendance in your "HR self service" offering. Cited in *Crosswind*. Retrieved September 2002 from http://www.crosswind.com

McAdams, J. (1996). *The reward plan advantage.* San Francisco, CA: Jossey-Bass.

McKenna, E..(2002). *Empowering employees.* Retrieved August 2002 from http://www.fcw.com/fcw/articles/2002/0107/tec-hr-01-07-02.asp

Nah, F., Lee-Shang, L. J., & Kuang, J. (2001). Critical factors for successful implementation of enterprise systems. *Business Processes Management Journal*, *7*(3), 285–296.

Nah, F. H., & Sieber, M. (2002). *A recurring improvisational methodology for change management in ERP Implementation.* Available: http://www.ait.unl.edu/fnah/sieberandNah.pdf

Netkey. (2002). *Unlocking the power of HR self service.* Retrieved September 2002 from www.netkey.com

Nolan and Norton Institute. (2000). *SAP Benchmarking Report 2000.* KPMG Melbourne.

Ordonez, E. (2002). *mySAP human resources: Human capital management for your business.* Retrieved July 2002 from http://www.sap.com

Ross, J., Vitale, M., & Beach, C. (1999). The untapped potential of IT chargeback. *Management Information Systems Quarterly, 23*, 215–237.

SAP. (2002). *SAP corporate profile*. Retrieved July 2002 from http://www.sap.com/company/profile_long.htm

Schein, E. (1988). *Defining organisational culture*. London: Jossey-Bass.

Schermerhorn, J. (1989). *Management for productivity*. New York: John Wiley & Sons.

Sheth, J. (1981). Psychology of innovation resistance. *Research in Marketing, 4,* 273–282.

Sohal, A. S., & Waddell, D. (1998). Resistance: a constructive tool for change management. *Management Decision,* MCB University Press, 543–548.

Somer, T., & Nelson, K. (2001). The impact of critical success factors across the stages of enterprise resource planning systems implementations. *Proceedings of the 34th Hawaii International Conference on System Sciences,* HICSS.

Stein, A., & Hawking, P. (2002). *Business improvement and ERP systems: an Australian survey 2002*. Industry report commissioned by the SAP Australian User Group 2002.

Turbit, N. (2002). *ERP implementation – The trap*. Retrieved July 2002 from http://www.projectperfect.com.au/info_erp_imp.html

Wagner, M. (2002). Saving trees and serving up benefits. *Internet Retailer,* June.

Walsham, G. (2000). Globalisation and IT: Agenda for research. In *Organisational and Social Perspectives on Information Technology,* (195–210). Boston, MA: Kluwer Academic Publishers.

Webster & Buchanan Research. (2002). *HR self service – The practitioners' view*. Retrieved August 2002 from www.leadersinHR.org

Wiscombe, J. (2001). Using technology to cut costs. *Workforce,* September. Retrieved August 2002 from http://www.workforce.com/archive/feature/22/29/82/index.php

Workforce. (2001).*HR Statistics, 79*(10). October, 54–61.

Yin, R. (1994). *Case study research, design and methods* (2nd ed.). Newbury Park: Sage Publications.

Zand, D. (1997). The leadership triad. *Soundview Executive Book Summaries, 19*(6), Part 1, 1–8.

Chapter IX

E-Government in Developing Countries: A Sri Lankan Experience

Ramanie Samaratunge
Monash University, Australia

Dianne Waddell
Edith Cowan University, Australia

ABSTRACT

Even though there is an emerging literature on information age reform of the public sector, research focused on potential and problems related to introduction of information-based reforms in developing countries is still limited. Thus in this chapter, experience in one developing country, Sri Lanka, is examined. Problems related to information-based technology is analysed and the lacuna in the literature is narrowed. It is argued that despite the great potential for IT in enhancing effective and efficient public sector in Sri Lanka, there are a number of difficulties hindering the development of computerised information systems. The upgrading of infrastructure facilities in Sri Lanka is long overdue. A lack of competent and committed individuals who could provide effective guidance in developing IT services in the public sector is another concern. The issues such as appropriate training, attractive promotion systems and remunerations for public officials need to be addressed urgently. Reforming existing organizational structures and changing officials' attitudes towards change are essential. The increasing public awareness of the potential of IT services enhancing the quality and timeliness of the public service is essential.

INTRODUCTION

The use of information technology (IT) in the public sector is increasing rapidly, with innovations including government web sites, electronic transactions such as electronic tax filing, and electronic kiosks. IT can have its greatest impact on the quality of government services by integrating what are often perceived as disparate functions. For this to happen, the public servants who manage these programs must bring about the integration and assimilation of such functions while being cognisant of the community's receptivity to these innovative practices. Thus, realising the potential of public sector IT (electronic government) is not merely a technical and organisational issue, but more a cultural issue, involving matters of both organisational structure/strategy and the management of change.

Electronic government (e-government) is the ability for government to provide access to services and information twenty-four hours a day, seven days a week. Governments are more broadly turning their attention and resources to providing information and services on-line, exploring digital democracy, and using technology for economic development. This is a broad definition, requiring a different mindset, and affects all customers of government, including the interactions between government and the public (G2P), government and business (G2B), government and other government departments (G2G), and between government and its own employees (G2E). While many current activities are predominantly G2P, an understanding of e-government is not complete unless it identifies and considers all of its customers. It must be stated that the definition of e-government will be different for each situation based on the community's values, goals and culture. Hence it is important to understand that e-government is much more than a web site, e-mail or processing transactions via the Internet.

Once there is a commitment to e-government, and a thorough understanding as to the ramifications of such a pathway, it is crucial for each country to define e-government for itself and its community, and to develop a strategy to move forward. This strategy is fundamental to navigating through the proliferation of e-government programs, re-engineering processes and procedures to support e-government, and implementing e-government initiatives.

E-GOVERNMENT IN DEVELOPING COUNTRIES

For obvious reasons, e-government has progressed farthest within the most economically developed nations. Now developing countries too are fast adapting these new technologies to their particular needs. But they also have the advantage of being considered as potential 'greenfield sites' where they can transform processes without being encumbered by past practices. Whether this is the case or not, there is an undeniable opportunity to instil an e-government approach with the benefit of utilising experience from more developed countries.

Research has shown that policy makers in developing countries, in particular, have become increasingly aware that gathering, storing, analysing and sharing information is crucial in public sector reforms leading to greater service efficiency and effectiveness (Heeks, 1999, 2001). It means facilitating a new government-citizen interface by making it not just efficient but transparent and accountable. This is the core idea of the widely discussed notion of information-based public sector reforms in recent years (Heeks, 2001). Given the high degree of enthusiasm for the development of e-government from various focus groups (politicians, administrators, academics and professionals) IT innovation to improve organisational efficiency and effectiveness became the focal point of government reforms in developing countries (Heeks, 1999).

Despite the growing awareness among policy makers about the prospects of the new technology in the public sector, the experience suggests that the quality and timeliness of the services provided by the information technology sector could best be described as poor. In particular, the effective use of e-government is far from satisfactory (Day, 2000; Bhatngar, 1988; Heeks, 1998; Peterson, 1998). The main stumbling block in this regard appears to be the government's inability to establish a foundation of information infrastructure such as modern telecommunication facilities. In fact, there is a huge gap between support and action with regard to IT sector development. As Day (2000, p. 302) points out, "there perhaps is support, but no direction; there are small initiatives, but nothing major".

Thus in this chapter, an attempt is made to examine the experience in one developing country, Sri Lanka. The country has much to offer as a case study in IT reforms due to two main reasons: first, Sri Lanka is blessed with a well-educated labour force which is a basic raw material for rapid technological change; second, the economic and administrative reforms introduced in the 1980s demanded an efficient and effective role of government in order to reap the full benefits of these reforms (Samaratunge, 2000). In keeping with the increased awareness and appreciation of the role of government in this context, the process of governance became stronger in favour of the use of information technology, and a new concept of e-governance emerged. The reforms demand new skills and attitudes from bureaucrats and politicians in the country. It is important to recognise the development of e-government initiatives in Sri Lanka and examine the potentials and problems with these initiatives.

THE PUBLIC SECTOR IN SRI LANKA: THE NEED FOR CHANGE

During the 1970s Sri Lanka experienced deteriorating terms of trade and increasing government deficits. When the policy makers in the country realised the imperative of economic and administrative policy reforms in addressing these issues, the emphasis was given to pro-market policies in trade and finance abandoning the inward-looking economic model. It also considered the intro-duction of decentralisation with a multi-layered administrative structure against the existing centralised administrative model. With an unprecedented increase of public sector reform, often sponsored by international financial institutions (IFIs), the reduction of government involvement in economic activities has become increasingly apparent. A new form of network between state, business and non-government sectors was instigated in order to provide services that used to be primarily government responsibility. Growing prominence of the private sector in economic activity and the IFIs, in particular the World Bank and the Asian Development Bank (ADB), forced the state to become more efficient and competitive. Flexibility and managing change were regarded as components in the public sector. In this regard, dissemination and sharing of information become a must. Introduction of e-governance is seen as a path to rapid improvement of efficiency in the public sector with much-needed transparency and improved accountability (World Bank, 2000). Large bureaucracies become outdated and a new set of competencies needs to be developed.

Compared to the existing administrative practices, information technology provides promising avenues to disseminate information and to obtain a speedy feedback from the public. It also allows administrators to connect "agencies, levels and data stores of government to strengthen capacity to investigate, develop and implement the strategy and policy that guide government processes" (Heeks 2001, p.5), which enhances the capacity to make decisions promptly at the local level. As customer-oriented benefits from Internet-based transactions have been a key focus in the information age, such efforts would reduce the differences between the local community, bureaucrats and political leaders on the performance of decentralisation initiatives and increase the people's participation in the process of development in the country. Computer-aided decision-making processes and electronic databases would provide an environment conducive to effective decentralised management in the country.

INFORMATION-BASED REFORMS IN SRI LANKA

Sri Lanka's attempts to improve IT facilities in order to increase the effectiveness of public policies can be looked at from two interrelated perspectives: the priority given to the better infrastructure for IT initiatives and computer education; and the growing awareness of the benefits of enhancing computer literacy in senior civil servants at the central and local government levels.

Having recognised the importance of information technology in the globalized world, Sri Lanka established the Computer and Information Council of Sri Lanka (CINTEC) under the Parliament Act of No. 10 of 1984. The main aim of the CINTEC was to identify the trend in the global IT industry and its implications for international trade (CINTEC, 2000). The Science and Technology Act No. 11 of 1994, which replaced the previous Act, further elaborated the functions of the CINTEC of Sri Lanka. The functions of the Council were: the promotion and development of information technology literacy; the development of the human resources necessary for the promotion of IT and the promotion of R&D in information technology (ICT, 2000). In the meantime, universities and government training institutes were encouraged to

introduce computer education courses. The private sector also actively partici-
pated in the provision of IT education. The result was that a large number of IT
institutes offered different certificate courses and degrees in IT for school
leavers and professionals during the last decade. The emphasis was given to the
increase demand for IT personnel, as a high level of computer literacy is a
necessity for employees in every organisation, public as well as private, in the
21st century (Daily News, 02/07/2003).

Increasing communication facilities has been a top priority in all governments in the country since 1977. The government greatly expanded the
telecommunication sector in the country. The privatisation of the Department
of Telecommunication in the late 1980s reduced the government monopoly and
hence a number of other private firms invested a substantial amount of
resources in this sector (Central Bank of Sri Lanka, 2000). In order to enhance
communication between the central and local level government entities, all
Pradeshiya Sabhas (provincial), Kachcheries (district) and Divisional Secre-
tariats (divisional) have been provided with fax machines and computers.
Short-term training programs for officers have been organised by the government training institutes such as National Institute of Business Management
(NIBM) and Sri Lanka Institute of Development Administration (SLIDA).
During a survey conducted by Samaratunge (2002) on the perception of
bureaucrats regarding the effectiveness of public sector reforms in Sri Lanka in
December 2001, most of the senior civil servants admitted that the failure or
ignorance of the government to understand the potential of new information
technology much earlier was one of the main reasons for the poor performance
of the public sector. They maintained that in the future the improvement of the
quality and timeliness of the public sector would mainly depend on computer-
based office systems, and therefore, the improvement of IT facilities in the
sector was a prerequisite in addressing the demand of devolution of power,
efficiency and greater transparency in the public sector. The Executive President, Mrs. Kumaranatunge, has also repeatedly emphasised the urgent need of
extensive use of information channels in policy making in order to improve the
quality of public service (Daily News, 14 Feb 2001). She further stressed that
unless the public service performs its role as an efficient facilitator for the private
sector, the projected economic and social targets could be jeopardised.

THE POTENTIALS AND CONSTRAINTS OF IT REFORMS

Despite this enthusiasm and awareness at the highest political and administrative levels and increasing the facilities for computer education and training, it appears that the public sector has not been able to realise the full benefits provided by information technology. The experience in the public sector shows that the provision of IT reforms has been largely restricted to installing a limited number of computers, fax machines in each ministry and short-term training programs for senior civil servants at the central level. At the local level, the use of computers and fax machines is still very limited; rather, they are treated as a status symbol in government offices. The sub-standard infrastructure services, such as unreliable electricity supply (since July 2001 due to the shortage of electricity power generation, a daily power cut has been a common phenomenon in the country), poor telecommunication facilities and a lack of trained personnel are the main factors responsible for this slow pace of change at the local level. Treasury directives that restricted the recurrent expenditure of government departments since 2000 greatly curtailed the use of telephones and fax machines and aggravated this problem.

At the national level, however, the quality of computerisation of the services in most of the key government institutions, in particular the Treasury and the Central Bank, is improving with the assistance from donor countries and IFIs such as the World Bank and the ADB. Some government departments, which so far have experienced difficulties in meeting the heavy service demand by the public, have also computerised their operations since the mid 1980s. The Department of Statistics and the Department of Examinations were the early initiators among the government institutions that introduced computers to their operations. The Department of Examination has significantly reduced its long delays it experienced in releasing examination results of the GCE Ordinary Level and Advanced Level examinations with more than 150,000 candidates. Other government departments such as Departments of Motor Vehicle Registration, Immigration and Emigration, and Personal Registration were under heavy criticism due to long delays in issuing passports, driving licences and national identity cards, respectively, which encouraged corruption. They have been able to streamline their services individually thanks to computerisation of application procedures but are unable to establish a developed network between these departments. Not surprisingly, the issue of fake passports, driver's licences and national identity cards is still a common phenomenon in the country. Even though the use of IT facilities is not necessarily preventing corruption (Heeks, 1998), the government has still not been able to use the opportunities provided by computerisation of relevant departments that strengthen the effectiveness of the procedure of screening applications for these documents at any significant level.

These examples demonstrate some benefits achieved by the public with the introduction of IT initiatives, but most of the government departments, particularly at the local level, are still adhering to the conventional office practices which inherited delays and bureaucratic red tape. Table 1 indicates the major sectors of the economy that use computers in their operations and demonstrates the finance and banking and the public sector as the pioneering customers in the IT sector. Globalized economic policies significantly increased the importance of private commercial banks and other financial institutions in the private sector. In order to face the strong competition from computerised private banks and financial institutions, state banks have been compelled to introduce computer-aided banking services and have gained a competitive advantage against others using inter-bank networks and Electronic Data Exchange (EDI) systems (ICT, 2000).

Table 1: Major customers in information technology sector in Sri Lanka

Categories	Percentage
Central government	47.1
Local government	41.2
Other public sector	58.8
Universities	47.1
Training institutes/schools	39.2
Other educational institutes	31.4
Construction	25.5
Manufacturers	47.1
Finance and Banking	58.8
Communication	49.0
Wholesale and retailer	47.1

Source: JICA study for BOI 1999-2000, quoted in CINTEC, 2000: 10-11

The increasing use of computers in the public sector does not necessarily imply that the sector makes use of full benefits provided by the IT service. As a recent survey on computer use in the country comments, despite all these initiatives in the IT sector, "it is hardly in use in an effective way in Sri Lanka, particularly in the public sector" (ICT, 2000, p.9). Even within the government institutions which introduced computers to their operations there is no developed networking system that would allow computer-aided policy formulation, coordination and decision-making within or between departments. In fact, computer-aided pooling, storing, analysing and sharing information are almost non-existent in the public sector.

Apart from the key government departments, most of the government offices are largely adhering to the existing practice of the public sector such as manual working in file maintenance and communication. Responding to the survey conducted by Samaratunge (2002) in December 2001 on the performance of the public sector in Sri Lanka, some officials were of the view that existing system of data collection, processing, record keeping and file maintenance is far more reliable than the computer-aided system. The existing system is slow and prone to bureaucratic red tape, but with proper management and incentive systems most of these problems can be overcome. The information technology may reduce cost and long delays, but given the poor infrastructure and training facilities it is unlikely that the introduction of computers would increase the efficiency of the public service. Poor maintenance of computers and lack of trained personnel may greatly weaken the advantages of computer-aided office work over the existing one. For instance, if office records are kept in computer files it is highly likely that dishonest officials may misuse computers to continue their corrupt practices. The more such officers obtain computer expertise, the higher their chances to misuse information for their own benefits. The majority of the officials interviewed were of the view that under a computer-aided office work system, monitoring of such malpractices would be much more difficult. Given the developing nature of computer-aided administration and lack of trained personnel in the country this phenomenon would be more prominent, they further added.

The lack of trained personnel in the computer field is a major problem that undermines the effectiveness of IT service in the public sector. Most of the officers are keen to obtain computer training not just because they can improve the system through computer-aided services, but because it is an added bonus to get their next promotion or find a well-paid job in the private sector. Compared to the attractive salary level and other fringe benefits that IT executives in the private sector enjoy, the remuneration for public servants is considerably inadequate. In fact, retaining skilled public servants has become a major problem. It is a general phenomenon, therefore, in Sri Lanka that civil servants who obtained good computer training are encouraged to leave the public sector for higher salaried-positions either in the private sector or abroad. Further, there is neither a systematic approach for training and development nor a specific plan that improves the link between strategic planning and human resource development in the public sector. These personnel rarely have sufficient time to improve their IT skills because their routine office work has been very time consuming.

As is the case in most developing countries (Heeks, 2001), IT initiatives in the public sector are either ignored or isolated from the main process of governance, resulting in no effective contribution and delays in decision-making and in implementing the country's development. In fact, it was pointed out that the sluggish decision-making process in the public sector was partly responsible for the country's slow economic growth (*The Sunday Times*, 14 December 2001). There is no significant partnership between the private sector and public training authorities, and virtually they "operate independently like closed systems in terms of planning, policy formulation and training" (Liyanage, 2002, p. 3). Making the necessary changes to achieve this policy integration will require a long-term vision with considerable political and administrative commitment. In the absence of such an assurance, little would change.

The lack of policy coordination in developing IT services is another common problem in the country (*Daily News*, 02/07/2003). Since the 1990s the availability of funds to develop computer facilities has increased significantly. However, there was no plan with regard to ordering computers from various sources, selection of proper computer systems for the needs of different government institutions or the provision of infrastructure facilities. In some instances, the installation of computers imported was delayed for several months because other facilities such as air conditioning and power supply were not readily available at the time. Misuse of funds set aside for IT sector development is also a problem in Sri Lanka. As is the case in many developing countries, malpractices in the government tendering procedure has been a common phenomenon in Sri Lanka. The increasing availability of foreign funds to develop the IT sector seems to provide ample opportunities for unscrupulous public servants to manipulate tendering process for their own benefits.

Public awareness of IT and its relevance to public service delivery and quality are key factors that increase the efficacy of IT services provided at the time. Availability of IT training facilities especially for school leavers and other professionals is a decisive factor in this regard. As indicated in Table 2, more

Table 2: Geographical distribution of IT training institutes

Region	Percentage
Colombo	30.7
Gampaha	10.0
Kurunegala	8.7
Kandy	6.7
Galle	6.0
Kalutara	5.3
Anuradhapura	5.3

Source: JICA study for BOI, 1999-2000, quoted in CINTEC, 2000: 12-13

than 40 percent of IT training institutes in the country are concentrated in the Colombo and Gampaha regions, which are the most urbanised districts in the country.

The lack of IT training institutes in rural areas suggests two factors that are relevant to the development of IT services. Firstly, rural youth are disadvantaged in obtaining training in a rapidly expanding field in the world and thereby weaken their relative competitiveness in the job market. It would prove to be a costly mistake when the inevitable failure to meet their expectations in this way would lead to youth unrest which in turn slows down the growth process. Secondly, it would contribute to the lack of awareness of the potential of IT services in delivering public services among the people in the rural areas. Without popularising the use of computers it is difficult to convince the people about the benefits available through IT services. Not only IT training providers but also other IT-based facilities are mainly limited to urban areas. For example, almost all state commercial banks have been computerised but ATM facilities are mainly limited to the urban areas. Most of the private banks provide island wide bank networking facilities for their customers, although their operations are also limited to urban and semi-urban areas.

Although problems of the use of computers in the public service mentioned above explain the ground reality of the country, they make no excuses to ignore the benefits provided by IT in increasing the efficiency of the public sector. The majority of the government officers are fully aware of the potential of IT facilities, but it seems that they are reluctant to change the status quo due to several reasons. Firstly, many top bureaucrats speculate that a computer-aided office work system would weaken their influence over their subordinates and undermine their dominant position in decision-making. Unlike in the existing system under which top bureaucrats can keep the key files that contain important data on a particular issue or project, a computer-based file system provides more opportunities to obtain data to other focus groups. This would challenge the authority of top civil servants in decision-making. Secondly, most of the central government officers hold considerable influence in key aspects of local administration and would not fully support computer-aided office procedures. For instance, the existing process of distributing subsidised goods and services, paying old age pensions and issuing various government permits and licences provide government officials ample opportunities to keep their influence in delivering these services. Computerisation increases public access to official documents and procedures and thereby weakens officers' influence on delivering public services.

Thirdly, many seem to believe that computers and fax machines are status symbols and should be used only by top-level administrative officers. The prevailing austerity measures in the government departments seem to encourage this line of thought. The use of fax machines was very limited in accordance with the cost saving directives. Expenses on telephone use are fixed and the relevant Head of the department or the supervisor is responsible for not exceeding this limit. In most offices, particularly in local offices, fax machines are kept switched off. Finally, where computers are used in general office works, it is treated as a superior substitute to a typewriter and is often limited to typing documents. In fact, while addressing a conference for senior civil servants in the country in February 2001 the President highlighted in her address the pathetic situation of the use of e-government and claimed that she had hardly seen any computer-assisted cabinet papers or ministry documents prepared by the public servants [even] in the central government (*Daily News*, 14 Feb. 2001). It could be argued, therefore, that on the surface, inadequate computer facilities, mainly in the provincial and local level offices, and the lack of computer literacy seem to be the main obstacles that prevent achieving the full benefits of IT facilities provided, but lethargy of senior officers to change the status quo might also be a key reason for poor performance of e-government.

Changing attitudes in the delivery of public service and convincing the public officials and the general public about the potential of the use of IT are the main challenges which lie ahead in improving the quality of the public sector. While accepting the fact that it is difficult to overcome the shortcomings of infrastructure facilities and financial constraints that limit expansion of IT facilities in the short run, the country would benefit if it could manage change in the public sector in order to make the best use of facilities available.

The provisions in IT legislation specified in the Science and Technology Act No. 11 of 1994 are limited to education, human resource development and R&D development. It is necessary to provide legal recognition for transactions carried out by means of electronic data interchange and other means of electronic communication. For instance, passing the Information of Technology Act of 2000 the government of India legally recognised the electronic records and digital signatures (Day 2000). Electronic data recording system has many advantages over the existing system. Paper work and file maintenance have always been under criticism because they allow bureaucratic delays. The IT initiatives with on-line information would enhance transparency and speed up the process. In Australia e-government is being used to improve the quality of social security while in China on-line information is used in the process of privatisation in special economic zones (Day 2000). These are the examples which Sri Lanka can follow as role models when the government designs the blue print of e-governance. It is the responsibility of the central government to provide an overall development plan for IT in the country introducing e-governance initiatives with a long-term vision in the global economy.

CONCLUSION

Parallel to administrative and economic policy reforms in the country, Sri Lanka introduced a number of IT initiatives in the public sector. The use of personal computers (PC) is just the beginning of an anticipated, and vibrant, network to get government processes online. The growing recognition of the new approaches of IT that emphasises the importance of e-government seems to have convinced the policy makers the timeliness of introducing the IT facilities in the country. Since the 1980s, Sri Lanka has initiated a number of IT reforms in public service delivery. The growing use of computers in various government departments, the establishment of inter-bank networks are clearly evident, but still the country has a long way to go in improving the IT facilities.

It is, therefore, argued that despite the great potential for IT in enhancing effective and efficient public sector in Sri Lanka, there are a number of difficulties hindering the development of computerised information systems. It requires competent and committed individuals who could provide effective guidance in developing e-government. The issues such as appropriate training, attractive promotion systems and remunerations for public officials need to be addressed urgently. Reforming organisational structures and changing officials' attitudes towards change are essential. It is of the utmost importance that the expansion of IT training facilities is carried forward not only for public officials but also for the rural youth.

This chapter has identified many of the challenges that IT and the Internet may place in the path of e-government in Sri Lanka and other developing nations. But there is enough evidence to suggest that such hurdles are not insurmountable. It is undeniable that the gains from moving towards an e-economy are substantial regardless of the country's status. E-government offers a remarkable set of opportunities to increase transparency of government operations, improve access to government services, reduce costs, and in the long-term (and most importantly) give the people a greater role in their own governance.

REFERENCES

Bhatngar, S. C. (1988). Productivity in public administration through computerisation: Manpower bottlenecks. *Indian Journal of Public Administration, XXXIV* (2), 284–293.

Central Bank of Sri Lanka. (2000). *Annual report.* Central Bank of Sri Lanka, Colombo.

Council for Information Technology (CINTEC). (2000). *National policy for Information Technology.* CINTEC, Colombo.

Daily News. (2001). *Challenges for public sector – President.* February 14, p. 1.

Daily News. (2003). *Information Technology will be taken to the grassroots – Minister.* July 2, p. 1.

Day, B. K. (2000). E-Governance in India: Problems, challenges and opportunities—A futures vision. *The Indian Journal of Public Administration, XLVI* (3), 300–313.

Heeks, R. (1998). Information Age reform of the public sector: the potential and problems of IT for India. *Information Systems for Public Sector Management Working Paper Series,* Working Paper No. 6, IDPM, University of Manchester, Manchester.

Heeks, R. (1999). *Reinventing government in the Information Age: International practice in IT-enabled public sector reform.* Routledge, London.

Heeks, R. (2001). *Understanding E-governance for development.* I-Government Working Paper Series, No. 11, IDPM, University of Manchester, Manchester.

Institute of Computer Technology (ICT). (2000). *Vocational education and training plan for the Information Technology sector.* University of Colombo, Colombo.

Liyanage, L. (2002). Why Sri Lanka needs a national policy in Information Technology. *Daily News [Sri Lanka],* July 24.

OECD. (1989). *Information Technology and new growth opportunities.* Paris: OECD.

OECD. (1995). *Governance in transition: Public management reforms in OECD Countries.* Paris: OECD.

Osborne, D., & Gaebler, T. (1993). *Reinventing government: How the entrepreneurial spirit is transforming the public sector.* Ringwood: Penguin Books Limited.

Samaratunge, R. (2000). *Decentralisation and development in Sri Lanka: a consolidated model of public management.* Ph.D. Thesis, Monash University, Melbourne.

Samaratunge, R., & Waddell, D. (2002). Information-based public sector reforms and the management of change in Sri Lanka. Paper presented and published in proceedings *Human Resource Development in Asia: Trends and Challenges,* Bangalore, India, October 28–29.

Sunday Times. (2001). *Delays in decision-making slows growth – ADB,* 9 December.

World Bank. (2000). *Sri Lanka: Capturing missed opportunities.* Washington, D.C.: World Bank.

Chapter X

Using Actor-Network Theory to Identify Factors Affecting the Adoption of E-Commerce in SMEs

Arthur Tatnall
Victoria University, Australia

Stephen Burgess
Victoria University, Australia

ABSTRACT

Just because e-commerce seems like a useful tool that may assist a small to medium enterprise (SME) do its business better, it does not necessarily follow that it will be adopted by this business. The implementation of an e-commerce system in an SME necessitates change in the way the business operates, and so should be considered as an innovation and studied using innovation theory. In this chapter we will argue that the decision to adopt, or not to adopt, a new technology, has more to do with the interactions and associations of both human and non-human actors involved in the project than with the characteristics of the technology. Information systems are complex socio-technical entities and research into their implementation needs to take account of this complexity. This chapter describes three case studies of adoption (or, in one case, of non-adoption) of e-commerce by small business. The chapter describes a research approach based on actor-network theory and innovation translation that we show can be usefully employed in many socio-technical situations involving technological innovation.

INTRODUCTION

Electronic commerce (e-commerce) is concerned with how computers, information systems and communications technologies can be used by people to improve the ways in which they do business. As e-commerce necessarily involves interactions of people and technology, any study of how it is used by a small business[1] must be considered in a socio-technical context. Although there is no universal consensus on what constitutes e-commerce, we believe that it contains elements of information systems, business processes and communications technologies. The complexity of studies in e-commerce is due, to a considerable degree, to the interconnected parts played by human actors and by the multitude of non-human entities involved. Small business managers, sales people, staff involved in procurement and warehouse operations, computers, software, web browsers, Internet service providers (ISP), modems and web portals are only some of the many heterogeneous components of an e-commerce system. In this chapter we will argue that the complexity of these systems will only be seen if it is reported in all its 'messy reality' (Hughes, 1983), and that research into their implementation and operation needs to take this heterogeneity into account and to find a way to give due regard to both their human and non-human aspects.

The implementation of an e-commerce system in a small business necessitates change in the way the business operates and we contend that it be studied in the light of innovation theory. The dictionary defines the process of innovation as "the alteration of what is established; something newly introduced" (Oxford, 1973), and "introducing new things or methods" (Macquarie Library, 1981). It thus involves getting new ideas accepted and new technologies adopted and used. In this chapter we describe a research approach to the study of technological innovation in small business that is based on actor-network theory (Callon, 1986b; Latour, 1986; Latour, 1996; Callon, 1999;

Latour, 1999; Law, 1999; Tatnall, 2002b; Tatnall, 2002a). We investigate the adoption, or non-adoption, of e-commerce by small to medium businesses in three separate situations: the use by a medium business of a business-to-business (B-B) portal designed for use by small to medium enterprises (SMEs) in a regional area of an Australian city; the adoption of e-commerce by a small academic publishing company, and the failure of a small chartered accountancy firm to make this adoption.

ACTOR-NETWORK THEORY AND INNOVATION TRANSLATION

One view of the adoption of an electronic commerce innovation by a small business suggests that decisions are made primarily based on its perceptions of the characteristics of the technology concerned. Innovation diffusion (Rogers, 1995) uses this approach, and is based on the following elements: characteristics of the innovation itself, the nature of the communications channels, the passage of time, and the social system. Using this sort of approach the researcher would probably begin by looking for characteristics of the specific e-commerce technology to be adopted, and the advantages and problems associated with its use. The next step would be to suggest that the adoption, or rejection, of this technology by the small business was due largely to these characteristics. We contend that while there may be some validity in such an approach, it is unlikely to provide the complete explanation, as it would miss other influences due to inter-personal and inter-business interactions, and to the backgrounds of the people involved.

We argue that actor-network theory (ANT) has much to offer in a situation like this. Researchers using an actor-network approach to study innovation would concentrate on issues of network formation, investigating the human and non-human actors and the alliances and networks they build up. They would investigate how the strength of these alliances may have enticed the small business to make the adoption or, on the other hand, to have deterred them from doing so (Tatnall & Gilding, 1999; Tatnall, 2000; Tatnall, 2002b). While some research approaches to technological innovation treat the social and the technical in entirely different ways, actor-network theory proposes instead a socio-technical account in which neither social nor technical positions are privileged. In order to treat both human and non-human actors in the same way, actor-network theory is based upon three principles (Callon, 1986b):

- Analytical impartiality towards all the actors involved.
- Generalised symmetry in explaining the conflicting viewpoints of different actors through use of a neutral vocabulary that works in the same way for both human and non-human actors.
- Free association that requires the elimination of all *a priori* distinctions between the technological, or natural, and the social.

Actor-network theory argues that interactions between actors are heterogeneous and denies that purely technical or purely social relations are possible. It considers the world to be full of hybrid entities (Latour, 1993) containing both human and non-human elements. Change, in the ANT view, results from decisions made by actors, and involves the exercise of power. Latour (1986) argues that the mere possession of power by an actor does not automatically lead to change unless other actors can also be *persuaded* to perform the appropriate actions for this to occur.

In our experience it is often the case that when a small business is considering a technological innovation it is interested in *only some aspects* of this innovation and not others (Tatnall, 2002b; Tatnall & Burgess, 2002). In actor-network terms, it needs to *translate* (Callon, 1986b) this piece of technology into a form where it can be adopted, which may mean choosing some elements of the technology and leaving out others. What results is that the innovation finally adopted is not the innovation in its original form, but a translation of it into a form that is suitable for use by the recipient small business (Tatnall, 2002b).

Callon (1986b) outlines the process of innovation translation as having four 'moments':

- **Problematisation:** in which an actor attempts to define the nature of the problem and the roles of other actors to fit the proposed solution.
- **Interessement:** is a series of processes that attempt to impose identities and roles, defined in the problematisation, on the other actors.
- **Enrolment:** will then follow leading to the establishment of a stable network of alliances.
- **Mobilisation:** occurs as the proposed solution gains wider acceptance and an even larger network of absent entities is created (Grint & Woolgar, 1997) through some actors acting as spokespersons for others.

It can be argued that research on SMEs should be practical (Burgess, 2001), and that innovation diffusion theory (Rogers, 1995), in giving considerable weight to the persuasive powers of the characteristics of technologies, is not best suited to explaining the manner in which *small businesses* adopt information technology. In many instances a small business proprietor will adopt e-commerce because a friend is using it, or because they know a competitor is using it, or because a son or daughter learned about it at school (Burgess, 2002; Tatnall, 2002b). The nature and size of each small business, the inter-business interactions in which they engage, and the backgrounds and interests of particular individuals in each are also likely to have had an important effect that would, most likely, have been ignored by the essentialist approach offered by innovation diffusion. Actor-network theory, in examining alliances and networks of human and non-human actors, provides a good foundation from which small business adoption and use of e-commerce can be researched. The ANT approach will be further amplified in the case studies that follow, particularly in respect of the identification of actors and networks.

THE CASE STUDIES

Each of the case studies that follow will include a discussion, under the umbrella of actor-network theory, of the approach taken by each of these SMEs to the adoption, or non-adoption, of e-commerce. In each case, data for the study was obtained through a series of semi-structured interviews with the proprietors and personnel of the businesses involved. A condition of each interview was that the businesses remain anonymous. The interviews were conducted between September 2001 and August 2002. The data were then subjected to an ANT analysis in which actors and networks were identified and interactions were traced. The approach used in ANT to identify and trace networks is to "follow the actors" (Latour, 1996, p.10) and investigate the leads each new actor suggests. This means that it is primarily the actors themselves, and not the researcher, that determine the direction taken by the investigation. The studies are:

- The use by a medium-sized business of a B-B portal designed for use in a regional area of a large Australian city.
- The adoption of e-commerce technologies by a small academic publishing company.
- The non-adoption of e-commerce by a small chartered accountancy firm.

Adoption of the Bizewest Portal (www.bizewest.com.au) by a Storage and Transport Company

In June 2000 the Western Region Economic Development Organisation (WREDO), a not-for-profit organisation sponsored by the six municipalities that make up the western region of Melbourne (Australia), received a government grant for a project to set up a business-to-business portal. This innovative project was to create a horizontal[2] portal, *Bizewest*, which would enable the whole range of small to medium enterprises in Melbourne's west to engage in an increased number of e-commerce transactions with each other. The western region of Melbourne contains around 20,000 businesses and is regarded as the manufacturing, transport and distribution hub of south-eastern Australia. The main objective of the Bizewest Portal project, in its initial stages, was to encourage SMEs in Melbourne's west to be more aggressive in their up-take of e-commerce business opportunities, and to encourage them to work with other local enterprises in the region also using the portal. Another important aspect of the development was youth involvement, and students from local high schools and colleges who were studying information technology-related subjects were to be given the opportunity to 'consult' with SMEs on a one-to-one basis in the development of their web pages for the portal. Bizewest became operational in June 2001.

The business to be considered in this study is a medium-sized Melbourne company, with about 50 employees, that stores frozen food and transports it to supermarkets and other locations around the country. The company was founded in 1985 and made its entry into e-commerce by doing some on-line stock control for its bigger clients, and on-line site-monitoring of its freezer plant. An interview with the general manager, who is also owner of the business, was conducted soon after his company adopted the Bizewest portal. When asked whether the company had already begun to make use of business-to-business e-commerce, he replied that they "do a little bit of it at the moment", and went on to describe how the company had only recently got all the computers in their office networked, and how this meant that they could now link all their staff to the portal.

Clients of the business include both small and large companies from many parts of the world, and it has dealt on-line with some of the larger ones now for over two years. In one case the firm is directly on-line with their client's stock so that they can facilitate all their freezing work. The general manager has found, however, that many companies are slow coming on-line, even some of the bigger ones. He suggests that this is because these companies are not really sure what systems they want to use: "The Americans don't like this and the English don't like that and the New Zealanders like this one and they don't like that." He goes on to add that he thinks that in some ways this may be in his company's interests as he can only talk from the viewpoint of what the business does: storage and distribution. The fact that a lot of their clients have not really determined what systems they want to use makes it easier for him not to seem backward.

The general manager has been involved with the local industry group for over twelve years and was no stranger to innovation and change. When approached by WREDO on whether he would be involved in the Bizewest project he indicated that he would. When asked if he had any specific expectations for Bizewest, he said that he did not, but that he thought it was "a really good idea". He indicated that he thought it was great for the region in giving local businesses a chance to work with one another and to get some benefits for one another. When asked about the benefits he saw in adopting the portal he stated these in terms of time savings and better service. "I think it will probably just give us a chance to give the client a quicker on-line communication to know where his stock is – when it is arriving, when it's gone out, and that it is the right stuff come and gone."

A major reason that the company adopted the portal was the hope that it would provide a better opportunity to deal with people in the local region. The general manager thinks that it is going to provide many benefits for everybody, not just his company, and this is important to him. "I think it's got a lot of terrific potential for the region to really build on one another, and if we can all keep building on one another we all keep enhancing our businesses in this region. If we do that, we'll attract more business and we'll be able to make more jobs available and hopefully have a really good future for the young people coming along. I think that's where there are a lot of benefits for this. Business grows on businesses in the region instead of companies in this region going outside to buy services or equipment or whatever. If we can help out people in the region, there are probably people who import products from overseas that can be manufactured here or supplied from here that we don't even know about." He thinks that use of the portal will change his business by enabling it to use people in the local region, and that "working together for the benefit of everybody" will be advantageous for the region.

Another factor that prompted the adoption of the portal was being able to involve school students in creating the company's web pages. With a long interest in the community and in education, the general manager saw this as important. "I want to see this area keep building and growing and driving and creating jobs. I suppose that while some minor advantage comes back to the company, that's 99% of what we do, and what I do is that I just want to see it a lot better for everyone around here."

Adoption of Electronic Commerce by a Small Publishing Company

The second case concerns a small publishing company where four people work on the production of textbooks and research publications. The company is a very small business with a relatively low turnover but a well-established market. Members of the company do much of the textbook writing themselves, commission authors for their research publications, consult with authors and potential authors, and perform all of the work involved in publication of their books except for the actual printing, which they send off to an outside printer. Most of the print runs are quite small and so the company makes use of a printer with access to Xerox printing technology rather than the more traditional offset printing. All those involved in the work of the company have other full-time jobs and do this work largely as a hobby, with the consequence that they do not have time to pursue growing the company into a larger enterprise. They are all highly computer literate and make good use of information technology. None of them, however, has much knowledge of graphics.

The company has long made use of computers and its members could not imagine writing without a word processor. It is currently based at two locations in Melbourne and uses four PCs, an Apple Macintosh, three laptops, two laser printers, several inkjet printers, two flatbed scanners, a slide and negative scanner, two fax machines and two modems. Each location has its own peer-to-peer network with Internet access.

The business has adopted some e-commerce technologies, but not others. Some time ago, it registered a domain name and set up its own web page, but only for informational purposes. The site shows details of the company's products and indicates how orders can be placed, but does not support sales or other business-consumer (B-C) transactions. It is interesting to note that the site has in the past not been updated frequently. When asked about this one of the directors said that it was really a matter of time: everyone was very busy. He acknowledged that the site needed updating and pointed out that the company was currently getting it completely revised and rebuilt by the partner of the other director's niece, who works with a graphic design company. He indicated that the new site would again be informational and would not include direct sales, as the company did not see these as fitting their main market, which was mainly for sales to bookstores and libraries, rather than the public.

The company makes use of Internet banking, mainly to save the company secretary the bother of getting to the local bank during the hours it is open and standing in queues. Its banking needs are quite simple: to deposit sales income into its account, to operate a cheque account for purchase and payments, and to transfer money to a credit card account used to make some other purchases. Except for deposits, all this could be done by Internet banking. Deposits are made at an ATM that the company secretary passes on the way home from work. Some of the company's larger customers have arranged to make their payments by direct credit, but this option has not been promoted to other customers.

As a publishing company, the main 'supplier' of the business is its book printer of long standing. When a new book is ready for printing, a copy of the book is delivered to the printer on Zip disk in PDF format. Apart from this, the transaction is traditional, with a paper order moving from the company to the printer, an invoice moving the other way and a cheque finalising the transaction. When asked why the company had not considered instituting a B-B e-commerce system with the printer, the director replied that they would like to do so, but that the printer was not really interested or geared up to get into this type of order.

Non-Adoption of E-Commerce by a Small Chartered Accountancy Firm

The last case is of a small chartered accountancy firm, which is a family business in the western suburbs of Melbourne. Employees of the business are the main accountant, who has a degree in accounting and is a Certified Practicing Accountant (CPA); the main accountant's father, who previously ran the business but, as he is not qualified, is limited these days mainly to supporting the taxation side of the business; another accountant (CPA); and a full-time secretary. The firm offers services that are typical of a small accounting business: advice on basic accountancy and bookkeeping for small businesses; preparation and lodgement of taxation returns; taxation advice; investment and financial planning advice and advice on the use of accounting software. Its clients include both individuals and small businesses. Apart from details about the business already known by one of the authors, information for this case study was gathered through a personal interview with the main accountant at the premises of the business.

For a while, some members of the business had been debating whether to set up a web site. The business does have an Internet connection, which they use for basic research and to connect to the web site of the Australian Society of Certified Practicing Accountants (http://www.cpaonline.com.au). The employees of the business are happy to interact via electronic mail with customers who wish to do so. All of the employees were comfortable with using computers, Microsoft Office software, accounting software, dedicated financial analysis software and with browsing the Internet.

The decision about whether or not to set up a web site seemed to come down to two major opposing viewpoints. The first viewpoint, held by the main accountant, was that a web site was 'the way of the future'; customers would expect it and some competitors already had one. The opposite viewpoint, held by the father, was that it would be a waste of time and money, that there was nothing you could put on a web site that customers would want anyway, and "who is going to do it?" Other members of the business seemed quite apathetic about the whole matter.

Undeterred, the main accountant investigated the cost of a web site with a few local ISPs, and found that the actual set-up of a simple site was relatively inexpensive. He also discovered a few new terms, such as domain name, URL, traffic costs and so forth, which were a little off-putting. One of the ISPs asked who would be responsible for uploading the web site content to keep it current, at which point the main accountant "felt a hot flush come over him". He found the terminology to be quite intimidating, even with his computer expertise. In the end, the final decision was to wait and see for another twelve months and then review the decision. In the meantime, the secretary was given the task of following up possible sources of expertise, either consultants or training materials, so that any future investigation may not seem so daunting.

ACTORS, NETWORKS, BLACK-BOXES AND TRANSLATIONS

ANT considers any human or non-human entity that can "make its presence individually felt by the others" (Law, 1987) to be an *actor*. While it is clear that a human entity may be able to do this, to those new to actor-network theory it is not so obvious that a non-human also can. The answer is to think of what lies behind an actor. If we consider the Bizewest portal as an actor, for example, then behind this actor we could find WREDO operational staff, an ISP, a web site, software, modems, computers, web browsers, telephone lines and many more things. When we speak of the portal making its presence felt and of *acting* to affect other entities, what we really mean is that some of the entities that make up the portal take actions that can be considered to be undertaken 'on behalf of the portal'. Therefore, when looked into carefully an actor itself consists of a network of interactions and associations. An actor is made up *only* of its interactions with these other actors (de Vries, 1995), and Law (1992) notes that an actor thus consists of an association of heterogeneous elements constituting a network.

An actor like this can, in many ways, thus be thought of as a *black box* (Callon, 1986a), the contents of which we can chose not to worry about. The details of its composition are then just a complication we can avoid having to deal with. We can consider this entity just as an actor, but when doing so it must be remembered that behind each actor there hide other actors that it has, more of less effectively, drawn together, or 'black-boxed' (Callon, 1987). When the time comes to open the lid of the black box and look inside, it will be seen to constitute a whole network of other, perhaps complex, associations.

Each of the businesses described were interested in some aspects of e-commerce, but not in all aspects of it. They each attempted, some successfully and some not so successfully, to translate e-commerce into a form they could adopt. They each attempted to choose some elements and to leave others out: to translate the technology into a form suitable for them.

The Company Adopting the Web Portal

It is clear from the study that the transport company has "not really been into computers", and has only recently started coming to grips with this technology. Although the manager had some idea of the benefits to his company of using the portal, he had no clear plan for using it. It was just "a really good idea". The reasons he adopted this innovation thus had little to do with the characteristics of this technology, and much more to do with his involvement with the local business community and because of his belief that the portal had the potential to improve business in the region. As someone with a long-term interest in education, he was persuaded by the use of school students in developing the web sites: he saw this as a good reason to get involved.

Among the actors contributing to this adoption are: the general manager himself, the local community, the local school students, the western region,

WREDO, office staff of the company, the company's larger customers, and the portal. The community and the region, in particular, should also be seen as networks that could be dissected into a large number of individual actors if this was required. As far as the general manager was concerned, the portal was definitely a black box, the contents of which he did not really want to investigate.

The general manager had a wider view of business than just his own, and was especially interested in fostering business in the local community and in the region. He saw the Bizewest portal primarily in terms of a means of achieving greater participation of business in the region and in getting SMEs in the region to work together for their mutual benefit. He certainly wanted to make use of a B-B portal, but his main interest was in one that would get the local business community working together. He was thus most interested in a translation of the portal to become a means of achieving greater business co-operation and community involvement within the western region.

The Publishing Company

In many ways, the publishing company is quite different from the storage and transport company. All members of the company are highly computer literate and understand the characteristics of e-commerce technologies, as well as the benefits and difficulties of using them in the business. The company makes extensive use of computers, but not full use of e-commerce. A significant factor is that it is a part-time business with all company members having full-time jobs outside. This means that company members are all very busy and needed to work efficiently, saving time wherever possible. The company chose to use just some e-commerce technologies (and not others), for several reasons. Firstly, to make use of B-B e-commerce takes two parties and most of the business' customers and suppliers were not yet ready to make use of this technology. Secondly, company members could not spare the time to do what they saw as secondary work, like updating web pages.

Adoption decisions within the company were influenced by the actions of a number of actors. Their own computer network was quite prepared and willing to engage in e-commerce transactions as required. The fact that the company did not engage in these to the maximum extent was not due to a lack of hardware or software. Their printer, their other suppliers and their customers were also important actors who had an effect by not pressing for the use of e-commerce. Their bank, on the other hand, effectively argued in favour of the company using Internet banking by not being open when required and in making greater charges for face-to-face transactions.

Updating of the web site, which is currently underway, has only really happened because of the intervention of another actor: the partner of a director's niece. The directors, who were all very busy people, were not prepared to commit the time to do this work, but when someone with graphic design skills became readily available then this changed things.

Adoption decisions of the company had more to do with the technological status of their suppliers and their customers than with the e-commerce technology itself. The company was interested in using those e-commerce technologies that its business partners used and those it considered useful or timesaving. What was adopted could be seen as a translation of an e-commerce innovation to include just these things.

The Chartered Accountancy Firm

In the case of the accounting company, the e-commerce negotiations were interesting. The initial conflict of interest between father and son produced a stalemate. The apathy of the other members, if anything, supported the argument of the father: "They don't care, so why bother?" The ISPs did not help themselves by failing to recognise that they had a potential customer who they turned away with technical jargon. It seems that in this instance, the web site was never given a chance to effectively negotiate its own position. It had to rely on human actors within the business who were not quite sure of its capabilities, and actors in the ISP who did not understand the needs of the main accountant. Another outcome of the negotiations was that the overall question: 'Would the web site result in extra profits for the business?' was never actually asked.

Although the decision has been postponed for the short term, have the accountants really helped any future negotiations by selecting the secretary to investigate further sources of information? The main accountant believes that the secretary is "very self-sufficient" and will "probably do it better than any of us could anyway". One of the problems in this case is that the operations of an ISP in setting up the web site fall within the notion of a black-box. The business has little idea of how the process operates, and probably even less now that they have spoken to the ISPs.

So, how is it that for the business the (potential) web site could not be 'translated' into a form where it could be adopted? In whatever form the technology actually ended up, it was not suitable for adoption from the viewpoint of the actors involved. The main accountant was the prime motivator in attempting to define the problem and to discover the solution: he defined the problematisation, but not well enough to gain acceptance of the innovation. Other human actors in the business failed to see that there was a problem at all, which made the process difficult from the start.

The main accountant also was a prime mover in attempting to impose identities and roles on the other actors, by initiating discussions with the ISPs. Attempts at interesting and attracting other human actors in the business by coming between them and the potential web site (interessement) failed somewhat. In addition, attempts by the ISPs to put themselves between the potential web site and main accountant failed miserably. There was never much chance of enrolment occurring once the ISPs were involved with the main accountant. He had enough difficulty trying to get other human actors in the business to yield before having self-doubts introduced by the ISPs.

ACTOR-NETWORK THEORY AND E-COMMERCE INNOVATION

The theory of innovation diffusion (Rogers, 1995) is well established and has been used as the framework of many studies. In most cases, however, the success of the diffusion model has been in explanation of innovation 'in the large' when the statistical effects of big numbers of organisations and individuals involved come into play. It has, typically, been less successful in explaining how particular individuals or specific organisations make their adoption decisions, and it is in situations like this that an innovation translation approach, using actor-network theory, is especially useful.

In offering a socio-technical approach to theorising innovation ANT provides a particularly useful tool to the study of innovations in which people and machines are intimately involved with each other. The adoption of e-commerce technologies certainly involves a consideration of the technologies themselves, but also of business organisations, business processes, and the needs and likes of individual humans. ANT, we suggest, is especially useful in researching innovations like these, and in particular, when considering individual adoption decisions.

Like any approach to research, actor-network theory is not without limitations. Perhaps the main criticism of ANT (Grint et al., 1997) is that it is not always sufficiently clear where the boundaries of a network lie or whose account of a network is to be taken as definitive. Grint and Woolgar (1997) note that the analyst's story seems to depend on a description of the 'actual' network as if this was objectively available. Radder (1992) expresses some concern with what he sees as the goal orientation of ANT: its tendency to look towards stabilisation, black-boxing, and control. He asks of the nature of the stabilisation process, and questions from whose point of view it is seen, pointing out a tendency in ANT to look at things from the viewpoint of the 'winners': the successful actors. He argues that a bias to do this is built into ANT's definition of an actor.

The main use made of any research approach such as ANT is in the study of past events, and ANT makes no claim to be able to predict what may happen in the future. We suggest, however, that ANT analysis can identify some pointers towards the successful introduction of an innovation, and the change management associated with this. ANT argues that it is not the characteristics of either the innovation itself or the potential adopter acting alone that are important, but rather the interactions of many actors. The key to successful change management, it would thus seem, involves allowing for these interactions and for the socio-technical nature of the process.

CONCLUSION

This chapter has offered a number of examples in which actor-network theory has provided a means by which adoption or non-adoption of technology can be explained. Situations that have arisen include:

- The desire of the general manager of the storage and transport business to adopt the portal so as to support development of the local region.
- The publishing company's reluctance to adopt more e-commerce technologies as their business partners did not use them, and they did not have the time.
- The accountancy firm not setting up a web site because they really just did not understand what was going on.

All of these situations point to the fact that decisions on the adoption of electronic commerce technologies are often made on the basis of more than just the characteristics of the technology, and that in many cases these characteristics are not especially significant in the decision-making process.

In each of these instances, the actor-network approach therefore offers a useful explanation of why a particular e-commerce initiative was or was not adopted. On the other hand, an innovation diffusion approach to investigating each of the potential adoptions would have looked for explanations for the uptake, or lack of uptake, primarily in the characteristics and properties of the technology in each case. It would not have considered as particularly important the human and non-human interactions described here. In our view, the decision to adopt, or not to adopt, has more to do with the interactions and associations of both human and non-human actors involved in the project than with characteristics of the technology.

ENDNOTES

[1]   For the purposes of this chapter SMEs (in the Australian context) are considered to be those businesses that have from 1-20 employees—small, and 21-50 employees—medium: Burgess, S. (2002). *Information Technology and Small Business: Issues and Challenges*. Burgess, S. Pennsylvania, USA, Idea Group Publishing.

[2]   Lynch, J. (1998). Web Portals. *PC Magazine* suggests that portals can be described as *horizontal* when they are utilised by a broad base of users across a horizontal market, and *vertical* when their content is tightly focused toward a particular audience such as a specific industry or group of industries.

REFERENCES

Burgess, S. (2001). *Business-to-consumer interactions on the Internet: A model for small Businesses*. PhD thesis. Business. Melbourne, Monash University, Australia.

Burgess, S. (2002). *Information Technology in small business: Issues and challenges*. Hershey, PA: Idea Group Publishing.

Callon, M. (1986a). The sociology of an actor-network: The case of the electric vehicle. In Callon, M., Law, J., & Rip, A. (Eds.), *Mapping the dynamics of science and technology*, 19–34. London: Macmillan Press.

Callon, M. (1986b). Some elements of a sociology of translation: Domestication of the scallops and the fishermen of St Brieuc Bay. In Law J. (Ed.), *Power, action & belief. A new sociology of knowledge?* 196–229. London: Routledge & Kegan Paul.

Callon, M. (1987). Society in the making: The study of technology as a tool for sociological analysis. In Bijker, W. E., Hughes, T. P., & Pinch, T. P. (Eds.), *The social construction of technological systems* (pp. 85–103). Cambridge, MA: The MIT Press.

Callon, M. (1999). Actor-network theory - The market test. In Law, J., & Hassard, J. (Eds.), *Actor-network theory and after* (pp. 181–195). Oxford: Blackwell Publishers.

Grint, K., & Woolgar, S. (1997). *The machine at work - Technology, work and organisation.* Cambridge: Polity Press.

Hughes, T. P. (1983). *Networks of power: Electrification in Western Society, 1880-1930.* Baltimore and London: Johns Hopkins University Press.

Latour, B. (1986). The powers of association. In Law, J. (Ed.), *Power, action and belief. A new sociology of knowledge? Sociological Review Monograph 32.* London, Routledge & Kegan Paul: 264–280.

Latour, B. (1993). *We have never been modern.* Hemel Hempstead, Harvester Wheatsheaf.

Latour, B. (1996). *Aramis or the love of technology.* Cambridge, MA: Harvard University Press.

Latour, B. (1999). *On recalling ANT.* In Law, J. & Hassard, J. (Eds.), *Actor network theory and after* (pp. 15–25). Oxford: Blackwell Publishers.

Law, J. (1987). Technology and heterogeneous engineering: The case of Portuguese expansion. In Bijker, W. E., Hughes, T. P. & Pinch, T. J. (Eds.), *The social construction of technological systems: New directions in the sociology and history of technology.* (pp.111–134). Cambridge, MA: MIT Press.

Law, J. (1992). Notes on the theory of the actor-network: Ordering, strategy and heterogeneity. *Systems Practice, 5*(4), 379–393.

Law, J. (1999). After ANT: Complexity, naming and topology. In Law, J. & Hassard, J. (Eds.), *Actor Network Theory and after* (pp.1–14). Oxford: Blackwell Publishers.

Lynch, J. (1998). Web portals. *PC Magazine.*

Macquarie Library. (1981). *The Macquarie dictionary.* Sydney: Macquarie Library.

Oxford. (1973). *The shorter Oxford English dictionary.* Oxford: Clarendon Press.

Radder, H. (1992). Normative reflexions on constructivist approaches to science and technology. *Social Studies of Science, 22*(1), 141–173.

Rogers, E. M. (1995). *Diffusion of innovations*. New York: The Free Press.

Tatnall, A. (2000). Innovation and change in the Information Systems curriculum of an Australian University: A socio-technical perspective. *PhD thesis*. Education. Rockhampton, Central Queensland University.

Tatnall, A. (2002a). Actor-Network Theory as a socio-technical approach to Information Systems research. In Clarke, S., Coakes, E., Hunter, M. G., & Wenn, A. (Eds.), *Socio-technical and human cognition elements of Information Systems* (pp.266-283). Hershey, PA: Idea Group Publishing.

Tatnall, A. (2002b). Modelling technological change in small business: Two approaches to theorising innovation. In Burgess, S. (Ed.), *Managing Information Technology in small business: Challenges and solutions* (pp. 83-97). Hershey, PA: Idea Group Publishing.

Tatnall, A., & Burgess, S. (2002). *Using Actor-Network Theory to research the implementation of a B-B portal for regional Smes in Melbourne, Australia*. 15th Bled Electronic Commerce Conference - 'eReality: Constructing the eEconomy', Bled, Slovenia, University of Maribor.

Tatnall, A., & Gilding, A. (1999). *Actor-Network Theory and Information Systems research*. 10th Australasian Conference on Information Systems (ACIS), Wellington, Victoria University of Wellington.

de Vries, G. (1995). Should we send Collins and Latour to Dayton, Ohio? *EASST Review, 14*(4).

Chapter XI

The Application of the Innovative Mobile Technologies in the Business Environment: Challenges and Implications

Nabeel A. Y. Al-Qirim
Auckland University of Technology, New Zealand

ABSTRACT

This chapter looks at mobile business (MoB) from technological, social, economical, and environmental perspectives. The issues that surround MoB and hence, influence its success at the wider scale in the long run, are dependent on significant factors addressed in this chapter. The chapter defines MoB and looks at different mobile technologies and standards that enable MoB. The chapter then looks at the different factors and contexts that would influence MoB success at a broader level, highlighting issues, gaps, and challenges. It is emphasised that unless such implications are addressed, the wide diffusion of MoB will not materialise in the near future. Despite the rapid technological development and the enthusiasm about the MoB innovation among researchers and professionals, the road toward true MoB is still a long one. What exist now in the market are just complementary solutions. At this level, at the lower end, MoB is the toy of the teenagers; at the higher end it is the toy of the rich or the executive who cannot tolerate to be away from his/her e-mail. There are indeed some useful business applications for MoB, especially in logistics and distribution, but the remaining potential masses that have tasted the beauty of Internet browsing are not yet prepared to compromise that with ill-specified mobile technologies, e.g., devices, wireless communications, and deficient and stripped down contents. Still, MoB stands strong as a futuristic direction and one day we will be there, wearing MoB.

MOBILE COMMERCE

Mobile commerce is defined as "content delivery (notification and reporting) and transactions (purchasing and data entry) on mobile devices" (Leung & Antypas, 2001). As suggested by Samaras (2002), mobile users can compute, engage in commerce and access information from anywhere, any time with mobile technologies. Mobile technology supported information exchange and transactions should take place in a convenient environment and setting. The users would be individuals or businesses and hence, mobile commerce enables business-to-business (B2B) transactions as well as business-to-consumers (B2C) transactions.

Referring to the opinions of Schneider and Perry (2001), and Turban, King, Lee, Warkentin, and Chung (2002) about the need to replace the term "electronic commerce" with the term "electronic business", as the former has always been accused of being limited to exchanges of monetary values only and with close trading partners only: this does not reflect the multi-faceted value-perspectives (monetary as well as non-monetary) that characterise the emerging new technological field. Therefore, the term "business" is envisioned here to be more encompassing and would achieve such an objective and hence, is used in this research interchangeably with "mobile commerce" to refer to mobile business (MoB) only.

Mobile business involves different stakeholders in the mobile industry such as mobile hardware manufacturers, mobile applications and portals developers, middleware developers and integrators, wireless network providers and carriers, intermediaries, and finally, services and content providers. In view of the different technologies that provide mobile commerce functionality, the following taxonomy depicts five main categories:

- Interactive or two-way pagers, which exchange short SMS (Short Message Systems) messages.
- Mobile phones that provide access to the web through the Wireless Application Protocol (WAP's WML *Vs.* DoCoMo's i-mode) or to SMS services.
- Personal Digital Assistants (PDA) with wireless modem (e.g., Palm).
- Wireless Internet access on laptop computers using IEEE 802.11a,b[1] radio frequencies (CSMA/CA not CD) standards.
- Wireless network devices such as those offered by Cisco, Symbol (e.g., wireless barcode reader/transmitters), and Proxim, using, e.g., infrared and radio frequencies and other wireless technologies including satellite, cellular and microwave communications.

There is increased hype among researchers and professionals about the recent emergence of technologies aiming at delivering remote or wireless commercial applications, mainly driven by the earlier hype about text-based mobile applications driven mostly by the wireless application protocol (WAP). The strength of this hype for mobile commerce among researchers and professionals is that the technology is promising to provide rich, personalised, localised, and real-time content on feasible handheld mobile technologies to users (usually very busy) anywhere, anytime, thus providing more convenience to traditional electronic commerce (e-business) buyers and suppliers existing in the wired marketplace. Let's not forget that mobile business is the result of this wired marketplace and pervasive computing, where mobile computing and communication capabilities are envisioned to be embedded in everyday activities of the different users (Lee, 2002; Samaras, 2002; Turban et al., 2002).

Despite the hype about MoB among leading operators in the U.S., where they expect the number of MoB subscribers to increase rapidly in the near future and the profit margins of wireless and voice communications to plummet drastically, these analyses are based on the wired subscriber-base (McCarthy, Zohar & Dolan, 2000). This perception among telecommunication carriers and operators that if the on-line consumer stake increases over the Internet this will lead to the increase in the mobile consumer stake that uses MoB-enabling technologies is quite misleading (McCarthy et al., 2000). Such positivism among carriers and operators about MoB success is plagued by the following major impediments:

- Bit rate: 9.6 Kbps: speed so far is the major barrier for the wide success of MoB and this relates directly to the existing operator/carrier (O/C) telecommunication infrastructure that exists in the different countries. Rather than providing at least regular 33 or 56 Kbps connection (as is the case with Internet subscribers) to domestic mobile Internet subscribers in order to provide full navigational and multimedia capabilities, O/C endeavours to provide a stripped-down version of some of the Internet content to cope with existing speed/bandwidth limitations in the wireless technology, and this represents a deficient process.

- Subscribers' interests and needs: despite the push from O/C for contents over MoB, recent statistics indicate that: (a) 82% of mobile consumers have shown no interest in mobile data services—Then, how about selling products and services over mobile technologies!?; (b) Small processing power and small mobile browsing screens are very hard to navigate, which makes the mobile browsing experience un-enjoyable to subscribers (Anonymous, 2000).

- Cost: ridiculous-costing schemes enforced by O/C to charge high profit margins—Driven mostly by fast Mobile Internet return-on-investments plans, and this in turn was encouraged by the lack of competition in the field (earlier players make most of the profits and dictate the roles of the game). However, with the introduction of more advanced and optimised technologies into the MoB arena (bandwidth, processing, etc.), increased subscribers base, and more competitors entering into the MoB field it is expected that prices will ultimately be drawn down.

Thus far, the results pertaining to the wide diffusion of MoB are not satisfactory and above all the comparison between Internet and mobile users is not a straightforward process, and the experiences of each medium differ fundamentally from the experience of the other! This necessitates a closer look at MoB in general and at subscribers and their needs alongside the mobile technology specifically in use.

Therefore, this chapter attempts to introduce and investigate the main issues influencing MoB success at the global level. The purpose of this chapter is to identify the main contexts and factors influencing MoB success and discuss ways where MoB could be progressed forward. Drawing that broader picture about MoB success or failure is very important. Building that holistic under-standing about main impending issues pertaining to MoB and addressing those issues is therefore very important in order for MoB to succeed in the different countries. Thus, tackling or focusing on specific issues with greater detail is not

an objective in the current chapter and it is left for future research to expand on
certain issues highlighted in this chapter. The chapter outcomes could assist
researchers, professionals and policymakers in understanding the main impending issues behind MoB success as an emerging, revolutionary technology
in a broader sense. Further, the current chapter represents a great opportunity
for the different stakeholders in the different countries to expand on some of the
main issues in this chapter that are more amenable to their countries and
contexts. In the following, each section attempts to address one unique aspect
pertaining to MoB in greater detail.

The Battle for Consumers

The recent emergence of e-business challenges many of the existing
marketing theories and models in the way businesses target their intended
consumers and segments. Earlier, most of the marketing strategies were
empowered by personal contacts (one-to-one) and mass media (one-to-many
(passive). In the mass media, however, promotional and marketing strategies
using broadcasting technologies such as the radio, newspapers, billboards, and
television have been designed to target a representative sample (the largest) of
the population. Thus, they could not customise their strategies to appeal to the
tastes of the different individuals in the population. e-business, on the other
hand, may represent many-to-one (search for information), one-to-one (async.
& sync. communications) and many-to-many (communities) media (Schneider
& Perry, 2001).

Driven by its digital nature, it is very easy to digitise products, services,
processes and even the delivery process within the e-business scenario. The
mass customisation aspect is unique to the e-business field. MoB is offering the
same but on a stripped-down version of the wired MoB, at least for the time
being, with the different technical limitations that plague MoB functionality. In
addition, the uniqueness of the MoB perspective is that mobile applications and
models could be designed to meet the tastes of individual consumers
(personalised services) existing within a certain region, city, village, block, etc.,
in accordance with the coverage provided by the wireless provider—thus
providing MoB businesses with more opportunities and hence, pushing the
mass customisation perspective to a climax.

However, the biggest challenge for mobile businesses, manufacturers, and
developers in grasping such immense opportunities and in developing a killer
mobile application is learning how deeper insights about consumers' behaviour

and tastes could be generated. This requires a complete change in the mindset of the different businesses working in the MoB arena in that they would need to optimise their marketing strategies to define consumers by their fundamental life intentions. Thus, in order to succeed in such a task, MoB businesses would require the assistance of different businesses that might not relate essentially to their businesses in the first place (network providers, wireless services providers, MoB providers, content providers, market research consultants) (Nohria & Leestma, 2001). Such open opportunities provided by MoB could lead to the creation of different players in the MoB area.

Intermediation, Dis-Intermediation and Re-Intermediation

As they control the underlying infrastructure and mobile subscriber-base (equipped with their mobile devices as well), network operators and carriers (O/C) are confident that they will not be dis-intermediated as in the case of the Internet earlier by, e.g., Internet services providers (ISPs) or by any new forms of intermediaries emerging in the new MoB arena (McCarthy et al., 2000). On the contrary, O/C envision making more profits as they know how and when their networks are being used and even charge traditional e-business vendors over the Internet commissions for sales executed over their mobile systems and networks. Further, mobile commerce operators and carriers expect to generate further revenues from MoB vendors by marketing their products over the mobile technologies. However, Geng and Whinston (2001), McCarthy et al. (2000), and Nohria and Leestma (2001) are highly suspicious of that.

We will have to wait and see the results of the battle between the O/C and the emerging MoB intermediaries for mobile subscribers and whether a new form of intermediaries will emerge over the new mobile arena! Whether the O/C will practice their ubiquitous monopolistic approaches and dominance over domestic markets and hence prevent traditional intermediaries (e.g., ISPs) from playing a role (re-intermediate) as mobile services providers (MSPs) is another issue! However, with more convergence in MoB, it is expected that O/C will loosen their grip on their services to other parties involved with MoB. The fear is that the huge costs involved in deploying 3G network-infrastructure and services mean smaller operators will diminish from the market unless they engage in alliances and mergers[2]. Let's not forget that according to the preceding section, it is highly suspected that the O/C would not be able to master all the MoB applications alone, and hence will need help from different players in the MoB area.

The Silky Route to Mobile Business

The low speed/bandwidth of the second-generation telecommunications infrastructure and the tedious services provided to mobile subscribers resulted in having small and infrequent users, and therefore, there was a need for a new technology that provides high-speed data service (Anonymous, 2000). Thus, migrating from the second-generation (2G) voice networks to the third-generation (3G) systems is what telecommunication companies are working on to build new broadband networks to transport data at high speed (Table 1). For instance, Europe has selected the wideband W-CDMA as the preferred air interface for its proposed third generation system (Tade, 1999). Third generation (3G) network infrastructure has been in Japan since 2001. Versions of 2.5G and 3G are rolling out across Europe and Asia during 2002. In Canada, the first phase of 3G has been introduced. It is expected to start in the U.S. by 2003 (Turban et al., 2002, backbonemag.com). However, it should be noted that each country has its own: macro circumstance (e.g., regulatory, social, political, economical, etc.), existing telecommunication infrastructure, and subscribers' needs, which would ultimately influence the selection of an optimal telecommunications infrastructure for that country. A number of wireless paths have been suggested and introduced in the marketplace to provide surrogates to the envisioned mobile subscribers, and Table 2 lists some of those available options.[3]

Table 1: The evolution of the wireless telecommunication infrastructure

	Wireless Technology Generations	Description
1	1G	Old Analog-based wireless technology.
2	2G	Wireless radio digital technology supporting text-based messages (TDMA (for GSM): 9.6-14.4 Kbps and CDMA).
3	2.5 G	A transition technology between 2G and 3G (next) (GPRS, EDGE), which support graphics.
4	3G	Non-IP-based wireless digital technology (W-CDMA, CDMA 2000, UMTS[4]) supporting up to 2 Mbps bandwidth supporting, e.g., video clips. With 3G mobile users are expected to be able to browse the web.
5	4G	End-to-end IP-based digital wireless technology (expected in 2006).

Table 2: Comparisons between different wireless telecommunication infrastructures

Specifications	HSCSD (High speed circuit-switched data)	GPRS (General packet radio service) 2.5G	EDGE (Enhanced data for global evaluation) 2.5G	W-CDMA (Wideband CDMA) 3G
Speed	57.6 Kbps	171.2 Kbps (theoretically) 115 Kbps (practically)	384 Kbps	- No more than 2 Mbps indoor - 144 Kbps for highly mobile service - 9.6 Kbps for satellite coverage
Infrastructure	Requires software upgrade to the existing GSM network		Extension to GSM: Enhanced modulation for GSM	Coexist with GSM networks
Functions	File transfer, applications require constant high bit rate, applications of 9.6 kbps	All major functions, point to point transfer of user data, internet and X.25 interworking, filtering functionality for security reasons, volume-based charging tools, and roaming between public and mobile networks, point to multipoint transfer	Good for network operators that don't have UMTS but wish to offer services similar with less cost Leverage TDMA and GPRS infrastructures.	- Changing bandwidth requirements of 3G systems - Access to advanced multimedia services during a call - Inherent spectrum efficiency - On demand services any time, any where
Advantages (functionality)	Not suitable for Internet because its not cost effective	Connect users at all time while on a call Its bursty nature is attractive for mobile applications, e.g., e-business.	Higher bit rates than GPRS per timeslot	
Advantages (Commercial)	Can be introduced without major investment in the existing network infrastructure, no extensive network element modification required	New nodes are needed to integrate into GPRS into the GSM network Bills by volume of data rather than by connection time		Protecting investment of existing GSM networks, customer base and bolstering existing relationships with vendors for continuous product development
Result	Fast return on investment, and faster data connections for the end user		Not yet fully specified and undergoing study	
Disadvantage	For wideband service is a waste of investment			

What influences the selection of an efficient wireless medium for MoB is the existing telecommunication infrastructure in the different countries. Upgrading/replacing the existing wireless telecommunication infrastructure to support MoB efficiently would require a huge investment and this would reflect on the existing regulatory procedure pertaining to providing and to billing wireless services. Therefore, it would be quite logical and advisable for each country to assess its current telecommunication infrastructure and avoid investing large sums of money on new trends such as MoB unless it is justifiable and financially feasible. On the other hand, it should be noted here that the development of "killer mobile" applications may not require 3G-bandwidth in the first place except, for instance, movie clips to kids, video conferencing, etc. Further, time and location-specific services are likely to be low in value and this makes the huge investment on 3G-communication infrastructure for small countries with small populations unjustifiable (Anonymous, 2000).

There are many good wireless solutions that could work or coexist seamlessly with existing telecommunications infrastructure such as the most common mobile phone GSM network, but O/C should consider the impact of other factors before progressing toward an optimal solution and those factors are mostly dictated by the market demand and whether the upgrading to the full-fledged 3G infrastructure would yield any justifiable profits!

Therefore, driven by the importance of being in the Mobile Internet arena, each O/C could pursue a very cautious approach in adopting a suitable mix/replacement to the existing telecommunication infrastructure, e.g., GSM network. The HSCSD is a readily available solution and requires software upgrades to work directly with existing GSM networks, but for operators wanting to offer wideband services, the HSCSD may not work out to be justifiable financially. Yet, the unpredictable consumer attitude towards the new technology will cast many doubts about the feasibility of introducing such technology and investors in turn would be quite reluctant to support such "risky" initiatives (Anonymous, 2000).

General Packet Radio Service (GPRS) provides most of the functions; however, many researchers suggest that the battle between GPRS and HSCSD will continue for a while, though at the end GPRS may win due to its superiority (Table 2), but with higher cost margins (Tade, 1999).

In comparison with other countries like the U.S. and Asia, the telecom companies in Europe are prepared to take this risk and adopt 3G systems quickly and at competitive prices to support both mobile telephones and the Internet. The driver for the European initiatives came about as a result of the European spectrum auctions, which resulted in a massive transfer from shareholders to governments. The Japanese, however, might get there as a result of their capacity shortages (Anonymous, 2000).

However, the fight for market share and for radio spectrum rights in auctions around the world is escalating among wireless providers. They do not anticipate any immediate payoffs from their huge investment on radio spectrum rights, equipment and marketing strategies; however, as highlighted earlier, they anticipate the introduction of the 3G wireless technology and powerful handheld devices soon will allow them to differentiate their value-added wireless services and offerings (Geng & Whinston, 2001).

The telecommunication sectors in general and the emerging MoB sectors specifically are highly competitive markets and the O/C that is willing to take the plunge into the fast developing MoB arena first would yield most of the profits. However, in endeavouring with MoB, O/C should balance among different options in adopting an efficient wireless telecommunication infrastructure such as the quality of service (QoS) required to support mobile applications and users, coverage and scope (multicast, unicast, broadcast, etc.), location management, standards, and roaming (including the coordination with the different local wireless providers) (Varshney & Vetter, 2001; Varshney, Vetter, & Kalakota, 2000).

Even with the high speed and bandwidth expected in these wireless systems, applications with extensive frames, colours, graphics, and animations will always be difficult to support in the near future. Due to these limitations and impediments, there is a need to design MoB applications that require minimal bandwidth and have a simple and friendly interface. One solution for content providers is to plan their applications to be character-based terminal applications with cursor and entry forms. One possible path is to migrate applications designed as an Interactive Voice Response (IVR) system to MoB, because it is designed for the phone keypad with minimal bandwidth (Leung & Antypas, 2001). There are future trends aiming at developing vortals, which change data to voice and communicate the information to us thorough our cell phones; however, this technology will not be readily available in the near future (Shulman, 2000; Turban et al., 2002).

Strategies and Best Practices for MoB

There are three basic differentiation strategies: horizontal (diversification), vertical (niche), and cross market differentiation by tying. With the expected revolutionary enhancement in 3G wireless and mobile devices and with the increase in number of subscribers in the near future, it is expected that wireless providers will not be able to differentiate their communication infrastructure services. Thus, providers are expected to adopt the third strategies and provide integrated services by tying with value added wireless application services providers (WASP) (Geng & Whinston, 2001), thus further endorsing the disintermediation perspective highlighted earlier.

However, let's not forget the monopolistic dominance of the different O/Cs in the different countries and how they enjoy slack resources and economies of scale, which could help them in developing such integrated services internally, especially at this initial stage of convergence with MoB, where there is not much high demand from consumers for mobile products, and mobile business models are still scant and premature. With the increase in the number of wireless providers and WASP in the near future, it is expected that market efficiencies will dominate, and hence, all stakeholders involved in the MoB business will be able to share fare profits.

Geng and Whinston (2001) summarise the forms of competition that might take place between wireless providers into three types:

- The first option is that providers engage in price wars, which ultimately would leave sellers without any profits.
- Engage in collusion activities, which are illegal and a highly penalised practice in many countries.
- Accumulate a large enough cash reserve to ride out a price war and bankrupt their competitors.

The preceding authors, however, envision that unless providers introduce different solutions and vary user experience so that consumers find it extremely difficult to switch to another service, they will not be able to survive, especially in the light of the new MoB technology.

The Battle for Prices

Wireless telecommunication providers have monthly plans that charge a flat rate based on restricted time usage of the radio spectrum. Prepaid flat-rate plans may tie consumers, and hence, most of the current plans would deter many consumers from freely going into/out of the service. However, most of the mobile phone services are usage-based. Usage-based pricing refers to charging subscribers based on connection time or traffic volume (e.g., e-mail and text messaging).

The promise of the 3G technology is that it will enable the delivery of various services at the same transaction-completion time but through different bandwidths. The preceding makes the connection time fee uneconomical to wireless providers, as it does not reflect the actual use of the bandwidth (radio spectrum usage, e.g., downloading video requires far more bandwidth than wireless web access) (Geng & Whinston, 2001).

The Battle for Location: *LMoB*

Traditional e-business over the Internet and other electronic mediums have always been accused of being too large, spanning across different continents and countries and fragmented, and hence plagued with yet unresolved global political, social, economical, and technological implications. Issues concerning taxation, legal prosecutions and litigations, and international trade over the Internet are far from being resolved and this in large resulted in slowing the rapid diffusion of MoB at the global level. Above all, the MoB environment is facing bigger problems pertaining to security and privacy of mobile users over the wireless medium.

The promise of MoB is that the emerging applications of MoB could target specific geographical regions. Thus, MoB applications could be developed and localised/customised easily to meet the needs of the different buyers/suppliers existing in a specific geographical region. Further, knowing the location of the mobile user in relation to a nearby trading outlet[5] or vending machine, more marketing and promotional messages (or a newly customised one based on the prior knowledge of the user's preferences) could be sent to that user encouraging him to grasp that bargain from a nearby outlet (for full details about the different uses and applications of MoB refer to Varshney, 2001).

The preceding would provide a more secure trading arena where O/Cs have more control over their mobile subscribers, and hence, could trace misuse/fraudulent activities more easily. Further, the current legislative/legal systems in place in that region could be extended or adapted easily to suit the MoB commercial perspective. Convenient shopping would be at its best driven by the above assurances, and hence, many businesses would be attracted to the MoB arena.

Mobile business is considered as distributed computing where users execute MoB applications while they are moving (Samaras, 2002). However, mobility, location of mobile users and sustaining the location of the mobile user at all times and with adequate accuracy levels (e.g., moving from one cell to another) still represent a big challenge for researchers (Samaras, 2002; Varshney et al., 2000; Varshney & Vetter, 2001).

Most of the existing location management schemes used in wireless networks deal with location information that is precise at a location area level (accuracy levels: existing networks: several kilometres and clusters: around one kilometre). This may not be sufficient for numerous MoB applications that require high precision location, e.g., let's say, within a few meters. Some possible solutions include the use of global positioning satellite systems (GPS), which use several base stations for triangulating the location, and mixed handset-network protocols for location determination (Varshney, 2001). If the GPS data (longitude and latitude) are integrated with spatial geographic information systems (GIS) data, the MoB provider can pinpoint the location of the mobile user in relation to a map, e.g., area, block, street, etc., thus providing more effective commercial services to mobile users by pinpointing them to a nearby bargain, vending machines, outlet, etc. (Turban et al., 2002). The tradeoff is that the overheads involved in optimising the MoB technology to locate mobile users accurately and to provide real time services are quite expensive. This depends completely on the type of the application, as stated earlier.

Another challenge is the ability to retain the association between the mobile user and his connection with the information source while he/she is moving from one location to another (Samaras, 2002). This entails investigating issues like the current wireless telecommunication infrastructure and how it handles mobility and location specifics. Measures and ratios like call to mobility (effectiveness in pinpointing a required location) depend on how frequently calls are made and how fast a mobile user is moving from one location to another (Varshney, 2001). Accordingly, the preceding implications would influence the developed middleware (content providers, services providers, developers, tools, technologies, etc.) and its success in hiding the underlying complex processes involved in tracking mobile users while delegating seamless MoB content and services. Figure 1 shows MoB architecture based on the WAP as the wireless communication protocol with the web. The wireless middleware provides a great opportunity for developers and content integrators to introduce different MoB applications and services across the Internet and the wireless medium.

Figure 1: Mobile commerce application infrastructure based on GSM network and WAP protocol

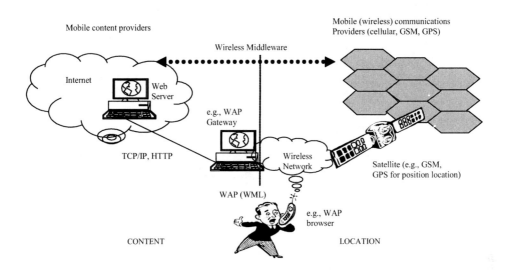

The Battle for Protocols

In overcoming bandwidth barriers, limited memory and processing power of mobile devices, and other bottlenecks as explained earlier, O/C, mBusiness researchers, hardware manufacturers and applications developers are adopting different mBusiness standards and protocols to deliver content more efficiently to mobile users. Further, those same stakeholders are attempting to offload part of the Internet content and integrate it to be part of the next generation smart mobile phones, equipped with primary user identification module (UIM) and integrated chip (IC) for secure on-line transactions. A secondary contact-less IC Reader/writer is also integrated, which could be used for off-line authentications and transaction processing such as buying a ticket, etc. Overall, the potential of loading lots of information and data seems quite promising on these next generation mobile devices. The challenge is to lower the cost overheads on the merchant side to support the local interfaces (e.g., readers for the contact-less IC or any other interfaces such as the IrDA, Bluetooth[6], etc. (Kinoshita, 2002)). On the other hand, dealing with different protocols and standards will only impede the rapid development of the mobile technology.

WAP

Formerly known as the handheld device mark-up language, Web Markup Language (WAP) is a new advanced intelligent messaging service for digital mobile phones and other mobile devices. It is an open specification based on IP and XML. WAP facilitates interoperability among different wireless networks, devices and applications. It specifies a micro browser (thin-client) using a new standard Web Markup Language (WML, a stripped down version of HTML) as the client software and supports texts, graphics, and standard Web content. WAP specifies a proxy server that acts as a gateway between the wireless network and the wire-line Internet, providing protocol translation and optimising data transfer for the wireless handset (Figure 1). It specifies a computer-telephony integration application programme interface (API), called wireless telephony application interface (WTAI), that provides interface between data and voice. On board memory on a WAP phone can be used for off-line content (address books, bookmarks, and text-input methods). WAP is expected soon to support video streaming, but so far, most of the WAP applications are text-based and simple black and white graphics.

DoCoMo

According to recent statistics, subscribers of DoCoMo mobile Internet access service "i-mode" exceeded 27 million in 2001 (Kinoshita, 2002). The reasons behind the success of the i-mode in Japan is attributed to the C-HTML (subset of HTML) that enable services providers to develop MoB applications and contents easily; charge is based on packet data volume instead of duration charge, and DoCoMo provides a billing system for services providers that reduces their billing cost. i-mode phones allow mobile users to send/receive graphics and photos, play music, and download/run small pieces of software.

Social and Environmental Impacts

There are many advantages of introducing mBusiness to our daily activities as highlighted in this research. People could work or execute large parts of their work from their offices (even between floors, out of the office, break, etc.), home, and even while driving from/to office during the rush hours in the morning and afternoon. On the other hand, there are several disadvantages that come along with mBusiness. The lack of convergence in the mobile devices represented here by displaying ads on mobile phones will prevent the user from using the mobile phone effectively. Issues like privacy and security, represented here by the ability to know the exact location of the mobile user anytime, anywhere, will put great strain on our personal lives. Since the mobile services provider or carrier already knows our profiles and personal details as subscribers, this will open up a large venue for customer profiling and direct personalised marketing campaigns. Intercepting the wireless communication spectrum by hackers is much easier than tapping into the wired medium. Stealing the mobile device with its valuable contents is another challenge. Unless a complete regulatory framework is put in place to regulate the mBusiness industry (national/ international) and to protect consumers' rights, the preceding impediments would stand high and wide against mBusiness progress. Learning from the earlier e-business experience is highly recommended here. There are developments aiming at increasing mobile devices' security by using smart cards (DoCoMo's smart phone) and a portable version of the Public Key Infrastructure (PKI) encryption solutions (c.f. Turban et al., 2002).

Still, serious issues like viruses are starting to surface on the mobile arena and need to be resolved. As the mobile devices get more sophisticated and multimedia enabled, more viruses will be able to penetrate the mobile arena, threatening to freeze the whole mobile network. How much overhead the mobile device can accommodate to guarantee confidentiality and integrity of transactions, authenticity of mobile users, and hedge against fraudulent activities among sellers and buyers, represents the biggest challenge for manufacturers and developers. Still, we expect the mobile device to have a convenient display, longer battery life, faster performance, buffer and bigger storages, and support multi-features (colours, tones, digital camera, voice recognition, roaming, etc.).

With the proliferation of different mobile technologies in the market and advancement in mobile technology, more business processes could be integrated very easily, enabling workers to squeeze more jobs within the one day. This "burnout" effect will create an environment of high expectations, and hence, puts greater strain on employees to increase their productivity, and this will have devastating social impacts on our lives in the long run, e.g., social ties, psychological problems, etc.

Recent research shows great health hazards to the human brain as a result of the radio spectrum and waves used by the different mobile operators and how receiving a mobile call by a user will increase the amount of waves around the mobile phone reception end, which is located near the user's head. Turban et al. (2002) confirmed the same and pointed to cellular RF emissions and to radiation emitting from mobile devices and how these effects could endanger our health and cause cancer. On the other hand, issues like getting rid of, or recycling, old or used mobile stocks are very important as they represent a great threat to the environment. However, getting rid of these stocks is very costly and requires conscious handling by the different countries.

DISCUSSION AND FUTURE DIRECTIONS

There are many drivers for MoB success as highlighted in this chapter. MoB business provides convenient communications and business services to mobile users anytime (24X7), anywhere (on the move) and everywhere (provided there is global coverage, roaming). Some governments such as the U.S. are realising the importance of MoB in tracing emergency calls and in pinpointing the location of a distressed person, and hence, followed a proactive approach toward MoB and have been working on a law that forces the local O/C to identify the telephone number and location of a mobile phone caller to the 911 emergency number (the law is called E-911) within 100 meters.

On the other hand, there are still many technical, psychological, social, and environmental challenges to overcome for MoB to succeed in the long run. It is expected that more challenges will surface as the technology diffuses in organisations, highlighting further organisational and managerial challenges. The wide macro-political, economical, social, and technological (PEST) impacts are not yet fully identified. The micro-impacts in relation to the nearby environment of the organisation are still not widely reported as yet. Forces like competition, rivalry, suppliers and buyers, substitute products and services and new entrants (Porter & Miller, 1985) are not widely explored as well and would prove to be quite challenging to researchers in revisiting the existing IS and e-business theories in relation to the new mobile technology perspectives.

The investments needed to upgrade the existing telecommunication infrastructure in the different countries to support the mobile environment are very high. The changes that are needed to go alongside such upgrades are enormous and expected to impact on the regulatory framework that runs the business of the different O/C, thus making the mobile experience across the different countries quite different. Recalling the earlier cries by the different researchers (Kalakota & Robinson, 2001; Turban et al., 2002) about the need to change our mindset and to think differently when appraising e-business, the same argument applies here to MoB. Complementary MoB solutions provided by the different O/Cs, manufacturers and developers in the different countries provide short and narrow bridges between e-business and MoB. The current biggest risk for those investors in MoB is that their initiatives would not materialise unless each country provides the 3G or even the 4G infrastructures in order to satisfy their subscribers and increase the mobile subscriber base. Even then, as highlighted in this chapter, this is not sufficient as there is no way to predict customers' behaviour toward the yet not fully blown wireless bandwidth and whether the customers are willing to compromise the rich Internet browsing from their PCs to MoB devices. It is agreed that with greater convergence of mobile technologies and a critical mass of mobile users occurring that MoB may flourish in the different countries. However, each country has it own circumstances, and hence, needs to carefully assess the strategic importance of MoB to their country setting and to the potential wireless subscribers' base.

The same preceding argument applies to equipment and mobile device manufacturers. Looking at the huge drive for MoB by mobile technology vendors and manufacturers, the different markets are flooded with different mobile devices that work with the different existing wireless telecommunication infrastructure, protocols, etc. Some are providing an external interface for a larger keyboard; others are providing Bluetooth capability, smart card integration, etc. Surprisingly, thus far there is no unified protocol that governs the interface between mobile devices and the Internet content. It is obvious that there are two main protocols fighting for dominance (WAP and I-Mode) and it seems the battle is still in its early stages. However, emerging technologies such as Java (J2ME) for MoB may further aggravate the battle for dominance among the different O/C and equipment manufacturers in the mobile battlefield.

There is no widely accepted standard for mobile applications as well, and hence, developers need to customise their applications to suit the operating systems and the browsing needs of the different mobile devices (e.g., PalmOS, Windows CE) and to work with the different wireless infrastructures. This "shooting in every direction" needs to be resolved and unless there are agreed upon standards to guide the conduct of business via mobile devices, valuable time, money and effort will be wasted and indeed could be directed to focus on more impending issues pertaining to MoB.

Finally, let's not forget that the strongest point in the mobile device is its portability and voice capability. The amount of overhead needed to support efficient and secure MoB transactions is quite large and this would increase the mobile device size and weight by incorporating more electronic components and circuitry into it, such as memory chips, processors, smart cards, storage, bigger battery, larger screen and keyboard, more provision for interfaces, etc. Compromising the size and the weight of the mobile device will only deter many of the existing and potential mobile buyers from buying into the technology. The solution is in the voice power of the mobile device, and hence, providing efficient voice solutions in conjunction with data will eliminate the need for most of the complementary and inefficient solutions that will only aggravate the mobile savvy and muster his/her resistance to the oversized and heavy mobile device. Voice portals, or vortals as they are called, provide basic voice-driven information retrieval tools and some basic interactivity. Some mobile devices are equipped with basic voice recognition systems to execute basic commands. However, the technology is still developing and has not yet matured. Further development in this direction and further integrating of voice recognition technology with intelligent software agents could prove a highly significant retrieval tool. However, providing rich and fast content on lightweight devices will represent the biggest challenge toward the wide success of MoB in the long run. There are indeed significant applications for MoB in situations where mobility is an advantage, e.g., sales, courier, logistics and dispatching, but thus far, at the lower end, MoB is the toy of the teenagers; at the higher end it is the toy of the rich or the executive who cannot tolerate to be away from his/her e-mail. With the witnessed development pace in technology, there is no doubt that MoB will have great impact on humanity, where eventually business will drive MoB technology, not teenagers!

ENDNOTES

[1]   802.11a (High-speed 54Mbps, 5GHz band), 802.11b (or called Wi-Fi; Low-speed 11 Mbps, 2.4GHz band)

[2]   Retrieved 15/7/2002 from the Web: backbonemag.com

[3]   Other wireless network standards including Mobitex, DataTAC, iDEN and CDMA/1xRTT.

[4]   Universal mobile telecommunications systems

[5]   Coca-Cola help customers with wireless Web phones find the nearest outlet that sells coca-cola. Retrieved April 15, 2002 from the Web: www.computerworld.com/storyba/

6   Mobile devices equipped with Bluetooth could exchange data (1 MB of data) automatically within a range of 30-35 feet on an ad-hoc basis.

REFERENCES

Anonymous. (October 14, 2000). Leaders: The wireless gamble. *The Economist, 357*(8192), 19–20.

Geng, X., & Whinston, A. (2001). Profiting from value-added wireless services. *IEEE Computer, August,* 87–89.

Kalakota, R., & Robinson, M. (2001). e*Business 2.0: Roadmap for success.* MA: Addison-Wiley Publishing.

Kinoshita, M. (2002). DoCoMo's vision on mobile commerce. *Proceedings of the 2002 symposium on applications and the Internet (SAINT'02).*(Retrieved June 31, 2002 from IEEExplore database).

Lee, H. (2002). Mobile commerce: Vision and challenges. *Proceedings of the 2002 symposium on applications and the Internet (SAINT'02).*(Retrieved June 31, 2002 from IEEExplore database).

Leung, K., & Antypas, J. (Sep/Oct 2001). Improving returns on M-commerce investments. *The Journal of Business Strategy, 22,* 5, 12–13.

McCarthy, A., Zohar, M., & Dolan, T. (May 2000). Mobile Internet reality. *The Forrester Report.* Forrester Research Inc.

Nohria, N., & Leestma, M. (Spring 2001). A moving target: the mobile-commerce customer. *MIT Sloan Management Review, 42*(2), 104.

Porter, M., & Miller, E. (1985). How information gives you competitive advantage. *Harvard Business Review, 63*(4), 149–160.

Samaras (2002). Mobile commerce: Vision and challenges (Location and its management). *Proceedings of the 2002 symposium on applications and the Internet (SAINT'02).*(Retrieved June 31, 2002 from IEEExplore database).

Schneider, G., & Perry, J. (2001). *Electronic commerce* (2nd ed.). Canada: Course Technology.

Shulman, R. (Dec 15, 2000). Is m-business ready for the world? *Supermarket Business, 55*(12), 27–28.

Tade, D. (February, 1999). Evolving wireless systems: Choosing a migration path. *Telecommunications Online.*

Turban, E., King, D., Lee, J., Warkentin, M., & Chung, H. (2002). *Electronic commerce: A managerial perspective 2002.* Upper Saddler River, NJ: Prentice Hall.

Varshney, U. (2001). Location management support for mobile commerce applications. *Proceedings of the ACM, First international conference on mobile commerce,* July.

Varshney, U., & Vitter, R. (2001). A framework for supporting mobile commerce applications. *Proceedings of the 34th Hawaii international conference on systems sciences (HICSS), IEEE Computer society.* January.

Varshney, U., Vetter, R., & Kalakota, R. (2000). Mobile commerce: A new frontier. *IEEE Computer: Special Issues on E-commerce*, October.

Chapter XII

The Evolution of Technology Innovation at Dakin Farms

Pauline Ratnasingam
Central Missouri State University, USA

ABSTRACT

The evolution of technology innovation by businesses using the Internet is transforming and reshaping the nature of inter-organizational commerce and relationships. This case proposes the evolution of technology innovation by a popular family-owned business situated in Vermont. It investigates the technology innovation at Dakin Farms applying the systems development life cycle methodology. The case analyzes phases of IT implementation and its influence on inter-organizational systems and relationships that in turn affects employees' morale and culture. The case contributes to research, practice, and education.

INTRODUCTION

Developing computer-based information systems is usually concerned as a rational process, intended to achieve identifiable and agreed upon goals that enhance its effectiveness. Virtually everyone is familiar with the concept of systems development life cycle. Kendall and Kendall (2001) define systems development life cycle (SDLC) as a phased approach to analysis and design of systems development through the use of a specific cycle of analyst and user activities. Hoffer, George and Valcich (2002) refer to systems development life cycle as a common methodology for systems development in organizations that features several phases marking the progress of the systems analysis and design effort. Similarly, Dennis and Wixon (2000) identify phases that are composed of a series of steps which rely on techniques that produce deliverables (specific documents and files that provide understanding of the project).

The common stages in the systems development life cycle include: initiation and investigation, systems planning, analysis, design, implementation and maintenance (Kendall & Kendall, 2001; Laudon & Laudon, 2000; O'Brien, 1999). The systems development life cycle was intended to ensure the translation of system objectives into operational systems within constraints of schedule and budget. It disciplines practitioners to respect the technical prerequisites. Robey and Markus (1984) suggest that implementing information systems is commonly acknowledged to bring about both technical and social changes to organizations. In this case we describe information systems implementation at Dakin Farms using a case study research method.

Case study research method was found to be useful as it allowed for in-depth information in a real setting that paved the way for further "how" and "why" types of questions, resulting in thicker descriptions and explanations. The author first conducted a series of interviews with the president of Dakin Farms. Each interview lasted between 1-2 hours. Then the author made arrangements for two groups of students—each group consisting of 4 students—to visit Dakin Farms and gather data about their systems implementation process as part of their group projects. Students had to present their findings in front of the entire class as an oral presentation assessment. This case presents the findings from both the author and the students. The next section presents the background information of Dakin Farms.

BACKGROUND INFORMATION
OF DAKIN FARMS

Dakin Farms is a Vermont company which produces maple syrup, cheddar cheese, smoked meats and other speciality foods. The central office is located in Ferrisburg, Vermont. In 1960, Sam and Joan Cutting purchased the 130-acres farm and relocated their family from Connecticut. At first the farm stand which had been added to the property was a family hobby which they operated during the summer months, where they mainly sold Vermont maple syrup. Then they began its business with a small roadside stand and sold pure Vermont maple syrup to tourists in 1980. Sam Cutting Jr., the president of Dakin Farms, manages all marketing functions in order to expand the mail order operations. The company mails out major catalogs, flyers, and newsletters once every three months. Their customers include individuals who purchase packages of products for their friends and relatives for special occasions. Other customers include those who respond to their direct mail advertising and tourists who stopped in at the retail store while visiting Vermont. Dakin Farms relies extensively on repeat business by retaining their customers. The smaller competitors located outside the metropolitan areas rely on attracting potential customers through traffic and mail order. Furthermore, regional and national companies have the advantage of making bulk purchases that in turn reduces the cost of goods.

Dakin Farms does not produce from scratch. Instead, they perform value-added processes by manufacturing a fairly substantial amount of their products themselves. They purchase their maple syrup from local Vermont producers, blend, and pack them into a consistent, high quality product. Furthermore, by operating their own smoke house, they are able to smoke meats using the company's choice of ingredients, thus ensuring product quality and unique flavors. They also produce selected cheeses. These and other procedures ensure that all perishable goods are properly stored, and marketed as "made in Vermont" products. Dakin Farms' products are competitive, ranging from local Vermont businesses (Cold Hollow, Cider Mill, and Harrington's) to national companies such as Hickory Farms. The number of employees in the company varies during the year. During the busy holiday season Dakin Farms employed over 100 people and shipped up to 4,000 packages a day. Eighty to ninety percent of Dakin's annual sales normally occur during the peak season. Dakin Farms' sales revenue for the year 1994 was U.S. $2.5 million and $4 million in the year 2001. Furthermore, the line of business has changed from selling syrup at a roadside stand to being primarily a specialty foods mail order business.

With the success of Sam's mail order strategy, the company was able to open two more retail stores in the Champlain Mill, a medium sized mall located in Winooski, just outside of Burlington, Vermont. At that store, customers could purchase food or fill out mail order forms for gifts to be sent to almost any destination. Sam developed three major strategic goals for Dakin Farms. They include: (1) to produce moderate growth (double sales revenues over the next 10 years), (2) to improve efficiency in the business processes, and (3) to control business costs.

Dakin Farms now has five avenues where it receives its profits. The first two are the retail stores at Ferrisburgh and Burlington in Vermont. The third sector comes from mail orders and the fourth is from their e-commerce web site. Finally, the last sector is via corporate sales. Revenues from these five sectors totaled U.S. $4 million for the year 2000.

The purpose of this case is to examine the evolution of technology innovation at Dakin Farms, applying the systems development life cycle. In particular, it examines how Dakin Farms evolves in IT innovation from a manual mail order processing system to a web presence in e-business. The study attempts to examine change management at Dakin Farms, by answering the following three questions:
1.   How did Dakin Farms evolve from a manual mail order processing system to a web presence?
2.   What were the lessons learned?
3.   How did it affect the morale of the employees in this change management process?

The next section describes Dakin Farms' old mail order processing system and identifies the problems they faced.

The Old Mail Order Processing System

Dakin Farms had been experiencing problems with the mail order processing system. Everything about the process from taking a customer order, picking the goods, packing the order, and sending it seemed to have inefficiencies. The mail order system increased labor costs during the peak season and was unable to handle the amount of orders during these times, thus contributing to the loss of return customers. Eighty to ninety percent of Dakin's annual sales took place during the four-week period. Dakin Farms was unable to handle all of the customers' orders it received and had to turn away an estimated U.S. $30,000 to U.S. $50,000 of business annually.

Some of the problems stemmed from the computerized order-processing system, which Dakin had in place to meet the needs of their business operations. The software program in the system was originally designed for a different company and had parts rewritten to suit Dakin Farms' business. It was a batch system, which meant that orders were recorded on paper, held or "batched" during the day, and then entered into the computer system in batches. The phases in the systems development life cycle examined at Dakin Farms include: initiation and investigation, planning, analysis, design, implementation and maintenance.

SYSTEMS DEVELOPMENT
LIFE CYCLE AT DAKIN FARMS

Phase 1: Systems Initiation and Investigation

With the company growing in the mail order business, its success demanded the implementation of an efficient method for generating and processing mail orders. The Rolodex file system required manual input and maintenance, which made it very inefficient. The manual storage and processing of customer orders also slowed the process substantially, leading to errors and delays. Sam negotiated with a developer, and acquired a mail order software package for Dakin Farms. Sam purchased a used Digital Equipment Corporation (DEC) PDP 11/73 minicomputer with four dumb terminals for U.S. $3,000 in 1983. The software was supposed to be an on-line order-entry system that would allow the Customer Service Representatives (CSRs) to service their customers with the required information while they were on the phone. The system was sluggish, littered with bugs, and could not respond fast enough for people who were trying to order over the phone.

Sam hired a programmer to modify the software by dropping a few modules and rewriting others. Eventually it looked like the original software package that was purchased. Rather than being on-line, the mail orders were processed manually on paper, and then entered in batches into the computer. The system was inefficient, but marginally sufficient for the volume of business that Dakin was doing in the late 1980s and early 1990s. These problems seriously affected the sales and profits of Dakin Farms. Sam Cutting commented:

> "Yes, it is safe to say that I had a lot of expectations from the new order processing system. I also had a lot of questions. We weren't exactly sure what we were getting into when we began the change management process. I only knew that we couldn't continue to operate the way we had been."

The problems in the old system include:

- **Inefficient management and inaccurate forecasting of stock**

   Communications between the Winooski store and the main office were handled by telephone and personal delivery. Customer orders (for gift sales) were recorded in a form that was signed by the customer. The forms were then collected at the close of business, and the store manager would drive to Ferrisburg and drop them off. The orders were then added by the staff at Ferrisburg. Requests for products to replenish the Winooski store inventory was handled by completing a form that was taken to Ferrisburg along with the customer order forms. Any emergency requests were handled by phone. The store manager would call up the Ferrisburg office and indicate that she needed more stock of a certain product before the regular delivery. Someone at the Ferrisburg office would load the required products and deliver them to Winnoski.

   Trying to determine how much of any given product to stock in inventory was a difficult decision, especially for the more perishable items. Sam had to order the products in advance for the busy season. With the maple syrup, for example, Sam had to order them in February for the following Christmas. The production process also required forecasting demand for certain products. There were opportunities to modify the processes as required; however, the measures were not taken accordingly. For example, if they were selling large numbers of maple-glazed hams, production could cut back on some of its smoked turkey flavors and increase the production of maple-glazed ham.

- **Failure of the system to handle large orders**

   The manual order recording over the telephone was time consuming and costly. Both customers and businesses lost money by using this system. The customers lost their money paid for extended toll call, and Dakin Farms lost important Customer Service Representatives (CSRs) time. Furthermore, this slow process discouraged customers from calling again. Additional problems occurred when customers changed their minds or wanted to verify the status of an order. The CSR receiving the call for information on a previous order would have to go through literally hundreds or even thousands of paper order forms, looking for the correct one. During the busy season, Dakin lost much valuable employee time on checking orders instead of processing new ones. In addition, the CSRs had no way of knowing exactly what was still in inventory at any given time. They may accept an order from a customer, only to discover later that the packer was unable to fill it. The CSR would then call the customer back, and ask if they would like to substitute an item.

- **Inefficient use of Packing Systems**
  The packing operations were inefficient, with no formal procedures in place. It relied on the personal preference of the packer. Considerable time was wasted during packing. For example, an order might come through that required a corn-smoked turkey which was located at the end of storage cooler, far from the final packing area. After packing this order, the packer moves to the next order and discovers that it too required a corn-smoked turkey. If he had known that in advance he could have picked two turkeys at the same time, thus saving a lot of time.
- **Failure to Manage Payment Information**
  There were inefficiencies in the payment systems, in particular in verifying the credit card payments. If the credit card purchases were not approved by the bank, they needed to be verified against the original telephone order form. The CSR would go to the basement and pull the packing list or pull the package from the cooler where it was awaiting pickup for verifying the order and customer's credit card information. The divergence of information flow created inefficiencies in the mail order process and purchase, for sometimes the order was already being packed by the time the CSR discovered it, and thus the time taken to pack the order was wasted. Furthermore, the order had to be unpacked as well.

Phase 2: Systems Planning

The problems and inefficiencies of the mail order processing were derived from a lack of planning that led to a drop in sales and profits. Three key areas of improvement were identified for a new system within a short time period. They included:

- Reduced labor costs;
- Increased sales (by being able to handle heavy seasonal orders); and
- Increased customer retention.

- **The Evolution of Dakin Farms' IT System**
  By implementing a new system, Sam had big decisions to allocate tangible costs for the system. It included the cost of creating it, which meant hiring designers, and covering their benefits and any costs they incurred in the process. The budget also has to be allocated for acquisition of new

computers. His intangible costs came from low employee morale and frustration along with the confusion from a few long-term employees who were not willing to learn the new system. Meanwhile his benefits, both tangible and intangible, seem to greatly outweigh his costs. While benefiting from an increase in customer satisfaction, he was able to recoup the $30,000 to $50,000 and retain more customers and receive better recommendations from his current customers. Thus, the new system, combined with a new packing room layout, was aimed to dramatically increase the number of orders packed in one day, as well as the timeliness of these processes. With the need to focus on the three key areas (namely, reduce labor costs, increase sales, and increase customer retention), the system was expected to reduce the cycle time from order to shipment and from order to payment. The reduced delivery time was also derived from the quality of customer services. Customers who received the orders on time were satisfied due to the quality of service and are likely to order from Dakin Farms in the future. The new system enabled temporary employees to be hired during the peak seasons. Furthermore, the automatic selling functions and the on-line product information made available by the computers in turn reduced the training costs.

Phase 3: Analysis

Efforts to improve the new order processing system and to redesign existing operations proceeded in a somewhat parallel manner. The president of Dakin Farms had two broad objectives: (1) to improve efficiency, and (2) to increase capacity. He wanted to expand capacity by about three-folds (from the current 1,000 orders to at least 3,000 orders) and do it without hiring more staff. In addition, he wanted to provide customers with immediate response to inquiries and reduce delivery of orders from the current several days to a maximum of two days. In order to achieve the objectives Sam focused his expectations on three operations. They included:

1.   **Customer Service**

    The on-line capabilities of Dakin Farms' web site aimed to improve the efficiencies of the customer service order entry time. The new system will contain pertinent information about customers in a database. Customer Service Representatives (CSRs) will be able to answer customer queries, and access product information on the screen, along with the technical descriptions of the products.

2.   Business Operations

Sam had high expectations for improving the efficiency of the existing operations. He wanted the new system to integrate the three existing operations processes, namely: the mail order process, credit card verification, and mail manifest. One goal is to achieve the automatic verification of credit card purchases, so that only orders for approved purchases could be printed to the packers, thereby lowering the risk of bad debt accumulation. The mail manifest (which calculates the amount of postage needed for the order) will be improved because the new system would show the CSR the approximate weight and cost of shipping on-line as the orders are taken. This in turn improves the customer service because it allows customers to know the full price (order total plus shipping costs) of their purchases immediately. Furthermore, the increased efficiencies in using phone time per customer enabled the CSRs to handle more calls in one day, thus decreasing the number of calls they could not answer during the busy seasonal period, which in turn decreased the number of CSRs needed during peak business times.

3.   Marketing

The new system aimed to efficiently produce sales, marketing strategies and distribute marketing materials (brochures) from mailing lists generated from files of customer purchases. Currently the CSRs are requested to write down where the customer heard of Dakin Farms and whether or not they had ordered from Dakin Farms in the past. This information was then tabulated manually from the paper slips, which was very time consuming. The accuracy of the data was an issue because during the busy periods, CSRs may skip these questions or make up answers. Furthermore, advertising was expensive, and Sam wanted to ensure that he was getting the most out of his advertising dollars.

Phase 4: Systems Design

Sam explains the design of their IT system in these words:

"The core of our system has to do with two servers. One is the mail server which runs the network of PCs on Microsoft Windows Operating Systems and Microsoft Office Applications. Files are shared between PCs at different security levels depending on a user's position in the company. All information is stored in the mail server where it is backed up nightly. The mail server

is connected to the Internet through a mixed use T-1 connection with 512K of bandwidth for data. The second server runs the order processing system which is called Quick Order Processing (QOP). QOP is the core of our business as the inventory is produced and is recorded in the QOP. As items are transferred from one store to the next, the QOP tracks the transfer. All points of sale are run by QOP including every cash register, every PC taking mail orders, and every dumb terminal taking mail orders. Plus there is an interface to QOP from our corporate sale department, remote call centers and the web. The satellite store at 100 Dorset St. in South Burlington is connected to the QOP and mail serves over the Internet. Therefore, every scan of a product on a cash register at Dorset St, for example, is running off the server located in Ferrisburg."

During the design phase the IT staff defined exactly how the system would work. The most important aspect of the system was the need to make information immediately accessible to the Customer Service Representatives (CSRs). Things like the weight of the product would be immediately available, which enabled the customer to know their shipping cost while, or directly after, placing the order. The system needed to be easy to use, thus saving time and costs from employee training.

Several rules had to be defined so as to cut back on human error as much as possible. This is important for both the customer service representatives and customers using the web site. For instance, one rule in the program includes the earliest data available for shipping. This way, when a CSR enters the delivery date, they cannot accidentally key in another date which has already being entered as the system locks in the date.

Phase 5: Systems Implementation

The implementation phase of the information systems at Dakin Farms took place in 10 stages. 1981 marked the phase one of the 10-phase process of IT implementation at Dakin Farms. During the first phase Dakin Farms outsourced an outside vendor to maintain the mailing list. Dakin Farms mailed their card files to a company in Albany who updated and entered the card files into the system. By outsourcing the mailing list, Dakin Farms was able to increase their number of mailings from once a year to five times per year and also reduce labor costs as it no longer needed individuals to type up labels to be mailed out. This was vital since many customers ordered through the mailings.

Phase two of the implementation process occurred in 1982. This step involved the purchase of Dakin Farms' first computer. It was a PDP11 and it had three users. The new system could process mail orders, produce packing slips, and post summary orders history to the customer's record. The only history that was kept in the system was the date of the order, the date of the shipment, and the amount of the order. In addition, payment information in terms of dollar amounts was kept for each customer and the details of the orders were kept in paper form. In order to look up an order it was necessary to look into the system and see when the order was shipped, then refer to the paper record to see the details of the order. This implementation allowed Dakin Farms to guarantee the delivery of its products on time. The system had its glitches and although it did increase efficiency, a certain level of reliability was lost.

In the mid-1980s, Sam decided that another step in IT innovation was needed for the business to flourish. The third phase of IT implementation at Dakin Farms involved the purchase of a Macintosh Apple computer which was popular at that time and Sam found it necessary to keep up with popular trends. A second Macintosh Apple was bought immediately thereafter. These two computers operated independently as they were not networked. They were used for word processing spreadsheets, and desktop publishing. The growing use and dependence on computer technology was difficult for some employees to handle, especially the more experienced ones who were reluctant to embrace changes. As a result of IT innovation, a few employees refused to adapt to the changing technology and so left the company.

The year 1987 marked the fourth phase where Sam aimed to minimize the errors and maximize the profits in the accounting department. This led to an automated accounting system using a PC. Shortly thereafter, the Macintosh Apple computers were sold and a PC network was installed. The fifth phase permitted sharing of information between end users. All of these users by now had management positions in the organization. There were now four Paces on the network and the orders were still processed on the PDP11.

Sam found the sixth phase to be a big one for his organization as it involved the purchase of a Quick Order Processing (QOP) system. Sam said that *"this was perhaps the biggest advance in information systems use that Dakin Farms has made to date."* The QOP automated the mail order processing system and kept complete details of all activities. There was no longer a paper trail that employees had to follow in order to get information about a certain customer or order. All of this valuable information was now right there at the fingertips of all CSRs in the mail order section of the business. Orders could instantly be looked up on the system and customers' queries were handled in a more timely and organized manner.

In 1991, the seventh phase included the implementation of a Point Of Sale retail system that kept track of retail sales and inventory. In addition, the Retail Information Management Systems (RIMS) was implemented. The RIMS system had its shortcomings because the system simply did not have the capabilities to provide real-time information, as customers were unable to know exactly where their packages were and when they would be receiving them.

In 1995, the eighth phase in the IT implementation took place. Sam was aware that this was the first step into the somewhat risky field of e-commerce. Dakin Farms implemented the Internet connectivity for their two PCs, and had to implement their first web site. With the help of a company called "Competitive Computing", they developed a small web site. With this new web site, customers were able to enter their own orders and pick a date for the goods to be delivered. Another aspect that was beneficial to the company is that the web builds file orders and transfers them to the Quick Order Processing (QOP) system. The file transfers are handled in batches and during Christmas the batches are run hourly.

The ninth step was to upgrade the QOP system onto an NT server, which added a frame relay Internet connection in 1998. This implementation provided all PC users the ability to run multiple sessions of QOP. The tenth and final stage bring us up to date with the IT innovation at Dakin Farms. This phase took place in the year 2000 when QOP took over the Point Of Sale and inventory functions from Retail Information Management Systems.

Phase 6: Systems Maintenance

Systems maintenance is the last phase in the systems development life cycle. The activities in this stage include monitoring, evaluating, and modifying the new system in the event that it is not running according to the business needs. The deliverable of this stage is an improved system. After the system has been implemented, the company will monitor its performance and collect feedback from employees and customers. The maintenance phase at Dakin Farms relied mostly on allocating human resources. Sam's office manager supervised the Customer Service Representatives (CSRs) and managed the business operations whenever Sam was unavailable. There was a packing supervisor (one for each shift, during the busy season) for the packers who filled and shipped the customer orders, as well as a supervisor who ran the production operations (smokehouse, cutting room, inventory control). There were two store managers at the Ferrisburg and one at the Winooski Mill retail outlets who supervised the store operations. A report was produced at the end of each week outlining the problems/issues that they experienced in the business operations.

Figure 1 presents a summary of the activities at Dakin Farms, applying the phases in the systems development life cycle. The figure identifies the activities, roles, and deliverables in each phase of the SDLC relating to IT innovation at Dakin Farms.

Description of Dakin Farms' Business Operations After IT Implementation

Dakin Farms now has five avenues where it receives its profits. The first two are the retail stores at Ferrisburgh and Burlington in Vermont. The third comes from mail orders and the fourth from their e-commerce web site (www.dakinfarm.com). Finally, the last avenue comes from corporate sales.

Figure 1: Systems development life cycle phases at Dakin Farms

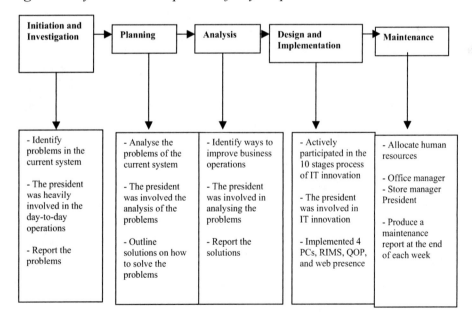

Revenues from these five avenues totaled U.S. $4 million for the year 2000. The next section describes the business operations at Dakin Farms on a typical day.

There are four ways by which customers could purchase products through Dakin Farms. First, by shopping at one of two retail stores, either at the Dorset street retail store in South Burlington or the retail store in Ferrisburgh. The next three ways are through mail order. Customers can order by mailing in a catalog order, calling in a catalog order, or order through Dakin Farms' e-commerce web site at www.Dakinfarms.com.

When a call comes in by a customer wanting to order from Dakin's catalog it goes to the offices at the Ferrisburgh retail store. The call is answered by a Customer Service Representative (CSR) or if they are all already on the line the call goes through to a call sequencer, which will hold the customer's call until the next CSR is available. The CSR then enters the data which he/she receives from the customer to the computer and specifically into the Quick Order Processing (QOP) system. The type of information that is entered into the computer includes customer-number, customer-last-name, customer-first-name, address, telephone-number, fax-number, e-mail-address, CSR-name, the date of the order, who it is being shipped to, the shipping address, the date that they wish the package to be delivered, and the products that the customer wishes to purchase. The order is stored in QOP until it is time for the package to be shipped so that it can reach the customer on time. The CSR also manually enters the data from the catalog orders that came in via mail.

Alternatively, orders taken on-line were slightly different. When customers visit the Dakin Farms e-commerce web site they browse through the products and choose the products that they wish to purchase. Order details such as order number, order-description, order-quantity, order-delivery time, payment-method, and CSR-name are recorded. The customer then enters all the information that Dakin Farms requires. The customer fills out the appropriate information and sends it to Dakin Farms' web site where it is stored in the QOP system, similar to the phone and mail in orders. This saves Dakin Farms a lot of time and money.

The next step takes place when it gets closer to the time in which the package must be delivered. The computer knows when the package must be shipped in order to reach the customer on time. QOP sends the open orders, which are due to be delivered to a printer. The paper orders are then physically taken upstairs to the picking, packing and shipping room. The room contains shelves and refrigerators filled with Dakin's products waiting to be shipped. The employees begin to pack the products. They pick each of the individual products from the shelves or from the refrigerator. They scan the product, which has a bar code to keep track of where a certain product came from and where it is currently located. By scanning the product the item is removed from the inventory list and it is then packed. While a few employees pack the boxes other employees are busy restocking the shelves and the refrigerators from the back.

The package is then sent to the Mail Room where the package is weighted and shipping details are filled out for the package to be shipped. Each package is scanned and given a UPS or FedEx tracking number. Other information such as shipping date, shipping company's name, shipping amount, and payment method are also recorded. This number allows Dakin Farms and their customers to go onto the UPS or FedEx web site and look up to see where exactly their package was located. At this point the customers are then charged for the package and the open order becomes an Ice file (which means that it has been shipped). As for the scanning of the products, each product is given a bar code in order to keep track of the products available at all times. When the meat, cheese, or maple syrup is produced, it is packaged, weighted and given a bar code. These records indicate where each product is at all times, whether it is in the production room or in one of the retail stores, in inventory, or being shipped off to one of Dakin's customers. The product is scanned when it moves from one department to another, thus updating the computer system on where the product is located.

LESSONS LEARNED

The lessons learned by Dakin Farms emphasize the importance of implementing IT at the right time and with functions that will not only solve the existing problems, but also will provide strategic directions for the future. Dakin Farms experienced the following problems from the old system.
- Inefficient management and forecasting of stock;
- Failure of the system to handle large orders;
- Inefficient use of employees time;
- Failure to manage payment information; and
- Change in employees' morale.

Sam commented that the lessons he learned from the past 22 years in the family business as to using a proven system and not trying to invent, and that some employees will be reluctant to use the new system. They need to be educated and well-trained in order to see the big picture and its importance. Eventually they will need to adapt to the new system or leave the company. Similarly, Robey and Markus (1984) conducted a study applying the systems development life cycle for implementing information systems projects. They found that information systems development involves both a rational and a political process. Their findings indicate that consequently developers may differ from users by their cognitive styles and personality differences.

DAKIN FARMS TODAY

Dakin Farms now uses an ECC (Electronic Commerce Connection) Order Integrator which is defined as "the module which interfaces with the e-commerce software and the catalog management system". The system takes Internet orders from customers and turns them into files which are then put with the rest of the orders as if they had been taken by the customer service representatives. Further, a bar-code database is created for the shipping department which is linked with the UPS and FedEx's databases for customers' convenience in package tracking.

Sam indicated that the current state of business at Dakin Farms included:

- We are moving forward with the construction of a pick/pack and ship facility, warehouse and a call center expected to be completed by the summer of 2003.
- This year (2002) we have temporarily opened a third retail location in Champlain Centers North Mall in Plattsburgh, New York.
- Web sales are currently running 70% ahead of last year (2001) and should represent approximately 40% of our direct marketing sales for the year.
- Our total payroll for the holiday season will settle between 110-115 employees for the year 2002.
- Our future plans include expanding our e-commerce business, mail order business, corporate sale and opening new stores, and
- The size of our business earnings is: U.S. $1.75 million from the retail stores, U.S. $1.25 million from mail orders, $U.S. .5 million from e-commerce, $U.S. .5 million from corporate sales, contributing to a total of U.S. $4 million in sales.

CONCLUSION

The new system which Dakin Farms implemented has dramatically increased the number of orders packed in one day, as well as the timeliness of the procedure. With these new improvements, the system is expected to reduce cycle time from order to shipment and from order to payment. The decreased delivery time was also tied in with customer service. The sooner the customers received an order the happier they would be and the greater chance they would order from Dakin Farms in the future.

The contributions of this case study pointing towards the lessons learned indicates that businesses should implement technologies not only to remain competitive but more importantly to meet their own organization's business needs and strategic goals. The study contributes to research, practice and education in the following ways. First, the case provides an avenue for researchers to examine IT adoption applying the systems development life cycle methodology which explicitly identifies each phase and stages of IT implementation, activities, roles and deliverables at each phase. As most previous research emphasized competitive advantages of IT adoption, it will be useful for future researchers to investigate antecedent and consequence factors in IT adoption. Second, the contribution to practice focuses on the increased awareness by businesses to emphasize best business practices and goals that meet their business needs and strategic directions rather than investing on IT just to be seen as was revealed in a recent study conducted by Morgan and Stanley (*USA Today*, 2002). Their study revealed billions of dollars that companies spent on much unnecessary software and IT. Furthermore, the rush and greed to make quick profits has led to corporate scandals and business malpractices derived from unethical, inadequate audit and accounting systems as was seen in collapse of large corporations such as Enron, Xerox, and Worldcom, that in turn affected the economic confidence of the nation, investors and employees. For example, IBM had to retrench 2500 employees (in April 2002) and in fact had to close down one of its plants in Vermont. Similarly, Adelphia, a provider of U.S. cable TVs and telecommunication lines, filed for bankruptcy in June 2002. The above examples have provided sufficient evidence for businesses to be aware of best business practices in IT adoption. Finally, this case contributes to education by providing a real-life teaching case applying the systems development life cycle for the MIS undergraduate curriculum in the business schools across the nation and world.

ACKNOWLEDGMENTS

The author wishes to acknowledge students' assistance in compiling the case study notes for this research project and the participants at Dakin Farms.

REFERENCES

Dakin Farms' home page: http://www.Dakinfarms.com

Dennis, A., & Wixon, B. H. (2000). *Systems analysis and design: An applied approach*. Wiley and Co.

Hoffer, J. A., George, J. F., & Valcich, J. S. (2002). *Modern systems analysis and design* (3rd ed.). Prentice Hall.

Kendall, K. E., & Kendall, J. E. (2001). *Systems analysis and design* (5th Ed.). Prentice Hall.

Laudon, K. C., & Laudon, J. P. (2000). *Management of information systems – Organization and technology in the networked enterprise* (6th Ed.). Prentice Hall.

O'Brien, J. (1999). *Management of information systems: Managing Information Technology in the Internet-worked enterprise* (4th Ed.). McGraw-Hill.

USA Today.(2002, May 22). *Company squanders millions in IT and unneeded software*.

Chapter XIII

From Cash to E-Money: Payment System Innovations in Australia

Mohini Singh
RMIT University, Australia

Betty Zoppos
RMIT University, Australia

ABSTRACT

With technological developments, and the changing needs of global and on-line businesses, innovations in retail payment methods have evolved progressively. The retail business has undergone a transformation from main street business to on-line business in the last decade due to globalisation, technological developments, application of the Internet and innovative business models. When commerce goes electronic, the means of paying for goods and services must also go electronic. Paper-based payment systems cannot support the speed, security, privacy and internationalisation necessary for electronic commerce. This chapter is an appraisal of retail payment innovations and changes in payment instruments in Australia in the last decade. It highlights continued primacy of cash for face-to-face payments, growth in payment by cards and other new developments to support evolving e-business models. The need for e-payment systems in e-business, an understanding of payment systems, market developments, payment risks and technological applications to payment methods are also discussed.

INTRODUCTION

The retail business has undergone a transformation from main street business to on-line business in the last decade due to globalisation, technological developments, application of the Internet and innovative business models. With technological developments and the requirements of global and on-line businesses, innovations in retail payment methods have also progressed. As suggested by Watson, Berthon, Pitt, and Zinkhan (1999), when commerce goes electronic, the means of paying for goods and services must also go electronic. Paper-based payment systems cannot support the speed, security, privacy and internationalisation necessary for electronic commerce.

This chapter is about retail payment innovations, trends and developments in payment instruments, providers and applications. With developments in e-business the need for e-payment systems, a better understanding of payment systems, market developments, payment risks and technological applications to payment methods is required. Recent trends in retail payments are generally common to most countries around the world; however, the discussion in this chapter is generally based on developments in Australia. It is focussed on recent trends in retail payment methods identified by Andrieu (2001), including:

- continued primacy of cash for face-to-face payments, despite a longstanding movement towards non-cash payments;
- growth in payment cards, primarily for face-to-face payments, and in direct funds transfers, especially direct debit transfers, for remote payments; and
- substantial changes in the market arrangements for providing and pricing the retail payment instruments and services delivered to end-users.

Changes in key supply and demand factors for retail payments including changes in relative prices, risk and convenience for existing instruments and increases in the general acceptability of newer instruments, have an impact on the application and use of certain retail methods. The development of new information technology (IT) is probably the most fundamental supply factor. This, together with regulatory changes in some countries, has supported the emergence of a broader range of instruments, such as payment cards, and significant changes in the delivery, pricing and processing arrangements for retail payments. The increased cooperation by payment service providers in developing and operating shared retail payment networks has also contributed to new developments in retail payment methods. These developments, along with market entry by non-financial institutions in some countries, have contributed to increased competition and an increased pace of change in payment services markets. An increased demand for on-line processing of payments for e-business, which is global and technology-based, has further demanded changes and increased the acceptance of electronic payment methods.

The discussion in this chapter is a review of literature supported with information from the Reserve Bank of Australia, the Australian Payment Clearing Authority and the Australian Bankers Association reports.

The APCA's role is to manage and develop the Australian payments clearing system and preserve the integrity of the system, identify and control settlement risk, improve the effectiveness and efficiency of the system, ensure principles of equity and competitive neutrality are applied in determining participation in the system, facilitate the co-ordination of payments clearing arrangements among providers of payment services, assist the community's understanding of the system and ensure that the public is well informed (www.apca.com.au).

In the commercial world there are a number of entities made up of organizations, individuals, intermediaries and institutions. The Australian Payment Control Authority (www.apca.com.au) refers to these entities as counterparties. For example an individual is one counterparty and an individual, firm or government agency can be the other. The counterparties can be engaged either in a transaction-by-transaction relationship involving one-time payment or in a contractual relationship involving recurring payments; either face-to-face or remote. To support this commercial relationship there are numerous payment devices. Different classes of vendors and customers may prefer different types of payment arrangements and accept or use only particular types of payment instruments. Retail payments generally entail higher volumes and lower average values than wholesale payments settled either in the same fashion as the wholesale payments or differently.

Cash retail payments are categorised as paper-based, and non-cash payments are generally electronic, or a transfer of value between financial institutions. Non-cash payment instruments are generally subclassified into cheque payments, direct funds transfers and card payments, all of which are based on certain rules and procedures. Each class may also involve more than one specific type of instrument, payment delivery mechanism or market arrangement for providing the payment services to end-users.

RETAIL PAYMENT INSTRUMENTS

The following discussion includes a description of some of the retail payment instruments, their applications and related issues.

Cash

Currency continues to be the most convenient and popular form of payment for everyday, low-value transactions. Cash payments are usually associated with face-to-face transactions of low value between individuals or between an individual and a retail firm. In most countries legislation or regulation enables the acceptance of currency for all types of transactions, subject possibly to minimum denomination limits. Cash payment transactions do not usually require further identification. It is an immediate and final transfer of value, and the currency received as payment can be reused by the recipient for further payments (www.rba.com.au). Andrieu (2001) adds that cash is still a popular payment instrument due to familiarity and simplicity and the fact that it can be easily withdrawn from automatic teller machines and is untraceable, satisfying the user's demand for privacy.

Cheques

The use of cheques has traditionally dominated Australian non-cash payments and they were, until the mid 1970s, virtually the only non-cash payment instrument (www.rba.gov.au). As reported by the Reserve Bank of Australia, despite the development of other payment instruments, cheques remain an important form of non-cash payment. In Australia cheques can be drawn on authorised deposit-taking institutions such as credit unions and building societies besides banks.

Direct Funds Transfers

Retail funds transfers include credit and debit transfers, both of which apply to remote payments. Instructions from either the payer or the payee prompt its payment service provider for transfer of funds from the payer's account at its financial institution to the payee's account at its financial institution. These transfers usually are scheduled payments to individuals, different individuals that have been grouped together in a file of electronic payment messages to the payer's service provider (www.apca.com.au).

Direct-entry payments entail direct computer-to-computer linkages, usually after payments have been bulked. In Australia since March 1994, banks and other financial institutions such as building societies and credit unions have been linked in an integrated but decentralised national system to support direct-entry transactions. Direct credits enable a paying institution to transfer funds to the accounts of a large number of recipients. These are useful to government departments and companies for regular payments such as social security benefits, salary and dividend payments. Direct debits are used mostly by insurance and utilities companies and like bodies for collecting regular policy premiums and payments, and by financial institutions to collect loan repayments (www.apca.com.au). Direct debit transfers are initiated by the payee, usually through a preauthorised agreement with the payer, and are generally processed in electronic form. Penny (2001) advocates that credit, debit and charge cards are the main payment instruments for goods and services bought on the Internet.

Credit Cards

Credit cards include charge cards, which involve a short-term fixed-period credit arrangement, and cards with revolving credit arrangements. With charge cards, the accumulated credits are settled at the end of the charge or billing period, generally around one month. Cards with revolving credit arrangements allow a minimum partial payment at the end of the billing period, with the balance of the accumulated credits charged to the cardholder's revolving credit line. In some systems the credit charges accumulated through the initial billing period are interest-free if the charges are fully paid at the end of the billing period or interest is charged only on the unpaid credit balances and on subsequent charges. Cash advances are also possible through credit card transactions, either from vendors directly or from ATMs. Interest is charged from the date of the advance and in some countries there is even a surcharge for cash advances (www.apca.com.au). Yu, Hsi, and Kuo (2002) are of the opinion that although using a credit card entails a fee, it is popular because of its acceptability in many foreign countries and also because it is a relatively safe method of payment. Credit cards are used in both on-line and off-line systems to initiate and authorise payment. On-line payments, which are either via the Internet or EFTPOS, involve a direct communications link through a network switch for real-time authorisation of the payment. At the point of sale the payer signs the merchant's credit card voucher to authorise the payment. Initiating the payment through to its clearing and settlement is fully electronic. Turban, Lee, King, and Chung (2002) suggest that the credit card is the most popular payment method for on-line shopping today, despite its vulnerability to security breaches when used on-line.

Debit Cards

Debit cards are usually used for non-recurring electronic funds transfers at the point of sale (EFTPOS) to initiate payment to the vendor with an immediate debit to the cardholder's account. Payment cards with a deferred debit arrangement are classified as credit cards in most countries and as debit cards in France (www.apca.com.au). In Australia, banks, credit unions and building societies are the main issuers of debit cards, which can be used in ATMs, cash dispensers, automated petrol dispensers, telephones and EFTPOS terminals.

Travel, Entertainment and Retailer Cards

These are also called charge, store and private label cards, and allow payment to be deferred from the date of purchase until the account due date. Accumulated balances are payable in full on receipt of the monthly statement. No interest is charged if payments are made on time, but there may be joining and annual membership fees. In some instances, the card may be linked to a separate line of credit through an account with a financial institution (www.apca.com.au).

EFTPOS

All electronic funds transfers at point of sale (EFTPOS) in Australia apply with PIN-based identification and authorisation. Most EFTPOS transactions debit customers' accounts in real time. Payment to the merchant is guaranteed by the bank which acquires its transactions, with a cash-back facility to cardholders making purchases. EFTPOS terminals operate whenever the merchant is open; for some merchants, such as petrol stations, this is 24 hours a day, seven days a week. Many EFTPOS terminals are integrated with retailer cash registers (www.apca.com.au).

Automated Teller Machines

Andrieu (2001) advocates that although automated teller machines (ATMs) are not money in many forms, they enable cash withdrawals, deposits, balance enquiries, transfers between accounts and ordering of cheque books and statements. There are no legal restrictions on the siting or number of machines financial institutions may install; however, operators have to meet standards established by Standards Australia covering design and placement. Most operate 24 hours a day. Some financial institutions also provide limited-purpose Cash Dispensers which can be used only for withdrawals and account balance enquiries. ATM and cash dispenser transactions are authorised by debit cards and certain credit cards with a Personal Identification Number (PIN) (www.apca.com.au).

Stored-Value Cards

The use of prepaid stored-value cards (SVCs), although available in Australia, does not have a widespread application. The major issuer is Telstra with its Phonecard, which is used for making calls from public telephones. Prepaid tickets have been used in urban transport systems for some time, and some tertiary institutions sell prepaid rechargeable cards for use by students in their library photocopying machines (www.apca.com.au).

There have been extensive trials of SVCs in Australia. The major operators and technology involved are MONDEX, VisaCash, ERG (using Proton technology) and Chip Application Technologies Ltd, a domestic operator. The cards have an electronic purse function which was recently "turned-on", but to date the take-up of this facility has been modest.

Yu Yu, Hsi, and Kuo (2002) are of the opinion that since smart cards have advantages of anonymity, payment between parties, and low transaction fee, it is possible that in the future this will be a preferred method over e-cash. Similar to credit cards and stored-value cards, smart cards function like magnetic strip cards, with different payment times. In on-line commerce, customers use smart cards by keying-in certain identification numbers that match the information stored on the magnetic strip. The amount of the product or service is then deducted by the card reader and the reader rewrites information back to the card. Many stores desiring micropayment mechanisms adopt the stored-value card payment system. In Taiwan, Software International issued Web Gold Services (WGS) for its on-line game players to make payments. The stored-value card can be either anonymous or identifiable. Anonymous cards have the advantage of being able to be transferred from one person to another, whereas identifiable cards are nontransferable (Greenstein & Feinman, 2000, cited in Chou, Lee, & Chung, 2002).

Chou et al. (2002) also explain that the smart card exemplifies the real-time payment method and is also capable of converting stored value back to real currency, have superior encryption technology, and are less vulnerable to security breaches than the credit card. It can also support peer-to-peer payment. However, Plouffe, Vandenbosch, and Hulland (2001) suggest that for smart cards to succeed, many consumers must use them for many products and services across many purchase occasions. At the same time, many merchants must adopt the required point-of-sale technology needed to process smart card payments from consumers. "If too few consumers adopt the technology, merchants will have little incentive to invest in the required equipment, to alter their business practices, or to train their employees in the system's operation. If too few merchants adopt the system, consumers will have little use for the cards. Thus, adoption must take place simultaneously within both groups" (p. 69).

Electronic Data Interchange

Electronic Data Interchange (EDI) is the computer-to-computer exchange of information in a standard format. EDI is most commonly used in the retail, transport, automotive and heavy engineering industries as well as some areas of the public sector, particularly Customs, the Reserve Bank and the Department of Finance and Administration (www.apca.com.au) settling business-to-business payments via inter-bank settlements.

Other Retail Payment Instruments

Other instruments for retail payments include *money orders*, *wire transfers* and *travellers' cheques*. A money order is essentially a direct credit transfer instrument involving a payment to a specified recipient. It can be used for both domestic and foreign currency remote payments. A money order is a paper-based instrument transmitted and processed as an electronic credit transfer, similar to a wire transfer. Retail wire transfers are electronic credit transfers sent through a proprietary communications system. Wire transfers entail a fee and enable quick transfer of funds between two parties. Travellers' cheques are essentially paper-based instruments issued in specific denominations for general-purpose use in business and personal travel. Travellers' cheques are available in domestic currency and selected major foreign currencies. They can be converted into cash only by their specified owner, and are generally accepted only by other issuers, large retailers, hotels and restaurants.

Third-Party Bill Payments

In Australia, the largest operator of third-party bill payments is Australia Post. There are around 3,900 post offices or agencies throughout Australia. Australia Post offers access to banking facilities as an agent for the Commonwealth Bank and for a range of other financial institutions through its giroPost network. While the agreement with the Commonwealth Bank is long-standing, giroPost was introduced in July 1995. It is an electronic banking and financial services network which provides post office access to card-based accounts of participating financial institutions. Customers of these institutions can open accounts, make deposits and withdrawals, pay bills and make balance inquiries. Post offices accept over-the-counter cheque and cash payments for over 300 principals (www.rba.gov.au).

A bank-owned service company, BPAY, recently established a new third-party bill payment service. BPAY is an electronic bill payment service owned by a consortium of banks. It allows customers of participating financial institutions to arrange for the transfer of funds from their bank account to issue payment instructions via telephone or the Internet. Fees are charged for payments made using the BPAY service (www.apca.com.au).

Building Societies

Building societies are organised to lend money mainly for housing. However, they also offer comprehensive retail payment services. Cheque-issuing arrangements with banks enable them to offer depositors access to cheque account facilities.

Credit Unions

Credit unions are mutual organizations that provide for deposits and borrowing by their members. Loans are mainly for the purchase of consumer durables, motor vehicles and housing. Most credit unions have an arrangement with a major national bank whereby depositors with the credit union are able to draw cheques on the credit union's account with the bank.

Credit and Debit Card Companies

There are three major credit cards issued in Australia. Banks and many building societies and credit unions issue cards which are affiliated with either the Visa or MasterCard schemes. Some banks also issue Bankcard, a local credit card used in Australia and New Zealand. American Express recently signed agreements with two banks to issue Amex credit cards. Many institutions issue proprietary debit cards for ATM and EFTPOS transactions.

Charge Card Issuers

American Express and Diners Club also issue charge cards in Australia. American Express cardholders have access to some bank ATM networks. Some other overseas card issuers have arrangements with Australian merchants to accept their cards.

Retailers

Retailers are not generally providers of third-party payment services. However, many stores and retail chains issue their own cards for use in their premises only, such as Myer and David Jones. Some oil companies issue their own cards, both credit and debit for commercial fleets.

TRENDS AND DEVELOPMENTS IN RETAIL PAYMENTS

The Australian Payment Control Authority (www.apca.com.au) predicts that in Australia the trend is:

- A movement away from cash towards electronic non-cash payments;
- A growth in payments made by cards;
- A greater use of direct debit transfers; and
- A greater dependence on technology to support real time transactions and Internet payments.

Factors predicted to have contributed to the changes in retail payment methods are:
- Growth and advancements in information technologies;
- Competition and cooperation between providers of retail payment services;
- Globalisation of payment services offered by individual institutions in international retail payment networks;
- Risk preferences of both payers and payees for specific instruments and services;
- Cost and convenience of various instruments to users;
- Acceptance and availability of alternative payment instruments;
- An increased application of the Internet for the sale of goods and services; and
- Introduction of e-payment services such as e-banking.

Chou et al. (2002) highlight that economic factors such as costs, monetary convertibility, customer base, peer to peer payment ability, anonymity, privacy, convenience and merchant acceptance influence the application, acceptance and innovations in payment systems.

Continuation of Currency as a Retail Payment Instrument

The continuing role of cash in retail payments may be attributed to the absence of credit risk, the anonymity associated with many of these transactions, and its immediacy and finality in transactions. Yet another contributing factor is legislation imposing an obligation to accept legal tender as payment (www.rba.gov.au).

The existence and growth of ATM networks is a contributor to lower costs and greater convenience in obtaining cash, as well as lower costs of supplying cash at traditional banking locations. ATMs now offer varied services and belong to a proprietary network offering a broader range of financial services other than just cash withdrawals. However, cash withdrawn from ATMs are an important retail payment instrument (Andrieu, 2001).

Information Technology and the Shift to Electronic Non-Cash Payment Instruments

Technology and its applications to payment services have facilitated innovation in retail payment instruments and services. With developments and applications of IT in the retail market there has been a movement away from cash and cheques towards direct funds transfers and card payments. While technological applications may create new payment instruments and services, it is the demand from a body of users, stimulating competition among providers that drives the development of markets. As users embrace new payment technology and instruments, other users become attracted. This has been particularly evident in credit and debit cards (www.apca.com.au). Existing cardholders benefit from the participation of new merchants, since they can use the card more broadly for transactions, attracting new cardholders to the system. Merchants benefit from the participation of new cardholders, since sales increase, encouraging more merchants into the payment card network, especially if devices required by different networks are interoperable. These "network economies" are often cited as critical to the success of new payment technology (Plouffe et al., 2001).

Increase in Card Payments and Direct Debit Transfers

Card payment growth is attributed to several factors, which include the substitution of cards for both cheques and cash at the point of sale and purchases from catalogues, telephone and on-line shopping opportunities, where cards are the primary payment instrument (www.apca.com.au; Plouffe et al., 2001; www.rba.gov.au). Since 1990 Australia experienced a decline in the relative use of cheques for non-cash transactions. The growth of card payments in all countries also reflects the development of network payment technology. New network arrangements have enabled providers to share the initial costs of payment card infrastructures and have given them a platform for developing new procedures and instruments. Andrieu (2001) indicates that credit and debit cards today capture a significant share of all retail transactions due to their convenience and the role they play in on-line transactions.

Figure 1: The changing pattern in payment methods in Australia (1994 – 2002)

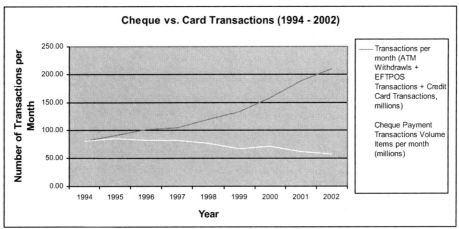

The growth of direct debit transfers indicates the rising awareness by users and providers of their convenience and relatively low cost. For payers, the convenience and attraction of direct debit transfers for recurring payments has been enhanced with the introduction of overdraft lines on deposit accounts. Direct debit transfers are convenient and useful for vendors since they provide greater control over the timing of cash inflows. The cost to service providers of processing recurring payments using direct debit transfers is sometimes lower than for other debit instruments, such as cheques (www.apca.com.au). It is anticipated that in the future these will have a more important role, with the ability to support peer-to-peer payments as well.

There has been an increase in payments by EFTPOS and credit cards, and a decrease in cheque payments in Australia, based on the Australian Payment Control Authority (www.apca.com.au).

RETAIL PAYMENT INNOVATIONS

New retail payment technology that has emerged over the past few years signifies the potential for developing alternatives to existing instruments and technology. Some involve entirely new instruments such as electronic money; others involve new electronic payment delivery and processing technology.

Electronic money, or *e-money*, is essentially value stored electronically in a device such as an IC chip or a computer's hard drive. Stored-value cards rely on tamper-resistant IC chips for storing and transferring value and information securely, while software (or network-based) money depends on encryption technology. Value is transferred electronically from one e-money storage vehicle to another, either at the point of sale or remotely. E-money is designed primarily for individuals to make small value payments. As a retail payment instrument, e-money is easily divisible into smaller units of currency value that are portable and potentially receivable (or deliverable) through different electronic devices. Hybrid products are also emerging that can be used in both card-based and network-based systems (www.apca.com.au).

Internet payment methods are new distribution channels for traditional payment instruments, designed for remote, computer-based on-line payments. They are modelled on existing banking arrangements and modified for application to open networks such as the Internet. *Internet credit transfers* are usually transmitted on-line from the buyer's payment service provider to the merchant's payment service provider, similar to how electronic data interchange (EDI) payments are used by business. *Internet debit transfers* are designed for remote transactions of variable amounts where the merchant obtains on-line authorisation for the payment directly from the buyer's financial institution. With *Internet payments*, financial institutions are centrally involved as payment service providers. *Electronic cheques* are payment instruments which are prepared by either the purchaser or the merchant for the purchaser's payment authorisation. Once authorised, the purchaser may route the payment on-line through its own financial institution to the merchant (as with a credit transfer) or transmit the authorisation back to the merchant for collection through its financial institution (as with a debit transfer) (www.rba.gov.au).

M-PAYMENTS

Portability of mobile phones makes them attractive access devices for purchasing goods over the Internet. Consequently, m-commerce is expected to complement e-commerce as the use of mobile phones becomes more widespread (Andrieu, 2001). Therefore m-commerce will require a range of payment mechanisms to support different transaction types and the diverse profile of mobile subscribers. Possibilities include payments aggregated by the network operator and added to mobile subscription bills, credit and debit card payments, and the use of an electronic purse such as that offered by Mondex (Andrieu, 2001). In Australia payments for parking meters and purchase of cokes via mobile phones are currently being trialed.

E-MONEY

E-money will become an important retail payment method if financial institutions as well as merchants have a strong vested interest in the gradual disappearance of traditional forms of payment due to their costs. E-money is able to cover a wide range of transactions. It is an excellent accounting unit, and can be converted from one currency to another, or transformed into bonds or stocks almost instantly. It takes up virtually no room, can be counted automatically, and never wears out, rusts or tarnishes. E-money is especially useful in distant transactions (Andrieu, 2001).

PEER-TO-PEER

Penny (2001) is of the opinion that the generic P2P business model requires P2P payment infrastructure and support. Almost all goods and services bought on the Internet are currently paid for by credit, debit and/or charge cards, although these are either not available to all, or not very appropriate for all e-commerce transactions. Generally, young consumers do not 'carry plastic' or do not qualify for a credit card. In consumer-to-consumer e-commerce, and on-line auctions where often neither party is an established business, P2P provides a safe, simple, fast way of settling small value transactions. Although the growth of the Internet and e-commerce has transformed many aspects of both the global financial services industry and individual domestic markets, its growth has lagged behind in payments. Andrieu (2001) states that the developments in credit and debit cards have not considered peer-to-peer transactions, a form of payment that is critical for the development of some forms of commerce such as on-line auctions.

However, as predicted by Penny (2001), with developments and acceptance in person-to-person payments services the need to use banking services and credit card providers to settle transactions will be reduced. The impact is expected to lead to:

- An expansion of P2P payments providers, products and services;
- Customers will tend to rely less on traditional banks, credit card companies and payments providers to meet their changing financial needs as they become comfortable in using P2P payments for the management and movement of their finances;
- With more of a customer's disposable money deposited in P2P payment accounts/pre-paid cards, the amount of funds in traditional banks will be reduced.

RETAIL PAYMENT RISKS

All types of retail payment instruments are subject to varying degrees of operational, security and fraud risks. Some, like currency and cheques, are perhaps more vulnerable to loss and theft than others. However, with card payments, security risks are a primary concern. Credit card payments for mail and telephone orders involve even stricter security standards than face-to-face payments. For example, retailers may be obliged to honour charge-back provisions that require them to refund immediately in the event of a repudiated payment (www.apca.com.au). The introduction of integrated circuit (IC) chips into payment cards could help reinforce the PIN as a security device. In addition, secure transmission standards have been developed for remote payments in which card numbers are transmitted electronically.

The immediacy and finality of *e-money* payments differ depending on the type of system and the laws and regulations applicable in different jurisdictions. Other payment risks depend on the technical design of an e-money system, its procedural rules and risk guidelines, the host country's laws regarding consumer protection and risk allocation, and the incentives for e-money issuers and distributors to comply with these rules (Andrieu, 2001). E-money also has the vulnerability of being stolen or used illegally. Transfers of e-money over computer networks can be intercepted and manipulated. Losses could also result from accidents or damage to electronic devices, or from operational error or malfunctions. Finally, consumers may also be exposed to financial losses, if the e-money issuer becomes insolvent (Andrieu, 2001).

Other risks of e-money identified by Andrieu (2001) are the open access character of the Internet, in which electronic transactions are likely to attract the attention of criminals. Such crimes can be expected to be particularly difficult to detect and prosecute. Moreover, even if law enforcement authorities know how a cyberspace crime is being committed, supporting evidence may be inadmissible because of lack of an adequate legal framework. Controversies regarding the relevant jurisdiction for investigating or prosecuting cyberspace crime may also arise. Finally, the difficulty in locating transactions will blur the distinction between legitimate and illegitimate businesses. Consumers may also be faced with financial losses if the issuer of e-money becomes insolvent or bankrupt or otherwise unable to honour payments made with its electronic money liabilities. Consumers could thus be left with claims on the assets of the issuer whose value might depend on various factors, including whether assets are segregated for the benefit of electronic money holders, the quality of the assets and whether any third-party guarantees apply (Andrieu, 2001).

Andrieu also explains that security issues of privacy violation can have a major impact on the development of e-money in the coming years. Privacy violations may rise with the volume of electronic transactions, as such transactions allow merchants and government agencies alike to collect vast amounts of information on individuals, information which can then be cross-referenced and processed to generate detailed profile data on individuals.

With *Internet payments*, the early stage of development and the cross-border aspects of e-commerce payments mean that the focus of attention has been on operational risks, legal risks, security risks and the risk of circumventing anti-money laundering legislation. A number of steps have thus been taken to address these issues. The various systems use, or are developing, procedural standards and protocols for authentication and security (message encryption, digital signatures, counterparty certification and payment confidentiality). Several jurisdictions have established, have introduced or are reviewing legislation and rules for the legal treatment of electronic documents, transactions and means of authentication (www.rba.gov.au).

DISCUSSION AND CONCLUSION

Although different electronic payment methods are available in Australia, educating consumers and business partners is necessary, especially in smaller organizations to build their confidence and intensify electronic trade. Electronic commerce will be enhanced if the users know that the electronic transaction is secure, that orders and payments can be traced and that it is cost effective (Singh, 2000).

As more organizations adopt e-payment methods it is important to ensure that these also work within the framework of the companies' existing banking relationships and systems infrastructure. This, as the many banks trying to develop their own Internet payment systems have found, is one of the keys to widespread adoption (Walsh, 2001). Proprietary, bank-specific payment systems require both seller and purchaser to have relationships with the host bank. However, this is rarely the case, and it is unlikely that a business will create a new account at a different bank simply to take advantage of a new way to pay. "A successful online payment system should be bank-neutral, with the system's host service taking ownership of the bank relationship" (Walsh, 2001, p. 34). All customers and business partners of an organization should be able join the network simply and easily, with their existing bank accounts.

There is more than one type of e-payment system in existence provided by different distributors. Therefore to increase the frequency of use of e-payment systems and the loyalty of distributors it will be useful for industries to support these by forming alliances for bill payments, including consumer points and discounts, supporting search, and other services to make it easy to use and one-stop shop for customers.

Yu et al. (2002) are of the opinion that with electronic payment if there is even the slightest possibility that the payment system may not be secure, trust and confidence in this system will erode, destroying the infrastructure for electronic commerce. Therefore Yu et al. propose that when designing an electronic payment system, the system's ability to adapt to users' changing needs, the effectiveness and security of each transaction, the degree of compatibility among other payment systems, and the complexity in adapting to the system all need to be taken into account. The degree of security should take into account users' security when depositing or withdrawing money and transmitting data, the security of application programs and database, the security during transactions and payments, the security of the Internet and system, and security maintenance and management. Yu et al. emphasise that among these, the security of transactions and payments is most important for companies and consumers. Transaction and payment security needs to satisfy the following requirements:

1. Authority: Also referred to as validity. This is one of the most important things to take into consideration. The purpose is to verify the claimed identities of all parties involved, and to prevent third parties from sabotaging information or making unauthorized transfers.

2.   Privacy: The purpose is to protect information that is sent via the Internet, and to prevent unauthorized personnel or company employees from accessing confidential information.
3.   Integrity: This includes the prevention of tampered transactions and making mistakes when sending information, and avoids accidentally sending a transaction twice, or accidentally sending a transaction with false information, and to prevent consumers and producers from denying their involvement in a transaction or from changing information in the transaction.
4.   Non-repudiation: The electronic payment system must be designed in such a way that consumers and companies will be unable to deny their participation in a transaction if they were involved. Therefore, records of details, such as the time of the transaction, the information involved in the transaction, etc., must be kept in a secure database" (Yu, 2002, pp. 332-333).

Chou et al. (2001) are of the opinion that for successful e-payments it is essential to win users' confidence by ensuring security; ensure that the system is reliable, supporting a 24 hour service with no failures; incorporates measures to ensure nonrepudiation and acknowledge payment; address latency by managing the frequency of clearing time so that customers and merchants use the system without noticeable delays; and ensure transaction completeness.

Costs in adopting e-payment systems include fixed and transaction costs. Fixed costs refer to those of installing payment equipment such as card readers and payment software. Transaction costs are those incurred by merchants and customers every time they undertake a business exchange. As many on line transactions involve micropayment, all fixed and transaction costs need to be incurred for the acceptance of the e-payment systems (Chou et al., 2002).

Monetary convertibility in an e-payment system for converting the value in a digital format back to real currencies also increases the utility of the system for end-users (Schmidt & Muller, 1997, cited in Chou et al., 2002). The Internet provides access to the same information and services around the world, making it a necessity to include the function of exchanging currencies in e-payment systems.

Customer base by and large determines the performance of e-payment schemes. For a payment system that represents a certain network, its adoption depends on the number of customers and merchants using it. This is the so-called positive network effect by Katz and Shapiro (1994, cited in Chou et al.,

2002). For instance, the utility of an e-payment instrument will be zero if only one participant is involved. Nevertheless, the utility will increase with the number of users who participate in the network (Shapiro & Varian, 1998). Unfortunately, positive network effects lead to start-up problems of a new payment network, as it must exceed a "critical mass point" in order to succeed.

It is desirable to have an e-payment scheme that also includes and addresses:

- Peer-to-peer compensation when customer-to-customer (C2C) business reaches its potential over e-commerce (Chou, 2002).
- Anonymity—although the ability to make untraceable transactions raises concerns in regard to tax evasion, money laundering, and other criminal uses, transactional anonymity is a basic right of consumers. The identity of a consumer should not be revealed to other parties if she is unwilling to impart this information. Anonymous transactions further protect consumers against price discrimination (Choi et al., 1997).
- Privacy—in addition to a user's identity, her spending patterns and income sources should not be revealed to other parties without her permission. The legal requirement of privacy protects a user's transaction information from being revealed to other parties (Schmidt & Muller, 1997).
- Convenience—Convenience refers to the ease with which users can spend, store, and transport a currency value via the payment system. The ability to operate e-payment systems on different platforms and network infrastructures (i.e., telephone, modem, or Internet connection) makes on-line transactions quicker and easier for users (Neuman & Medvinsky, 1995, cited in Chou et al., 2002).
- Merchant acceptance—as use of the payment scheme becomes more widespread, network effects increase the utility of the scheme for users (Neuman et al., 1995).

Technological developments have enabled international and ubiquitous Internet access from WAP, televisions, mobile phones and other portable devices. As consumers limit the use of personal computers to access the Internet, it is important to enable e-payment from other technologies as well, including digital televisions, personal digital assistants, and other wireless installations. This is a trend for future electronic payment systems.

For the success of new innovative payment services it is essential to include the implementation of more effective pricing of payment services, abolishing the physical presenting of cheques and liberalizing access to central clearing and settlement facilities (Andrieu, 2001). E-money and payment systems will gain a greater acceptance if governments decided to declare it legal tender. The feasibility of doing so has been assessed in some countries such as Canada, Singapore and Japan. As electronic forms of payment become ubiquitous in the future, the use of cash is likely to decline in the general society. This will have an impact on the buying options of those who rely exclusively on cash payments such as the young and the poor.

Security measures will contribute to improving the transactions and the confidence of consumers and merchants in the e-payment system. However, effective implementation will take time because of both the costs involved and the complexity of many of the issues to be addressed. Also, because of the rapid rate of technological change, there is a danger that many of the solutions found may become obsolete even before they are implemented. Moreover, the way they are implemented may introduce socio-institutional obstacles to the acceptance of e-money by consumers and merchants alike (Andrieu, 2001).

REFERENCES

Andrieu, M. (2001). The future of e-money: Main trends and driving forces. *Foresight, 3*(5).

Chou, Y., Lee, C., & Chung, J. (2002). Understanding m-commerce payment systems through the analytical hierarchy process. *Journal of Business Research, 5802*, 1–8.

Neuman, B. C., & Medvinsky, G. (1995). *NetCheque, NetCash, and the characteristics of Internet payment services*. Paper presented at MIT workshop on Internet Economics. Retrieved July 2003 at the URL: http//:www.mit.edu

Penny, J. (2001). The payments revolution: The growth of person-to-person and 'Generation Y' payments services. *Journal of Financial Services Marketing, 6*(2), 190–201.

Plouffe, C. R., Vandenbosch, M., & Hulland, J. (2000). Intermediating technologies and multi-group adoption: A comparison of consumer and merchant adoption intentions toward a new electronic payment system. *Product Innovation Management, 18*, 65–81.

Schmidt, C., & Muller, R. (1997). *A framework for micropayment evaluation*. Retrieved July 2003 at the URL: http//:macke.wiwi.hu-berlin.de/IMI/micropayments.html

Shapiro, C., & Varian, V. R. (1988). *Information rules: A strategic guide to the network economy.* Boston: Harvard Business School Press.

Singh, M. (2000). Electronic commerce in Australia: Opportunities and factors critical for success. *Proceedings of the 1st World Congress on the Management of Electronic Commerce* (CD-ROM), January 19-21, Hamilton, Ontario, Canada.

Turban, E., Lee, J., King, D., & Chung, H. M. (2000). *Electronic commerce- a managerial perspective.* New Jersey: Prentice Hall International Inc.

Walsh, P. (2001). The B2B payment problem. *AFP Exchange,* Jan/Feb.

Watson, R. T., Berthon, P., Pitt, L., & Zinkhan, G. (1999). *Electronic commerce.* Orlando, FL: The Dryden Press.

www.apca.com.au. (2003). The Australian Payment Clearing Authority. Retrieved July 2003.

www.rba.gov.au. (2003). The Researve Bank of Australia. Retrieved July 2003.

Yu, H. C., Hsi, K. H., & Kuo, P. J. (2002). Electronic payment systems: An analysis and comparison of types. *Technology in Society, 24,* 331–347.

Chapter XIV

Security Management in an E-Business Environment

Mohini Singh
RMIT University, Australia

ABSTRACT

Ensuring security for e-business information exchange is essential as it entails exchange of sensitive information. E-business transactions entail transfer of funds with buyers, sellers and business partners. Vulnerabilities and security incidents in the digital environment require an understanding of technology issues and security challenges for privacy and trust in an online environment. Technological developments over the past few years have made significant contributions to securing the Internet for e-business. This chapter is a discussion of managing security in an e-business organization. It illustrates the differences in security policies for traditional businesses and online businesses, introduces basic security concepts, provides an understanding of security incidents in e-business and briefly explains some basic security tools. More importantly the chapter highlights e-business security management by highlighting the need for organization-based security policies, procedures and practices. Trust and privacy issues in e-business have been addressed by highlighting the need for effective management of security in e-business.

INTRODUCTION

The Internet is a worldwide collection of loosely connected networks that are accessible by individual computer hosts in a variety of ways, including gateways, routers, dial-up connections, and Internet service providers. It is a self-regulated network connecting millions of computer networks around the world (Turban, 2002). It is ubiquitous, enabling individuals and organizations worldwide to access the network without regard to national or geographic boundaries or time of day. Therefore, as suggested by Napier et al. (2001), a private computer network system is exposed to potential threats from anywhere on the public network. E-business operates in a networked environment supported by the Internet and other network technologies. Hence e-businesses are in need of stringent security measures for protection of data transmitted, databases, all electronic exchanges of information and other types of cybercrime. A lack of privacy, integrity and confidentiality can cause tremendous damage to an organization and its business, along with its system slowdowns and downtime. It is imperative that e-businesses put in place organizational, architectural and procedural approaches to ensure that the business operates in a secure and reliable environment. E-business security embraces the complete business transaction not only from the IT infrastructure inside an organization's network, but also outside, connecting all consumers and suppliers. However, "growth of e-commerce has made the Internet an enticing playground for hackers and crackers" (Turban, 2002, p. 544).

Ensuring security for e-business information exchange is essential, as it entails exchange of sensitive information. Technological developments over the past few years have made significant contributions to securing the Internet for e-business. However, challenges remain in this area, and combined with the business and legal requirements security remains a substantial barrier to e-business development.

Security, as defined by Adam et al. (1999), is:
- Measures taken to guard against espionage or sabotage, crime, attack or escape;

- Freedom from danger;
- Freedom from fear or anxiety; and
- Protection from unwanted attacks.

In society, ensuring security involves police and security guards, locks and alarms, but in a commercial environment protecting sensitive data and information, transactions involving financial information, corporate secrets and proprietary information need to be protected. Security for electronic commerce faces several challenges that are inherently not as challenging in paper-based commerce. Some intrinsic characteristics of paper-based signed documents in commerce that guarantee their security but are absent in electronic commerce are properties of the ink, the letterhead, characteristics of the printing process, watermarks, signature biometrics, timestamps, and ability to detect modifications. However, these attributes are not inherently built into e-commerce technologies.

Potential threats and attacks to which commercial activities in networked environments may be susceptible are accessing unauthorised network resources, destroying information and network resources, altering, inserting or modifying information, disclosing information to unauthorised people, causing networking services disruptions or interruption, stealing information and network resources, denying services received, claiming to have provided services that have not been administered, and claiming to have sent or received information not given (Adam et al., 1999).

This chapter highlights the importance of security in a networked environment, describes security incidents and risks and how to manage security in an e-business environment. It discusses the change from security of a physical environment to the security of an on-line environment.

BASIC SECURITY CONCEPTS

Security concepts in an e-business networked environment are authentication, authorisation, auditing, confidentiality, integrity, availability and nonrepudiation (Adam et al., 1999; Turban, 2002; Napier et al., 2001).

Authentication involves the ability of an individual, organization, or computer to prove its identity. Security systems accomplish authentication by verifying information that the user provides against what the system already knows about the user. Authentication methods include:

- Demonstration of knowledge of some type of proprietary information, such as password;
- Possession of some type of proprietary object, such as key card;
- Demonstration of some type of biometric characteristic, such as fingerprint; and
- Evidence that a trusted third party has already established authentication of the claimant.

To prove a user's identity these factors are typically considered in combination with each other, rather than relying on any single component. Some common methods of authentication include passwords, personal identification numbers (PINs), digital signatures and certificates.

Authorisation involves the control of access to particular information once identity has been verified. Authorisation is meant to limit the actions or operations that authenticated parties are able to perform in a networked environment. These limitations are based on the security level of the identified party for:

- Creation or destruction of documents;
- Reading, browsing or writing;
- Content addition, deletion, or modification;
- Export or import;
- Execution.

Audits include information on access of particular resources, using particular privileges or performing certain security actions. It identifies the person or program that performed the actions.

Confidentiality involves the secrecy of data and/or information, and the protection of such information from unauthorised access. For electronic commerce, confidentiality is of utmost importance in the protection of an organization or company's financial data, product development information, organization structures and various other types of information. Time related information such as a price list or confidential report can be crucial and needs to be kept confidential until a certain time. Policies regarding the release of information must be included in confidentiality, as well as authorisation services. Confidentiality policy must ensure that:

- Information cannot be read, copied, modified, or disclosed without proper authorisation;
- Communication over networks cannot be intercepted.

Integrity is the protection of data from modification either while in transit or in storage. E-commerce and e-business systems must have the capability of ensuring that data transmissions over networks arrive at their destinations in exactly the same form as they were sent. Integrity services must protect data against modifications, additions, deletions, and reordering parts of the data.

Information can be erased or become inaccessible, resulting in *loss of availability.* This means that those who are authorized to get information did not get what they needed. Availability of information is an important attribute in service-oriented businesses that depend on information (e.g., airline schedules). When a user cannot get access to the network or specific services provided on the network, he or she experiences a *denial of service.*

Nonrepudiation involves protection against a party involved in a transaction or communication activity that later falsely denies that the transaction or activity occurred. Nonrepudiation services must be able to demonstrate to a third party:

- proof of origin;
- delivery;
- submission;
- and transport of the data in question.

The need for these services reflects imperfections in any communications environment. In a networked environment security mechanisms are critical for transactions and communications to take place smoothly.

Why Care About Security?

A breach of security can compromise important confidential information about an organization leading to damaging impacts on business. The consequences of a break-in in the business network system can be a minor or major loss of time in recovering from the problem, a decrease in productivity, a significant loss of money or staff-hours, a devastating loss of credibility or market opportunity, a business no longer able to compete and legal liability. Data security is vital in the e-business environment as critical information is exchanged electronically between business partners. E-business operates in a networked environment with automated and electronic transmission of data, business information, payments and negotiations. All data transmission and storage thus need to be well secured. Even computers with nothing stored on them should be secured, as they can become a 'weak link' allowing unauthorized access to the organization's systems and information.

NETWORK SECURITY RISKS

A *network security incident* is any network-related activity with negative security implications (Napier et al., 2001). Security incidents on the Internet can come in all shapes and sizes, launched from specific systems or networks. An intrusion may be a comparatively minor event involving a single site or a major event in which tens of thousands of sites are compromised. A typical attack pattern consists of gaining access to a user's account and using the victim's system as a launch platform for attacks on other sites. The following are other examples of security risks in the network environment.

Hacking

Hacking is any attempt by an intruder to gain unauthorised access to a computer system. Activities carried out by hackers can include denial of service (DoS), dumping, port scanning and sniffing. *Denial of service* (DoS) prevents or inhibits the normal use or management of communication facilities. The attacker can redirect or suppress all messages to a particular destination (Minoli & Minoli, 1998). DoS attacks are initiated with software and can be launched by rival businesses or individuals with little or no computer skills (NOIE, 2002). Internet *'dumping'*, more applicable to small businesses, is when someone utilises the company's modem to place calls to high-cost premium rate or international numbers. This can be achieved by inducing users (often by promising adult content) to download new Internet dialer software, replacing their ISP connection. Proving that dumping was conducted without the user's knowledge can often be difficult. To prevent dumping, telecommunications companies can place a bar on all premium calls starting with 190 (e.g., 1900, 1901, 1902, etc.) and on international phone services. If business computers are not equipped with modems, dumping should not be a problem (NOIE, 2002).

Port Scanning and Sniffing

Port scanning scans a range of TCP (Transport Control Protocol) port numbers, UDP (User Datagram Protocol) port numbers, or both for a single host IP (Internet Provider) address in order to identify services running on the host computers (Panko, 2003). Sniffing programs can be installed on computer systems to observe traffic, storing information (ID/Passwords) that can be used to access other systems. Sniffer software tracks data travelling over the Internet or a corporate network. Unauthorised sniffers can compromise a network's security because they are difficult to detect and can be inserted almost anywhere.

Viruses

A computer virus is a program that can infect other programs by modifying them to include a copy of itself. A virus can be transmitted through an attachment to an e-mail, and by downloading infected programs and files either from web sites, floppy disks or CDs. Depending on the code in the virus program, some will activate as soon as the file is opened, while others will lie dormant in the computer system until activated by a trigger such as a specific date, execution of a particular key on the keyboard or activation by a particular function such as forwarding an e-mail to another user in the organization. Similar to human viruses, computer viruses can grow, replicate, travel, adapt and learn and consume resources (Minoli & Minoli, 1998).

Other virus-related attacks include worms. Worms, described by Panko (2003), install themselves on a machine, and actively seek to send themselves to other machines to infest those machines. Without any human action worms can spread more quickly than viruses. On January 25, 2003 a worm called Slammer spread with an astonishing speed on the Internet. Within ten minutes the Slammer had infested about 90% of vulnerable hosts on the Internet. Although it was controlled within hours, it had achieved its aim of infesting all vulnerable servers before the world even realised what was happening. The best protection against computer viruses is to use anti-virus software installed on all computers, and updated regularly.

Flaws in Technology and Software or Protocol Designs

If systems obtained from vendors are not aligned to the organization's security system it can lead to easy break-in to networks. When software and systems are first installed they come in a number of default settings, sample programs, and templates that are vulnerable to attack. Ignorance of implementation details by system administrators, sometimes due to a lack of time, a lack of expertise, or improper management also sacrifices security (www.softheap.com). Protocols define the rules and conventions for computers to communicate on a network. If a protocol has a design flaw it is vulnerable to exploitation no matter how well it is implemented. With software implementations, if security is added on later, it sometimes does not respond to security checks as planned, leading to unexpected vulnerabilities.

S-HTTP is exactly what its name suggests: a security-enhanced extension of the Hypertext Transfer Protocol. S-HTTP works at the application level, encrypting the contents of messages relayed between a browser and a server, allowing client and server to negotiate the strength and type of encryption to be used (Larson, 2003). S-HTTP supports end-to-end secure transactions by incorporating cryptographic enhancements to be used for data transfer at the application level (Minoli & Minoli, 1998).

Intruders' Technical Knowledge

For an intruder to achieve access to a system, he or she would have to have a good understanding of network topology, operations, protocols, databases and information management structures (Berbee, 2002). Intruders can examine source code to discover weaknesses in certain programs, such as those used for electronic mail. Source code sometimes is easy to obtain from programmers who make their work freely available on the Internet. Programs written for research purposes (with little thought for security) or written by naive programmers become widely used, with source code available to all (Berbee, 2002).

It is difficult to characterise people who cause security incidents. An intruder may be an adolescent who is curious about what he or she can do on the Internet, a college student who has created a new software tool, an individual seeking personal gain, or a 'paid spy' seeking information for the economic advantage of a corporation or foreign country. A disgruntled former employee or a consultant who gained network information while working with a company may also cause a security incident. An intruder may also seek entertainment, intellectual challenge, and a sense of power, political attention, or financial gain.

SECURITY TOOLS AND TECHNOLOGIES

The following taxonomy is useful in understanding the security systems, technologies and authentication tools widely available to support secure transmission and storage of information in a networked e-business environment.

Firewalls

Firewalls are used to keep a network secure from intruders. A firewall is a network node consisting of both hardware and software that isolates a private network. In order to understand how a firewall works, one should have an understanding of packets, IP addresses and DoS attacks. However, very simply, it is explained with Hazari's (2000) description:

> *"A firewall is like a bouncer in a nightclub. Like a bouncer in a nightclub the firewalls have a set of rules, similar to guest list or dress code, that determine if the data should be allowed entry. Just as the bouncer places himself at the door of the nightclub, the firewall is located at the point of entry, where data attempts to enter the computer system. As different nightclubs might have different rules for entry, different firewalls have different methods of inspecting data for acceptance or rejection"* (Turban et al., 2002, p. 565).

Authentication

Where services are provided on-line, agencies will need to reassess how they authenticate users. Flaws in authentication can lead to situations such as the illegal transfer of funds, unauthorised ordering of goods or the mischievous alteration of data. Authentication enforces confidence in electronic transactions and is a vital component of e-business (NOIE, 2002).

These can be implemented in the following ways:

Passwords, PINs and User IDs

A password is a code or more often a common word used to gain access to a computer network. Passwords are the most common method of authentication for computer systems today. Systems should be designed to include expiration of passwords at regular intervals. If a user has access to more than one system or database at the organization, he or she should apply different passwords to access different systems. The more often a password is changed, the more secure the account becomes. Login attempts should be limited to two or three times and passwords should not be written down. As described by NOIE (2002), under a password system, a client accessing an agency's electronic application is requested to enter a 'shared secret' such as a password with their User ID. The system checks that password against information in a database to ensure its correctness and thereby 'authenticates' the client. Multiple passwords and password encryption can be used to strengthen this technique. User IDs are usually used in combination with passwords. The User ID is not necessarily kept private and may be made up of several simple pieces of information. For example, Shirley Jones may have the User ID 'sjones'. User IDs may also contain numbers to help distinguish between clients with similar or identical names, e.g., 'sjones637'. Typically, password-based authentication requires no third party products or services. It is cheaper to implement and guarantees a limited degree of authentication, and relies on users keeping their passwords secret.

For some applications it is suitable to include a one-time password where the system generates a unique password to be entered each time the application is accessed. Challenge and response systems also authenticate by asking a user to respond to a random challenge that is based on information in their client record, or on 'secret' phrases lodged with the agency. For example, when entering a challenge and response web site, the user will first be asked for a User ID and password. They would then be asked for unique information, such as the middle name of their second child. If all data matches, access is granted http://www.rsasecurity.com.

Cookies

A cookie is a piece of information that allows a web site to record one's comings and goings. It can act as a form of authentication to identify the user when he or she next enters the same web site. Not only can cookies help web sites recognise returning users, they can provide access to specific resources, track on line purchases or provide customised web pages. Properly used, cookies can greatly enhance the user's experience of web resources and increase convenience. However, misuse of cookies raises obvious privacy and security issues. If cookies are used, it should be mentioned in the web site privacy statement. Although cookies are useful for users as well, they have raised concerns over privacy with web sites collecting private information such as users, preferences, interests and surfing patterns (Turban, 2002).

Biometrics and Authentication

A biometric control is the verification of the identity of a person based on physiological or behavioural characteristics (Turban, 2002). The most common biometrics are photos of face, fingerprints, hand geometry, blood vessel pattern in the retina of a person's eye, voice, signature, keystroke dynamics, iris scan and other facial thermography. With biometric technology, the physical characteristic is measured (by a microphone, optical reader or some other device) and converted into digital form. This information is then compared with a copy already stored in the computer and authenticated as belonging to a particular person. If they match, the software will accept the authentication and the transaction is allowed to proceed.

Biometric applications can provide very high levels of authentication, and can be applied to identify students undertaking online exams from a remote location, fraud recipients of government entitlements, authorised buyers and sellers, and person undertaking the interviews for employment. Applications for biometrics include automatic teller machine access, personal computer network logon, time and attendance, enterprise-level data security, physical access and customer verification. Biometric authentication is also suitable for access to individual devices. It is less suited for authentication to software systems over open networks such as the Internet (www.biomet.org).

Encryption

Encryption is the coding of information by using a mathematically based program and a secret to produce a string of characters that are jumbled. It consists of an algorithm and a key for encoding and decoding of text. The system uses a secret key, which is a computer file that includes a mathematical value. This is used in conjunction with an algorithm to encrypt or decrypt a message. Conventional encryption is used for both encryption and decryption of information, and can be performed very quickly by modern PCs.

Asymmetric cryptography also authenticates users. For example, clients would be issued with a private key on a hardware device. The associated public key is securely held by the agency. When logging in, the client would enter his or her User ID and password. The agency would then automatically send a random number for the user to key into his or her device. The device employs the private key to process the random number and produces a result which the user enters into the agency's log-in process. If the agency is able to retrieve the original random number by reversing the process with the corresponding public key, then the client is authentic (http://webopedia.internet.com/TERM/C/challenge_response.html).

Public Key Cryptography (Digital Certificates)

Public key encryption is a form of asymmetric cryptography. It ensures the confidentiality and privacy of a message as it moves across a network by scrambling or encrypting it so that it is difficult and time consuming for an unauthorised person to decrypt the message. Public key cryptography uses separate pairs of keys for authentication (or signing) and encryption (or confidentiality). The key pairs are referred to as public keys and private keys. An application of public key cryptography as described in the NOIE report (2002) is:

> *"Authentication (or signing). When using an authentication key pair, the public key is published to the world while keeping your private 'signing' key secret. Anyone with a copy of the public key can decrypt something encrypted ones private 'signing' key. This will provide them with a level of assurance of ones identity. On its own, the public key cannot be used to sign a document; it can only be used to verify who has signed it.*
>
> *Encryption (or confidentiality). In the same fashion, to use an encryption key pair the public key is published while the private key is kept a secret. Anyone with a copy of this published public key can then encrypt information that only the sender can read. The information encrypted with the public 'confidentiality' key can only be decrypted using ones private 'confidentiality' key."*

Several prominent authentication solutions make use of public key cryptography. These include PKI, PGP and SSL.

Public Key Infrastructure (PKI)

PKI is a set of procedures and technology that enables users of a network such as the Internet to authenticate identity, and to securely and privately exchange information through the use of public key cryptography. To achieve this, public and private keys and a digital certificate can be obtained through a trusted third party authority, known as a Certification Authority (CA). The CA links the public key to the digital certificate and vouches for the identity of the key holder. Registration Authorities (RAs) collect and manage the appropriate levels of Evidence of Identity (EOI) from applicants for digital certificates. Dependent upon the PKI business model employed, appropriately accredited RAs may also create keys and certificates (NOIE, 2002).

Pretty Good Privacy (PGP)

PGP is a security software application that enables two known parties to exchange information securely with each other. PGP can be utilised for small communities or businesses who know each other and wish to communicate securely. In these instances it is easy to manually exchange diskettes or e-mails containing each owner's public key rather than publishing public keys to the world. Each member of the group holds a copy of each other's public key.

Difficulties associated with holding large numbers of public keys means that PGP is practical only to a certain point. Beyond that point, it is necessary to put systems into place that can provide the necessary security, storage and exchange mechanisms for co-workers, business partners or strangers to communicate if need be. PKI systems (discussed above) provide these kinds of features (http://www.pgpi.org).

SSL and TLS

The Secure Sockets Layer (SSL) protocol is a set of rules governing authentication of servers (such as web servers) and encrypted communication between clients and servers. It operates at the TCP/IP layer and supports a variety of encryption algorithms and authentication methods. The protocol was developed to secure the transmission of data over the Internet. The authentication process under SSL uses public key encryption, and digital signatures do not authenticate the user but confirm that a server is in fact the server it claims to be. Once the server has been authenticated, the client and server use symmetric key encryption to encrypt the information exchanged electronically. A different session key is used for each transaction, impeding a hacker's ability to decrypt messages. However, SSL and Transport Layer Security (TLS) only provide confidentiality and integrity for the server (http://www.dsd.gov.au/infosec/publications/SSL_policy.html).

SET

A crypotographic solution that is designed to handle the complete trans-action is the secure electronic transaction (SET). In order to fulfil credit-card payments on the web, both Visa and MasterCard needed a protocol that could safely link the Internet to existing bank-card processing networks, and the two went head-to-head with competing solutions (Turban, 2002). This enforces trust in e-business because of the involvement of reputed companies. Regard-less of which protocol comes out on top, customers' confidence in security of transactions on the web is enhanced by names like Visa and MasterCard. The converged protocol that the ensuing collaboration produced is known as Secure Electronic Transactions, or SET. Like any other secure-channel protocols, SET provides public/private key authentication and message integ-rity and is specifically designed for credit-card transactions, in that sensitive information is encrypted throughout the card-processing network. SET's configuration allows merchants to access only the data they require to fulfil the order, making it more secure. The customer's credit-card data remains encrypted until it reaches the appropriate financial institutions. All of the major companies involved hope that SET is the protocol that will finally instil confidence in the Internet as a safe space in which to conduct e-business (NOIE, 2002).

SECURITY POLICY

It is essential that all e-business organizations put in place a security policy at the time of implementation of technologies that will support the on-line business. A security policy is a documented high-level plan for organization-wide computer and information security (Minoli & Minoli, 1998). It provides a framework for making specific decisions, such as which defence mechanisms to use and how to configure services, and is the basis for developing secure programming guidelines and procedures for users and system administrators to follow. Because a security policy is a long-term document, the contents avoid technology-specific issues.

A security policy, according to Napier et al. (2002), generally covers the following:

*   high-level description of the technical environment of the site, the legal environment (governing laws), the authority of the policy, and the basic philosophy to be used when interpreting the policy;

- risk analysis that identifies the site's assets, the threats that exist against those assets, and the costs of asset loss;
- guidelines for system administrators on how to manage systems; and
- definition of acceptable use of guidelines for reacting to a site compromise (e.g., how to deal with the media and law enforcement, and whether to trace the intruder or shutdown and rebuild the system).

Factors that contribute to the success of a security policy include management commitment, technological support for enforcing the policy, effective dissemination of the policy, and the security awareness of all users (Singh, 1997). Management assigns responsibility for security, ensures that the security personnel are trained, and allocates funds to security equipment and management. Technological support for the security policy moves some responsibility for enforcement from individuals to technology.

Security policies must address technology as well as the personnel in the organization. Physical security of technology, access policy of data and equipment access are initial considerations. Having a physical security policy for IT and e-business equipment is vital for protecting confidential data. Issues included in the physical security policies generally address:

- ensuring the workplace technology supporting e-business is stored in a secure and lockable location;
- keeping up-to-date logs of all equipment;
- taking out appropriate insurance policies and developing emergency repair plans;
- putting extra measures in place for notebook computers (such as encrypting all data stored on them); and
- making sure all staff are aware of security policies and report any suspicious activities.

As mentioned earlier, sometimes internal staff can pose a greater security threat than external hackers, since they already have access to sensitive information. Policies to minimise internal risks should include:

- making sure passwords and access systems are revoked when staff resign;
- not giving any single member of staff complete access to all data;
- keeping logs of and documenting access to key business information;
- implementing and maintaining a strong password policy; and
- conducting regular internal security audits.

SECURITY CHALLENGES

Despite advances in security technologies, securing confidential and proprietary information has become more interesting and challenging than ever. In an attempt to keep pace with the onslaught of security woes, new technologies are often unleashed and implemented before due diligence and real understanding of these technologies occurs in the real world. Though understanding security technologies is noble, and certainly a diligent undertaking, the recent trends in corporate technology deployments have shown that most organizations do not have the resources and time to fully understand the technologies that they are deploying (Larson, 2003).

Security is not black and white. A firewall, if configured properly, will keep out 95% of the trouble-makers. Time and again it has been shown that it only takes a few bad apples to create a lot of work for everyone else. That wee 5% is a powerful force that only needs small trinkets of security holes to invade the corporate immune system, and anyone who has worked as part of an incident response team knows that once security has been violated, repairing the damage is time-consuming and often creates liabilities with alliance partners, suppliers, and customers.

Asking a small security team to secure an entire enterprise compromises some of the security implementations. Clearly users need to play a larger role in organizational security; thus it is important for the IT management to choose security technologies that are simple to use and understand. Users need secure e-business technologies that are so intuitive that using them and implementing them can be done with little to no training on things like complicated cryptographic authentication principles (Taylor & Hamilton, 2002).

The Internet is a public network consisting of many private computer networks exposing it to potential threats from numerous sources as indicated by Napier et al. (2001). Protection against these and other threats discussed above require businesses to have stringent security measures in place.

DISCUSSION

Ensuring security for e-business is a fundamental prerequisite before any commercial activities involving sensitive information can take place. Security is a leading barrier in the e-business industry. Technological developments over the past few years have made significant contributions to securing the Internet for e-business; however, challenges remain in this area, and combined with the business and legal requirements security remains a substantial issue for the development of e-business.

In an off-line business environment, ensuring security involves police and security guards, locks and alarms, but in a commercial environment protecting sensitive data and information, transactions involving financial information, corporate secrets and proprietary information need to be protected. Security for e-business faces several challenges that are inherently not as challenging in paper-based commerce. Some intrinsic characteristics of paper-based signed documents in commerce that guarantee its security but that are absent in electronic commerce are properties of the ink, the organization letterhead, characteristics of the printing process, watermarks, signature biometrics, timestamps and the ability to detect modifications. These attributes are not inherently built into e-business technologies.

Potential threats and attacks to which commercial activities in networked environments may be susceptible are accessing unauthorised network resources, destroying information, altering, inserting or modifying information, disclosing information to unauthorised people, causing networking services disruptions or interruption, stealing information and network resources, denying services received, claiming to have provided services that have not been administered and/or claiming to have sent or received information not given. These services reflect imperfections in any communications environment, whether it is networked or not. Proper security mechanisms are needed for critical transactions and communications to take place smoothly.

CONCLUSION

Security management involves the control of liability in digital transactions as well as the establishment and enforcement of security policies to ensure that the requirements for security services be met in order for a security system to achieve its objectives. Effective management of security will become an essential enabler of e-business.

Just as individual consumers tend to avoid businesses that do not protect their transactions, business partners will certainly avoid companies that don't take adequate measures to protect their databases and information. Findings from three independent polls in 1997 (Ernst & Young, FBI and Computer

Security Institute) indicated that on an average 46% of all corporate Internet sites have been broken into (Kalakota & Robinson, 1999). Security management needs must receive adequate subsidisation and support from e-business participants for their technology based commercial initiatives to be successful.

A business security policy clearly defining the scope and type of security measures to be used for the e-business strategy needs to be put in place in consultation with internal personnel, IT directors and business partners. A security policy should define the limits of acceptable behaviour within a system, determine what actions should be taken in case of a security violation, and may even specify protocols and permission to be used within a security system. An organization's business processes will determine its security policy. For example, banks, non-profit organizations, educational institutes and governments will each have different security policies due to their fundamentally different processes. Security audits are essential components of e-business controls.

Trust in a digital environment is closely related to authorisation requirements. Trust for e-business systems is closely linked with privacy issues. Web sites and vendors that alert individuals to the level of privacy protection that their web sites and services offer are rewarded by the establishment of a level of trust with consumers that is unattainable through other methods.

REFERENCES

Adam, N., Oktay, D., Gangopadhya, A., & Yesha, Y. (1999). *Electronic commerce technical, business and legal issues*. New Jersey: Prentice Hall.

Berbee. (2002). *Data security*. Retrieved on September 24, 2002 from http:llwww.berbee.com/"applications/datasecurity.htmi

Bria, R. (2001). *e-Commerce security—Public key infrastructure: Good practices for secure communications* (pp. 120–130). ISAW Board of Trustees, Minnesota.

http://www.dsd.gov.au/infosec/public/SSL_policy.htm. Retrieved July 2002.

http://www.rsasecurity.com. Retrieved July 2002.

Internet software consortium. (1997). *Internet domain survey*. Retrieved on October 30, 2002 from http://www.isc.org/ds/

Kalakota, R., & Robinson, M. (1999). *e-Business, roadmap for success*. Canada: Addison-Wesley Longman, Inc.

Larson, D. (2003). *The race to secure cyberspace.* http://www. webdeveloper.com/security/security_race_cyberspace.html

Minoli, D., & Minoli, E. (1998). *Web commerce technology handbook.* New York: McGraw-Hill.

Napier, H., Judd, P., Rivers, O., & Wagner, S. (2001). *Creating a winning e-business.* Canada: Thomson Learning.

NOIE (The National Office for the Information Economy) Online Authentication. (2002). Australia, July.

Panko, R. R. (2003). *Slammer: The first flash attack work.* University of Hawaii, February.

Piper, R., Blake-Wilson, S., & Mitchell, J. (1999). *The business case for user provisioning ROI model for eTrust admin: Digital signatures: Security & controls.* Computer Associates International, Inc.

Singh, M. (1997). *Effective implementation of new technologies in the Australian manufacturing industries.* PhD Thesis, Monash University, Melbourne, Australia.

Taylor, L., & Hamilton, J. (2002). *Security.* Retrieved on October 11, 2002 from http://www.intranetjournal.com/articles/200012/se_12_27_00a.html

Turban, E., Lee, J., King, D., & Chung, H. M. (2002). *Electronic commerce—A managerial perspective.* New Jersey: Prentice Hall International Inc.

www.softheap.com. Retrieved July 2002.

Chapter XV

Ethics and E-Business: An Oxymoron?

Dianne Waddell
Edith Cowan University, Australia

ABSTRACT

This chapter attempts to give an outline of some of the contemporary ethical issues related to technological innovation associated with e-business, in particular the notion that e-business and ethics is an oxymoron ('a figure of speech ... seeming self-contradiction'). The question is, has innovation in e-business resulted in unethical behaviour because of the new media and technology and the fact that businesses are embarking on something new therefore the old rules do not apply? Is it easier to behave unethically over the net? The author reviews the various methods used for dealing with on-line security and investigates the notion of trust which is implied in on-line transactions and business dealings. Also typical e-business ethical dilemmas are proffered as a catalyst for further debate.

The author concludes that as e-businesses deal with intangible products and services over the Internet, the potential for ethical dilemmas and shonky practices to develop is far higher than a bricks-and-mortar business. The challenge is for e-businesses to establish trust based on consistent good ethical practice and an industry approach to abusers of the system. Ethics and innovation are not mutually exclusive and will continue to challenge e-businesses.

INTRODUCTION

"For some people, the Internet is an anarchic space in which even the criminal can roam freely. For others, it is a place of liberty in which citizens can swap information and ideas free from risk of censorship by any vested interest. At least for the time being, there is neither corporation nor government capable of controlling the 'net'" (Longstaff, 2003).

The system of moral principles—or ethics—is a set of rules determining right and wrong behaviour (Delbridge et al., 2001, p. 645). Ethics can be applied to any human action and the study of business ethics is a growing phenomenon. Given the relatively new concept of e-business, and the rate of change that is measured in months rather than years, the rules are constantly changing and ethical dilemmas have become common. A literature search on e-business ethics will produce references to corporate collapses and mismanagement, spam, the illegal use of intellectual property and abuse of privacy laws, to name just a few. There are many articles available that discuss the science of ethics and the business ethics approach of understanding the social responsibility of e-businesses beyond legal implications. Many of the theories and studies are beyond the intention of this chapter, which attempts to give an outline of some of the contemporary issues related to technological innovation associated with e-business. The references supplied at the end of the chapter are a starting point for a more detailed analysis of e-business ethics.

IS THERE A NEED FOR ETHICS IN E-BUSINESS?

Harrison (2001, p. 40) refers to the individual's moral development as opposed to the corporation's. He mentions the years of debate about whether the modern corporation should be deemed responsible for immoral acts and collective responsibility and puts forward the notion that as "corporations are owned, managed and staffed by individuals who are morally responsible beings" then it follows that yes, modern corporations should be held responsible. The debate is taken further but for the purposes of this chapter, it is enough to assume that like individuals, ethics is a fundamental part of the corporate culture. Like traditional corporations, e-businesses are also made up of individuals (albeit sometimes only one) and these individuals also have moral responsibility.

At least a few references on the e-business ethics topic returned the concept that e-business and ethics is an oxymoron ("a figure of speech by which a locution produces an effect by a seeming self-contradiction", Delbridge et al., 2001, p. 1369). Is it a widely held belief that ethics and e-business is a contradiction? Sama and Shoaf (2002) say that "in the absence of normative ethical behaviour to guide decision-making in this new realm, rules of the game are being forged by special interests, such as company lawyers, eager entrepreneurs, and overnight millionaires seduced by the ease and rapidity with which they can amass their fortunes."

Sama and Shoaf (2002) also refer to peer scrutiny (in the new media) as being less than that of traditional businesses and cited a study by Tenbrunsel in 1998 (investigating how incentives and temptation play a role in ethical decision-making) which indicated that "mutual perceptions of unethical conduct trigger a cycle of more unethical conduct...where competitors and customers alike engage in unethical practices on the basis of others' unethical practices." This sounds a little like the used car salesman stereotype that these businesses are all alike in their lack of ethics. They argue that this is likely because many e-businesses are modelling themselves on 'pioneering' firms that may not be altogether virtuous. So innovation has resulted, according to these authors, in unethical behaviour because of the new media and technology and the fact that businesses are embarking on something new; therefore the old rules do not apply?

Interestingly, Sama and Shoaf (2002) also believe that web-based commerce or e-business consist of organisational cultures that have 'weak ethical climates'; that is, a low 'moral intensity' (a concept that relates to influences on ethics), and they refer to the *perception* of moral intensity—so this relates back to organisational culture in that marketing decisions have a perceived low moral intensity, which just continues the climate of unethical behaviour.

THE CHANGING NATURE OF E-BUSINESS: ETHICS AND TRUST

E-business has many definitions, but it is essentially "the use of networks and information technology to electronically design, market, buy, sell and deliver products and services worldwide" (Maury & Kleiner, 2002). Maury and Kleiner (2002) also suggest that e-business is in its "infancy" and that it is currently taking its first steps which are "tentative" and "unsure". This is perhaps a little dated in some respects because the e-business rate of change would suggest that it is growing up quickly, albeit with ethics trailing behind somewhat. There is still a great deal of excitement and buzz about e-business, perhaps due to its unregulated nature—"a free marketplace for the exchange of ideas and products" (Maury & Kleiner, 2002).

All businesses operate in a climate of insecurity, be that financial or otherwise, and are under increasing pressure to report on the 'triple bottom line'—"in which financial performance must be matched by environmental sustainability and social responsibility...and so on" (Longstaff, 2003). In traditional businesses, an element of trust is apparent - from dealing with other businesses, to suppliers and even customers. The notion of trust is tied to the ethical framework of the business because trust implies individual morality and values and a business is made up of individuals. To have trust in an individual and to be trusted in return is a part of society's expectations.

With the speed at which e-business is developing, "trust is becoming increasingly harder to establish and maintain" (Daughtrey, 2001). The lack of face-to-face interaction in transactions and the anonymity of the Internet result in an impersonal style of business where trust must be implied but is not necessarily there. Daughtrey (2001) notes that deliberately falsified information is also more difficult to detect.

Again on the subject of trust in e-business, Daughtrey (2001) refers to the conditions consumers expect when conducting business with or purchasing from the Internet:

- Generalised reputation or perception of supplier.
- Customer expectations for security, privacy and confidentiality.
- Assurances provided by supplier (such as certifications or guarantees).
- Reports of other customers. If the customer has a history of prior transactions, additional factors may be:

o   Accuracy of order fulfilment.
o   Timeliness of order fulfilment.
o   Nature of any interactions with customer relations.
o   Resolution of any disputes.
o   Subsequent communications from the supplier.
o   Any communications from other suppliers with whom customer information was shared.

Also, good media and the 'name' and 'logo' can be valuable for building trust (such as magazine promotions, etc.) wherever there is a third party advising customers—this can be a huge trust indicator. Amazon.com quickly became the leading on-line book retailer because it was referred to by the media and articles were written on its success. Also, successful on-line businesses are those that were once traditional businesses; that is, they have already built the business and are now transferring to the new business environment—these companies have a head start in terms of consumer/customer trust.

The level of insecurity regarding on-line transactions is interesting given that many face-to-face transactions are just as insecure, if not more. Take a restaurant bill for example; when a credit card payment is made the receipt kept by the establishment has both the credit card number and the signature included. While these receipts are often kept in secure locations, a great deal of trust is required in the establishment to ensure the details are not used fraudulently. On some occasions and with certain e-businesses, it may even be *safer* to transmit payment information on-line due to the security measures in place (encryption, secure web sites, etc.). To further highlight this advantage, consider the postage of cheques and money orders in the 'snail' mail and consider the number of potential dangers that mail will encounter during its delivery.

The use of credit cards is a perfect example, as mentioned above, where there has been much concern about giving credit card details over the net. On this note, it is safe to say that credit card fraud tends to happen in every business environment—it is not particularly an Internet issue alone. For example, credit card numbers appear on shop receipts and so does the signature. This allows the risk of a staff member or customer potentially having access to the details. Again, as mentioned above, transmitting this kind of information over the Internet is possibly safer than the traditional method of handing over the card. There is talk now of assigning pin codes to credit cards for Internet transactions, so credit card fraud is being addressed. Also, due to security concerns, many businesses will continually monitor security and increase security measures as any fraudulent actions could potentially cripple the business in terms of consumer trust.

Methods for dealing with on-line security: without delving into technical detail, e-businesses are constantly dealing with new security risks and hence having to develop advanced methods of minimising these risks. Actions taken include encryption, and developing digital certificates or signatures (to identify the consumer so he or she can proceed to enter data). The Australian Taxation Office now allows tax returns to be lodged on-line (called e-tax). In order to ensure the lodger is the person they claim to be, questions are answered to which only the ATO should be able to verify. In this way, the return can then be lodged with confidence.

E-businesses who apply good ethical principles are aware of the notion of trust implied in on-line transactions and business dealings. Keeping up to date with privacy and security issues and ensuring good authentication practices are maintained on the web site indicate that the e-business is an ethical one. It would be too simple to say that the company is merely trying to reduce the likelihood of financial loss. The author believes that a company that puts into place these elements is behaving ethically.

It may be worth adding that there are other factors involved in building trust in on-line environments. Consider web site design and layout; often a very attractive and well planned web site gives the indication that the company is around for good and invests in good communication methods, hence trust is implied. Even for companies with excellent reputations, a poor web site can actually repel customers.

THE TYRANNY OF ANONYMITY

"There is less questioning of the source of information [on the web] because all buyers and sellers are essentially anonymous in cyberspace. The consumer and the seller of goods and services are not "known" to each other in the traditional sense. They are transparent, and place-holders (i.e., easily replaceable with other buyers/sellers). Lack of any real contact with consumers contributes to a sense of distance and anonymity, and competitors compete primarily on the basis of price" (Sama & Shoaf, 2002).

Sama and Shoaf (2002), while agreeing that the lack of face-to-face contact results in less of a *relationship* between customer and e-business, say that there is less questioning and that "many customers using the Web to conduct transactions are lulled into believing they are in possession of perfect information...full and accurate when, in fact, large information asymmetries between buyer and seller exist." So perhaps customers are too trusting and do not consider or appreciate the range of information available and are not in the position to ascertain its value or accuracy. They trust that it is right. Do e-businesses exploit this? And in the process, abuse the trust so needed in new technological innovation?

Why then, is it easier to behave unethically over the net? Sama and Shoaf (2002) feel that it is related to immediacy; that is, unethical behaviour is easier to live with if the 'victim' of the behaviour is distanced from the perpetrator. The anonymity of the net ensures the victim is not seen or heard, whereas in traditional businesses the customer has a face and can walk into the store or business place and physically confront the abuser of trust. Maurer and Kleiner (2002) refer to business ethics over recent years as having become "a rather fluid and uncertain subject when applied to multinational transactions and venues". They liken it to the Wild West where formal laws were often disregarded in the push to expand and argue that the 'niceties' of business ethics have been pushed aside.

There is also the notion that 'if everybody else is doing it why can't I?' Like tax avoidance, it becomes easier to justify if a lot of people are attempting it. People tend to desire an even playing field even if that playing field is unethical. Sama and Shoaf (2002) refer to the anecdotal evidence of the Machiavellian nature of many e-business leaders (i.e., "being or acting in accordance with Machiavelli's political doctrines, which placed expediency above political morality, and countenanced the use of craft and deceit in order to maintain the authority and effect the purposes of the ruler") (Delbridge et al., 2001, p. 1145).

THE CONCEPT OF ETHICAL GOVERNANCE

"In the new economy, where knowledge, not equipment, drives profits, employees can no longer be considered 'outsiders'. They are the source of competitive advantage" (McGarvey, 2001).

Most organisations (be they e-businesses or more traditional businesses) utilise labour. There are many ethical implications and responsibilities when dealing with labour. Ethical issues arise in the areas of equal opportunity, equity, disability, anti-discrimination, racial vilification, privacy of employees and whistleblowing. E-business has to contend with these issues just as a traditional business would.

There have been huge cases of corporate collapse in recent times. Derrick Heywood (2003) states that criticism has been levelled at CIOs (Chief Information Officers), external auditors and CEOs (Chief Executive Officers) and other executives (who often make a large sum of money even if the company is underperforming). Heywood (2003) says that Directors should also be made accountable for their actions and that of their appointed CEO and that they have escaped much of the blame in these recent collapses. So in an e-business, is it the Directors who must establish a code of ethics that is appropriate for the technological bent of their company? Should they be conversant with the evolution of ethical dilemma in congruence with technological innovation? Or can it be the individuals, the staff, etc.? The author argues that with technological innovation, it may take somebody who knows the technology to establish and monitor the ethical issues that may arise. Non-technical staff, even those who have high moral standards and a knowledge of business ethics, may no longer have the technical expertise to determine ethical issues and resulting dilemmas.

There are many e-businesses currently operating; some large, some small. In all types of businesses, there are the 'shonky' operators—those who operate to obtain profit at the expense of consumers and perhaps employees. Many of these operators shut down before products can be returned or action can be taken, never to be heard of again. Think of perhaps a retailer selling sub-standard computers—the computers are sold and when the buyer realises they do not work properly, the retailer is long gone. So this happens anyway. The transition to e-business can increase the numbers of these operators simply because the Internet is difficult to regulate. Fraud and scams are a part of life on the Internet. And the fraudsters can be very difficult to trace, often operating internationally. There are obvious scams, such as the Nigerian money transfer scam (whereby e-mail recipients are advised that they can potentially make millions of dollars simply by providing a Nigerian 'government official' with their bank details) to those where the scam is not so evident; perhaps selling faulty or dangerous goods, etc.

There is a reluctance of legislators to hinder the growth of e-business by overly regulating it, but they are also regulating something that they may not understand fully, if at all:

"... the development of legislation that is supposed to prevent the worst excesses of Internet culture and usage. However, legislation enacted for this purpose is almost totally ineffective and therefore, largely meaningless" (Longstaff, 2003).

It is useful to acknowledge that not all unethical behaviour is illegal, and this is perhaps the most fundamental problem with e-business and the Internet. With legislation often lagging behind innovation, the choice between right and wrong is not made easier by using the law as a guide. Some behaviour falls into the basket whereby there is no legal ramification, but there is an effect; to shareholders, to staff and to customers. The decision rests with the individual. What happens if that individual has a different moral stance or a different upbringing than another individual? What if there are cultural differences in their ethical decision making?

The importance of the global nature of e-business should be stressed, dissolving traditional boundaries, so that while the boundaries of ethics are dissolving, so are the borders of trade and commerce. The transfer of business to an on-line environment has ramifications for customers used to the traditional face-to-face business transactions. Some have resisted quite strongly the request to transmit personal information over the Internet. There is a feeling that the information is put 'out there' to float around available to any person interested. This insecurity could perhaps explain why even today, on-line retailers' business has steadied somewhat—some have even had negligible sales increases in 2001 and 2002 (Howarth, 2002).

What about the international basis of e-business? Wouldn't some businesses have different moral codes than others due to the makeup of staff or origin of the business? Attitudes toward work and business vary country to country. With e-business eroding these borders somewhat, do the borders of moral intensity and upbringing also dissolve or are they much the same?

TYPICAL E-BUSINESS ETHICAL DILEMMAS

Cyberpirates

While not as pressing an issue now as a few years ago, Cyberpirates are still operating. Cyberpirates register well-known trademarks for business or financial gain. While traditionally, more than one business can use a trade name (with certain restrictions), on the net only one domain name can be registered (as it is an 'address'). The opportunity to make some money will always be pursued by some, and as established business made the move to an on-line environment, these opportunists registered the names of those established companies as domain names.

Maury and Kleiner (2002) note that while action can be taken in some cases (such as Hasbro vs. Candyland where a pornography site deliberately used the word Candyland in its address to gain site traffic), at other times it may not be successful because the 'cyberpirate' may have a legitimate use for that domain name.

As demonstrated in the Hasbro case, Cyberpirates can utilise a 'respectable' company's name as a veneer for a pornographic web site. Therefore, unsuspecting web users can be led to pornographic material while searching for a company name. What this shows though is that in the first instance before any test cases or government intervention, this practice was able to occur without any legislative control. Unethical businesses could trade on the reputation of another. They could also use the name as a form of bribery (cybersquatting).

Cybersquatting

A well-known case of a cybersquatter is Dennis Toeppen, who registered the name of Panavision with the intention of selling it back to its namesake (Maury & Kleiner, 2002). Panavision sued. Mr. Toeppen's case centred on the fact that he was not using the name to sell goods and services through his web site (in order to get around the Trademark Dilution Act) but the court ruled in Panavision's favour because the act of obtaining money from the sale of the domain name was in fact profiting from the name. This example shows that legislative intervention is incredibly important, albeit slow to catch up. Mr. Toesppen's intentions were unethical and needed to be tested in law before his actions could be thwarted. The opportunity to make money overruled moral decency. Maury and Kleiner (2002) also note an alternative strategy, 'reverse domain name hijacking' whereby a strong, powerful company uses their considerable financial reserves to force a small company to hand over a name. This is particularly worrying when both companies have equal claim to the name (especially evident where the name is a common word).

What is interesting though is that these authors suggest that companies are now being advised to register all the possibilities such as 'org' and 'net', etc.

And also possible insults (they use the example of acmesucks.com). So it would become someone's dedicated task within an organisation to predict what a cybersquatter may come up with (Maury & Kleiner, 2002).

Patents

Patents for a 'process' can be received for a computer program, just like they can be received for designs for an article of manufacture, asexually reproduced plants and so on (Maury & Kleiner, 2002). 'Business Model Patents' are granted by the Patent and Trademark Office in the United States for new processes on the Internet. Some examples of e-businesses that have taken advantage of patents are Priceline and CyberGold, with the name-your-price shopping method and using incentives to reward customers being the respective methods patented.

A very well-documented patent user, Amazon.com, sued Barnes & Noble when B&N started to use a similar method of on-line shopping, the 'one-click' method (B&N called it the Express lane). Maury and Kleiner (2002) in their article discuss the ethical implications arising from patents, with particular reference to the Amazon case.

They argue that patents on computer methods, while supposedly enhancing and encouraging innovation, actually do the opposite. Patents allow large (wealthy) companies to monopolise an industry—especially those concerned with computer methods such as on line retailers. As the Amazon case demonstrates, a patent can be held on a shopping method—the one-click method—which basically allows the shopper a more simplified check-out system. Even though B&N called their method something different (the Express Lane), Amazon argued that the process was the same, thereby ensuring that no other on line retailer could simplify and streamline their check-out processes.

An appropriate analogy here would be to compare the on-line book retailers with their more traditional counterparts, the humble bookstore. If there were two bookstores in the same street, and one store introduced a method whereby customers earned points on each purchase redeemable for a voucher at a later date, it would be reasonable to assume that the other store may try to offer a competing 'loyalty program'. This is the nature of competition, and the consumer benefits from the choice of two offers. As long as the competing store did not steal intellectual property (i.e., the name given to the program or the artwork or logos) then the competition would be legal. If these bookstores operated on line and the first bookstore had a patent on their loyalty program, the other bookstore would be unable to compete and probably lose customers.

Patents like the one held by Amazon are simply 'bullying tactics' by powerful companies to ensure competition remains minimal and could be considered as unethical.

Internet Start-Ups and Fraudulent Activity

The case of a fake press-release that cost an electronics company billions of dollars. This type of action is stock manipulation and is probably more effective with e-businesses because of the reduced consumer trust and not understanding the processes of e-business (Daughtrey, 2001). There are significant examples of venture capitalists and the over-valuing dot.coms, particularly new ones.

Deep Linking

This is linking to other sites without making it apparent—so perhaps using the information that another site provides without acknowledging the source (e.g., the weather forecast). The site may continue to do so if they licence the material; for example, on an Australian site where you can view maps of where you need to go, the site licences maps from Melways or Sydways or UBD, but the maps appear with the new site's logo. Expensive, but ethical in terms of intellectual property and copyright.

Meta-Tagging

Meta-tagging refers to the embedding of unrelated keywords into sites, so that when someone undertakes a site search, unrelated sites could be shown. It is obviously beneficial for pornography sites where many people would not choose to search for them—they have attempted to get people in by 'mistake'. How does this happen? Perhaps black text on a black background? You cannot see it but the search software can as it does not differentiate between colours. This can be extremely frustrating to customers/users and to search engine administrators. Why, because their business is searching and their product is seen as unreliable.

Advertising Practices

There has been recent controversy over the concept of 'cash for comment', whereby journalists make reference to a service or product without acknowledging that they are being paid to do so (this form of advertising being highly unethical due to the idea that a journalist cannot be 'bought').

'Cash for comment' transcribes to the Internet easily. A number of web sites contain book reviews or health advice and many of them have an 'arrangement' with the provider of goods and services related to the review. For example, the *New York Times* web site links book reviews directly to Barnes & Noble's web site. The Times and Barnes & Noble have an 'arrangement' (Outing, 1999).

The editor of WineToday.com, Bruce Kyse, is concerned about the "ethical considerations of combining e-commerce with quality journalism" (Outing, 1999). Linking articles with retailers can lessen the impact of wine, or any other product reviews and gives the consumer a feeling that the two could be colluding.

Intellectual Property

Sama and Shoaf (2002) refer to this dilemma as respecting rights as opposed to providing 'free' promotional goods and/or 'stealing' competitors' intellectual property.

> *"The embattled US music industry disclosed aggressive plans today to escalate its fight against Internet piracy, threatening to sue hundreds of individual computer users who illegally share music files online"* (M/X, 2003, p. 13).

The music sharing issue has been around for some time, but solutions have been few and far between. The article referred to above notes that the Recording Industry Association of America intends to search the web to identify individuals who have substantial collections of MP3 files available for downloading. The ethical dilemma here is twofold: consumers are distributing the intellectual property of artists to others without a fee being contributed to the artist, and the record industry is acting in a heavy-handed way to curb what is essentially the sharing of music between 'friends'. While on the one hand, the Internet encourages file-sharing and free speech, on the other it enables intellectual property to be uncontrollably distributed on a scale never before seen. Unlike copying a record on a tape to give to a friend, the Internet allows thousands of people to take a copy. The record industry is probably not acting in order to ensure the concept of intellectual property is respected—it is more likely that they are pursuing lost profits; however, the threat to artists is present and very difficult to control.

Discrimination and Offensive Material

Le Menestral et al. (2002) refer to the legal case that involved Yahoo! Inc and its French subsidary in 2000 regarding the sale of Nazi items on auction sites—dubious web site content. Issues raised by this case include: "multi-jurisdictional compliance, the technical specificity of the internet, opposing conceptions of freedom of expression, the nature of e-business, coordination between headquarters and a foreign subsidiary, leadership, and relations with domestic and international media".

The issue revolves around the concept of freedom of information. On the one hand, the Internet provides the most accessible way of obtaining a range of information. The range of information is not censored and can include pornography and opinions that may not be considered appropriate. There are also sites on the Internet that host the opinions of groups advocating hate and intolerance toward other sections of the community. What are the ethics involved in an auction site that sells Nazi propaganda or pornographic material? Is it the responsibility of the auction site to censor certain products? Or should the ethical responsibility lie with the person/s who post the item to the site? More specifically, can the auction site be held legally responsible (and hence liable) for discrimination or racial vilification or even advocating pornography? What about servers that host sites that deal with paedophilia? Again, with servers hosting thousands of sites, where does the responsibility lie and who needs to be held ethically responsible?

Le Menestral et al. (2002) note the various reactions by groups concerned about such hate sites on the net. They speak about the United Kingdom's Internet Watch Foundation (IWF), an industry self-regulatory group, who investigates complaints related to hate materials on the Internet, and the German Chancellor Gerhard Schroeder who asked for international cooperation to keep neo-Nazis off the Internet.

So as a method of distributing propaganda, the Internet provided the means lacking beforehand. Le Menestral et al. (2002) note that the groups always existed and always distributed their propaganda and met with each other—much like paedophiles. But the Internet has made the swapping of material and the organisation of events much easier. The anonymity is also a plus for this type of behaviour. Should Yahoo! have acted as a political censor? Should we be able to access this information? What about personal choice and responsibility?

Spam

Spam, or the sending of unsolicited marketing e-mail advertisements, is the subject of heated debate and it is only getting worse. Type 'spam' in any search engine of choice and your query will hit thousands of sites—mostly 'anti-spam' sites. One such site, www.spam.abuse.net, defines spammers as "… the mutant spawn of a bizarre reproductive act involving a telemarketer, Larry Flynt, a tapeworm, and an executive of the Third Class mail industry".

Not everybody finds spam so annoyingly funny however—Bill Gates of Microsoft has 'declared war on spam' (Maney, 2003) and is employing special groups of researchers to identify ways to tackle the problem, even suggesting programs that will add to the time it takes to send a spam message, thereby increasing the operating costs of spammers and perhaps encouraging them to apply a more selective method of targeting spam recipients (instead of targeting any active address they can get hold of). There is also talk of getting spammers to pay recipients for opening the spam, although how this could be done remains a mystery (especially considering the dubious nature of many spammers).

But why does unsolicited e-mail cause so much angst? To the consumer and/or employee, spam wastes time. Much of the content is a reference or link to adult porn sites or 'get rich quick' schemes. Therefore the most common action taken is to delete the e-mail. The time factor becomes apparent when thirty or so spam messages are received each time the mailbox is checked by the recipient.

On a more surreptitious level, spam senders often try to mask their messages (by not showing the true subject in the subject line—viewable without actually opening the message). This forces the consumer to open the message in curiosity, often leading directly to an adult site (some of which are difficult to navigate out of). Some spam message subject lines are deliberately worded so as to 'trick' the recipient (e.g., Hi. How are you?). The recipient is led to believe the e-mail is from a friend. More annoying still is the fact that the return e-mail address often bounces back, indicating that the true sender's details are not available.

While spam is clearly not ethical, it is usually sent by companies without a reputation to protect, companies that have been set up in the face of the new e-business revolution. Ethical behaviour is not high on the agenda. Because they are not 'respected' companies, they do not have to align themselves with retailing codes of conduct nor do they particularly worry about industry condemnation.

Some of the effects of and concerns about spam are listed below:

- *System Overload* - servers can become overloaded with what are essentially 'rubbish' e-mails.
- *Privacy* - privacy laws are often disregarded by spammers. If a recipient wishes to remove his or her details from the spammers' e-mail database and replies to the e-mail, the spammer confirms that the e-mail address is 'active' and thereby quite valuable. So rather than obliging the recipient by removing his or her details, they on-sell the 'active' address and the recipient receives even more spam. The moral to this story is to never reply to a spam message.
- *Exposing children to unsolicited material* - there is a high risk of children accidentally accessing pornography and/or disturbing hate sites by opening a spam message. Some messages link to sites that are so extreme as to even offend an adult recipient. Before the Internet, there were magazines; however, these were a great deal more difficult for children to access.
- *Costs to business* - businesses spend a great deal of time and money either blocking spam or paying staff to delete hundreds of spam messages during the course of their working day.
- *Fraudulent and misleading advertising* - People who are easily led to believe marketing claims by spammers may find themselves the victim of fraud or faulty products. As the source of the message is often masked or an address of the business is not included, fraud is common. Some sites may be entirely made up of false claims. Some people will take the information at face value and trust the sites' claims implicitly.

Privacy

Privacy is perhaps the most well-documented and potentially harmful side effect of e-business. At its most serious form, invasion of privacy on the net can lead to cyberstalking and physical harm. There have been instances of stalkers documenting their obsession on their freely accessible web site (Ardito, 2003). Sama and Shoaf (2002) argue that the benefit of accumulating customer information is that marketing can be tailored to certain groups ('niche' marketing).

Many corresponding annoyances such as spam (previously mentioned) and cookies are related to the privacy issue. A cookie is a piece of information sent by a web server to store on a web browser so that the browser can remember some specific information. This basically means that a web user need not enter the same information all the time and it increases efficiency while surfing. As a side effect of this idea, cookies can be used to track users' web use, what sites they have visited, etc. This was a boon to marketers of products. Web user outrage at this invasion of privacy led to the 'option' of whether or not cookies are enabled. However, many sites would not allow access or had restricted access to those who had disabled the cookie function—thereby reducing that choice to a catch-22, or ultimatum.

Many sites provide a privacy policy. This is an attempt to show that the principles of privacy are followed by the company, but as Sama and Shoaf (2002) point out, these policies are subject to change and the onus is on the consumer to periodically check back on the policy for updates. They refer to this as a protection primarily for the 'dot.com'; however, it is actually a realistic way for a legitimate e-business to adjust to new legislation and keep up with new technology. We must remember that there are positives to e-business and these businesses must be encouraged to tackle privacy issues and policies. Many privacy policies provide an e-mail address for a privacy officer, so questions regarding the policy can be raised.

Privacy issues are tied to the problem of spam. Privacy legislation in Australia enables customers to have access to and the right to update information held about them. This, however, would only apply to companies that legally abide by the privacy regulations. Spammers are often unable to be traced and ensure that this is so. So consumers will never be able to see or change or remove the information on them being held.

ETHICAL GUIDELINES OR CODES OF CONDUCT?

The ethical climate of an organisation 'refers to perceptions of the firm's practices and procedures that have ethical content. Manifestations of a positive ethical climate may include written ethics policies or codes of conduct, ethics training programs, and the installation of an ethics officer or ombudsman to assist employees in resolving ethical dilemmas' (Sama & Shoaf, 2002).

The code of ethics that establishes ideals and responsibilities of the e-business profession protects both customers and professionals. It should improve the profile of the profession by motivating and inspiring practitioners, raising awareness and consciousness of issues and improving quality and consistency. Since codes of ethics standards are not obligatory, their ethical values are culturally relativistic. Nevertheless, Johnson (1998) argues that Internet service providers, e-businesses, on-line services and civic networks should have a code of ethics, known as netiquette, to serve new users in cyberspace.

Computer Professionals for Social Responsibility (CPSR) have made an attempt to construct guidelines to identify ethical behaviour for both employees and employers of e-business (Woodbury, 1998). In their opinion defining what is ethical in terms of level of e-mail and voicemail monitoring is different from looking at laws and their enforcement. The level of monitoring can be legal and unethical at the same time, or illegal and ethical. Consequently, CPSR indicates that ethical use must be defined and enforced. If created as a policy, with the contribution of employees, it would become an integral part of the organisation and its culture. Otherwise, it may impose unexpected negative consequences on and from employees.

In Weber's (2000) opinion, a code of conduct is a sign of a mature profession. Hence, the Software Engineering Code of Ethics and Professional Practice, developed by a joint committee of the Association for Computing Machinery and IEEE Computer Society, indicates maturity of the software engineering profession. However, this profession, in spite of claiming its maturity, has still unsolved problems of privacy erosion as mentioned before. In particular, the Software and Information Industry Association Company argues that privacy rights erosion is inevitable in collecting consumer data. Further, without such consumer data, companies cannot develop the competitive products and services.

The strategic partnership between the InternetCommerce.com and WebAssured.com is worthy of attention (Travis, 2000). This partnership empowers consumers with easier access to retailing business and performance history. Retailers who agree to join WebAssured have to follow exact standards for security, privacy, integrity, and customer satisfaction in their business practices. As such they gain the benefit of preferential listing in ShopGuide.com's search directory. An icon next to the retailer's name highlights its WebAssured standards of ethics simply by being linked to the retailer's business track record. In regards to this partnership, Amazon.com has announced formation of the strategic alliance with Wal-Mart e-commerce supplier (Bloomberg, 2001).

Strategies for self-regulation suggested by Sama and Shoaf (2002) include:

1. "Focus on consumer welfare as a top priority; that is, measure consumer satisfaction as a gauge for 'how we are doing' rather than putting such an emphasis on the capital market as a driver for firm behaviour

2. Emphasize accountability as a means of ensuring more ethical conduct on the part of decision-makers. Those whose work requires them to be responsible for the consequences of their moral decisions are more likely to have advanced moral cognitive development

3. Encourage firms to perform a stakeholder analysis when gauging the true benefit/harm ratio of decisions' consequences. Analysis would consider impacts of decisions on ALL Stakeholders, including customers, employees, lenders, communities, government and competitors, not just investors and top executives. Even the most well-intended decision-maker may make an unethical decision when one or more impacted stakeholders are omitted from the analysis.

4. Avoid insular thinking bred by boards heavily dominated by insiders, and decision-making that is top-down rather than participative.

5. Consider increased public regulation of dot.coms in areas where self policing is not producing efficient market outcomes or is so lax as to invite fraud. Currently, privacy experts estimate that the law is about ten years behind the technology. Certainly regulation must be tempered by a concern with market efficiency.

6. Frame ethical issues analysis so that latent harm is clearly in evidence. Given that most managers rely on utilitarian thinking for ethical decision-making, the consequences of a decision become critical in resolving a moral dilemma. Yet, too often full consequences are not identified. It is therefore important to frame the issue so that potential moral harm is in evidence, including physical, economic and psychological harm. Training must include building sensitivity to all these facets of harm, and how they might be produced."

In the short term, it seems that strategic partnerships clarify the significance of having developed e-business codes of conduct for successful e-business organisations. If supported by ethical rules developed at a national level, e-business organisations would perhaps overcome more easily the many ethical dilemmas that they face at the present. Since this is still not the case, e-business organisations as global organisations per se should rely on both developed global ethical codes and codes of professional societies.

CONCLUSION

"Australia's company directors and executives are flocking to business ethics courses, which are booming after the spectacular collapses of high-profile companies HIH and One.Tel, and WorldCom and Enron in the United States" (Marino & Webb, 2002).

The 'hit-and-run' approach to e-business and the view that long-term viability of the firm is not a goal (Sama & Shoaf, 2002) indicate that e-business will confront ethical dilemmas continually as new innovations arise. The value of traditional businesses lies in the cultivation of customer relationships and an implied trust in the tangible nature of its primary business, service or product. As e-businesses deal with intangible products and services over the Internet, the potential for ethical dilemmas and shonky practices to develop is far higher than a in a bricks-and-mortar business. The challenge is for e-businesses to establish trust based on consistent good ethical practice and an industry approach to abusers of the system. The media continues to provide opportunities for unethical practices to be exposed as does whistleblowing and good corporate governance. But ethics and innovation are not mutually exclusive and will continue to challenge e-businesses.

With the Internet, we now "…cannot 'outsource' our ethical obligations to the government. Instead, they remain with us and we are, in a sense, forced to take responsibility for how we engage with the medium and the content that it carries … the unintended consequence of the anarchy of the net may be an increase in our general ability to deal not only with 'virtual ethics' but also with the here and now issues that confront us on a daily basis" (Longstaff, 2003).

REFERENCES

Ardito, S. (2003). Information brokers and cyberstalking. *Information Today*, Medford, May.

Bloomberg. (2001). Amazon in talks with Wal-Mart. *The Age,* March 5.

Daughtrey, T. (2001). Costs of trust for e-business. *Quality Progress*, October. Milwaukee, Wisconsin.

Delbridge, A., Bernard, J., Blair, D., Butler, S., Peters, P., & Yallop, C. (2001). *Macquarie Dictionary –Revised third edition.* The Macquarie Library Pty Ltd.

Harrison, J. (2001). *Ethics for Australian Business.* Australia: Pearson Education.

Heywood, D. (2003). Directing blame. *Australian CPA*, July.

Howarth, B. (2002). Shoppers click off. *Business Review Weekly*, November 28-December 4.

Johnson, J. (1998). Netiquette training: Whose responsibility? *CPSR Newsletter, Summer 16*(3), 14–18.

Le Menestral, M., Hunter, M., & de Bettignies, H. (2002). Internet e-ethics in confrontation with an activists' agenda: Yahoo! On trial. *Journal of Business Ethics*, August, Dordrecht.

Longstaff, S. (2003). *Corporate social responsibility.* St. James Ethics Centre, Retrieved on June 2 from: www.ethics.org.au

Longstaff, S. (2003). *Ethics of the Internet.* St. James Ethics Centre, Retrieved on June 2 from: www.ethics.org.au

Maney, K. (2003). Gates, Microsoft look for ways to zap spam. *USA Today*, Retrieved on June 2 from: www.usatoday.com/money/industries/technology/2003-06-25-gates_x.htm

Marino, M., & Webb, R. (2002). *Suddenly, ethics is a booming business.* July 28, www.theage.com.au

Maury, M., & Kleiner, D. (2002). E-commerce, ethical commerce? *Journal of Business Ethics*, March, Dordecht.

McGarvey, R. (2001). New corporate ethics for the new economy. *World Trade*, March, Troy.

Outing, S. (1999). *The old rules don't apply on the Web.* Editor and Publisher; New York.

Sama, L., & Shoaf, V. (2002). Ethics on the Web: Applying moral decision-making to the new media. *Journal of Business Ethics*, March, Dordrecht.

Travis, M. (2000). WebAssured.com: InternetCommerce.com and WebAssured "the dot.confidence company" form strategic partnership;

Partnership empowers online consumers with easier access to merchant business and performance history. *M2 Presswire,* October 24.

Waddell, D. (2002). *E-business in Australia: Concepts and Cases.* Australia: Pearson Education.

Weber, A. (2000). Ethics? Not interested. *Software Development,* 7–9.

Woodbury, M. (1998). Email, voicemail, and privacy: What policy is ethical?www.cpsr.org/-marsha-w/emailpol.html

About the Authors

Mohini Singh is an Associate Professor of Information Technology and E-Business in the School of Business Information Technology at RMIT University, Australia. She earned her Ph.D. in New Technology Management from Monash University, and has published widely in the areas of e-business and new technology and innovation management. Her publications include books, book chapters, journal and conference papers. She is the principal editor of *E-Commerce Diffusion: Strategies and Challenges*, Heidelberg Press, Australia. She was the founding director of the E-Commerce Research Unit at Victoria University (1998-2000). She supervises Ph.D., DBA and Research Masters research projects and teaches in the Master of E-Business program at RMIT. Her research interests are in the areas of e-business management strategies, B2B e-business issues, virtual communities, reverse logistics and IT innovation management. She has also taught in the Master of Information Systems, MBA and DBA programs at Victoria University and in the MBA program at IESEG Graduate School, Catholic University, France, http://www.rmit.edu.au/bus/bit/mohini_singh.

Dianne Waddell is an Associate Professor and Director of Graduate Management Programs at Edith Cowan University, Perth, Australia. She is responsible for the development, implementation and evaluation of postgraduate courses, including the MBA, and teaches in the areas of quality management, change management and strategic management. These subjects are offered both on-campus and off-campus. She holds a Ph.D. (Monash), Master of Education Administration (Melbourne), Bachelor of Education (Melbourne) and Bachelor of Arts (LaTrobe). She has published and presented papers on resistance to change, leadership, e-business, quality management and forecasting for managers. Her publications include two textbooks, *Organisation Development and Change* (Nelson-Thomson Learning) and *E-Business in Australia: Concepts and Cases* (Pearson Publishing). She has taught in both public and private education systems for many years, as well as presenting specifically designed industry-based courses.

*   *   *   *   *

Nabeel A. Y. Al-Qirim is a Lecturer of Information Systems and Module Coordinator of e-Business in the School of Computer and Information Sciences, Faculty of Business, Auckland University of Technology (AUT), Auckland, New Zealand. He has a bachelor's degree in Electrical Engineering, Certificate in Tertiary Teaching, a Postgraduate Diploma in Information Systems (Hons. with distinction), MBA, and is currently a Ph.D. candidate. His research interests and publications are in IT and e-commerce in small business supply chain management, mobile commerce, health informatics and telemedicine, e-Business in NGOs and in developing countries. He worked in the IT industry for 12 years as a consultant and in managing total IT solutions with multinational companies: IBM, Compaq, Data General, Group Bull, and Siemens Nixdorf.

Valerie Baker is a Ph.D. student at the University of Wollongong, Australia. Her research interests are e-business and IT strategic management. She has completed research projects with organizations such as BHP Steel and E-Steel Australia. Valerie has presented papers at both local and international conferences. Valerie also has experience in the area of educational multimedia, working on projects within the UOW Education Multimedia Lab for the Department of Education and Training.

Stephen Burgess (M.Bus RMIT, Ph.D. Monash) is a Senior Lecturer in Information Systems at Victoria University, Melbourne, Australia. He has a bachelor's in Accounting and a Graduate Diploma in Commercial Data Processing, both from Victoria University; an M.Bus. (IT) from RMIT, Australia, and a Ph.D. at Monash University, Australia, in the area of small business-to-consumer-interactions on the Internet. His research interests include the use of IT in small business, the strategic use of IT, B2C electronic commerce and management IT education. He has recently edited a book through Idea Group Publishing titled, *Managing Information Technology in*

Small Business: Challenges and Solutions, and is track chair in the area of small business and IT at the IRMA international conference (www.irma-international.org). Dr. Burgess is a co-founder of the IRMA Special Research Cluster on Small Business and Information Technology (www.businessandlaw.vu.edu.au/sbirit/).

Tim Coltman is a Lecturer at the School of Information Technology and Computer Science, University of Wollongong, Australia. During his Ph.D. candidature at the Australian Graduate School of Management, he has completed research projects for organizations such as the Smart Internet CRC, Westpac and the SAS Institute. He has published articles in leading journals such as *California Management Review* and *Communications of the ACM*. He has presented papers and addresses at internationally recognized conferences in the US, Europe, Asia and Australia. Tim has more than 10 years experience in the IT industry, having worked as a project manager within consultancy, government and higher education.

Joan Cooper is Professor and Pro Vice Chancellor Academic at Flinders University, Australia. She was the foundation professor of Information Technology at the University of Wollongong (UOW). She is the Dean of Informatics and has more than 25 years experience within the Information Technology field. She is the Co-ordinator of the Centre for Electronic Business Research and her most recent work is in electronic commerce and health informatics. Dr. Cooper is a member of the NSW Privacy Advisory Committee, established as part of the NSW Government's Privacy and Personal Information Protection Act of 1998, and is one of the three founders of Australia's first inter-university electronic commerce research and consulting group, CollECTeR (Collaborative Electronic Commerce Technology and Research).

Owen Cope is a Consultant with Accenture (Australia), a leading world management consulting and technology services company. He is currently managing a health informatics software development and implementation project within the South Australian health system. His thesis, titled "Leading Change in E-Commerce", investigated the Australian manufacturing industry and the relationship between levels of change and leadership styles. He holds a Bachelor of Commerce Honours and a Bachelor of Economics from Monash University. In 2000, he was name the Young Achievement Australia's National Tertiary Business person of the year. He has had a paper presented and published on leadership and e-commerce.

Susan Foster is a Lecturer in the School of Information Systems at Monash University, Australia. She has qualifications in Information Technology, teaching, and psychology. She has a strong interest in change management and has written a number of papers and book chapters related to this. She is an affiliate member of the ERP Research Group.

Paul Hawking is Senior Lecturer in Information Systems at Victoria University, Melbourne, Australia. He has contributed to the *Journal of ERP Implementation and Management* and *Management Research News* and contributed many conference papers on IS theory and practice. He is responsible for managing the University's strategic alliance with SAP and is coordinator of the University's ERP Research Group. Paul is immediate past chairperson of the SAP Australian User Group.

Byron Keating is a Lecturer at the Central Coast School of Business at the University of Newcastle, Australia. His research interests are in the area of relationship marketing, electronic business and social marketing. His Ph.D. research explores the impact of relationship marketing in the on-line and off-line contexts of the retail sector. His work has been published or is forthcoming in *Managing Service Quality, Australasian Marketing Journal*, and the *Journal of Doing Business Across Borders*. He has also published several book chapters and is a regular presenter at international conferences.

Ali Quazi is the Discipline Head of Marketing and International Business within the Newcastle Business School at the University of Newcastle, Australia. He received his Ph.D. in Marketing from the University of New South Wales, Australia. His research interests are in the areas of marketing ethics, corporate social responsibility and governance, green marketing, services and relationship marketing in an international context. His articles have appeared in numerous academic and professional journals including the *European Journal of Marketing, Australasian Marketing Journal, International Journal Managing Service Quality, Management Decision, Journal of Business Ethics, Business & Professional Ethics Journal*.

Pauline Ratnasingam is an Assistant Professor of the Computer Information Systems Department at Central Missouri State University, Missouri, USA. Pauline Ratnasingam received her Bachelors in Computing (Information Systems) and Honors in Information Systems from Monash University, Melbourne, Australia. She received her Ph.D. titled "Inter-organizational Trust in Business to Business Electronic Commerce" from Erasmus University, Rotterdam School of Management, The Netherlands. She lectured on topics such as project management, management of information systems, and electronic commerce in Australia, New Zealand, Europe and America. She is an associate member of the Association of Information Systems, and is a member of the Information Resources Management Association (IRMA) and Academy of Management. Her research interests include business risk management, Internet-based business-to-business e-commerce, organizational behaviour, inter-organizational-relationships and trust. She is the recipient and principal investigator of a National Science Foundation Scholar Awards Grant for $60,000. (Grant Number: 01227550. Research project title: *Inter-Organizational Trust in Business-to-Business Electronic Commerce.*) She has published several articles related to this area in national and international conferences and refereed journals.

Robert Rugimbana is Deputy Director of the Newcastle Graduate School of Business at the University of Newcastle, Australia. His research interests are in the areas of consumer behaviour, marketing education, technology diffusion, and cross-cultural business. He received his Ph.D. from Macquarie University in the area of consumer behaviour and innovation preference in a cross-cultural context within the financial services sector. His work has been published in the *Journal of Consumer Behaviour, Leadership and Organisational Development, International Journal of Bank Marketing, Journal of Managerial Psychology, International Journal of Education Management*, and other journals. He has also published an edited book on Cross Cultural Marketing, and is the current editor of the *Journal of Doing Business Across Borders*.

Ramanie Samaratunge is a Lecturer in the Department of Management at Monash University, Australia. She is currently teaching management of change and international management. Her scholarly interests are in public management, international management and management of change. Her recent publications include *New Public Management: Challenge for Sri Lanka* (2002) and *The Evolving Role of Trade Diplomacy in Multilateral Trade Negotiations: Experience of Agricultural Trade Liberalisation* (2002).

Sushil K. Sharma is currently Assistant Professor in the Department of Information Systems & Operations Management at the Ball State University, Muncie, Indiana, USA. He received his Ph.D. in Information Systems from Pune University in India. Prior to joining Ball State, Dr. Sharma held the associate professor position at the Indian Institute of Management, Lucknow (India), and visiting research associate professor position at the Department of Management Science, University of Waterloo, Canada. Co-author of two textbooks (*Programming in C* and *Understanding Unix*), Dr. Sharma's research contributions have appeared in many peer-reviewed national and international journals, conferences and seminar proceedings. He has extensive experience in providing consulting services to several government and private organizations including World Bank funded projects in the areas of information systems, e-commerce, and knowledge management. Dr. Sharma's primary teaching and research interests are in e-commerce, networking environments, network and information security, ERP systems, database management systems, and knowledge management.

Andrew Stein is a Lecturer in the School of Information Systems in the Faculty of Business and Law at Victoria University, Melbourne, Australia. He has contributed to the *International Journal of Management*, *Journal of Information Management*, *Journal of ERP Implementation and Management*, *Management Research News* and has contributed many conference papers on IS theory and practice. His research interests include enterprise systems, e-procurement applications, e-marketplace business models and reverse auction systems. He is a member of the university's ERP Research Group and the Australian SAP user group.

Arthur Tatnall is a Senior Lecturer in the School of Information Systems at Victoria University in Melbourne, Australia. He holds bachelor's degrees in Science and Education, a Graduate Diploma in Computer Science, and a research Master of Arts in which he explored the origins of business computing education in Australian universities. His Ph.D. involved a study in curriculum innovation in which he investigated the manner in which Visual Basic entered the curriculum of an Australian university. His research interests include technological innovation, information technology in educational management, information systems curriculum, project management and electronic commerce. He has written several books relating to information systems and has published a number of book chapters, journal articles and conference papers. He recently chaired the 13th Australasian Information Systems Conference, and is currently editing a book on Web Portals.

Fang Zhao is a Lecturer in the School of Management, Faculty of Business, RMIT University, Melbourne, Australia. She also supervises a number of

Doctor of Business Administration (DBA) and MBA projects on various management issues. She has published widely, contributing to management knowledge via refereed book chapters, journal articles and conference papers. Her research interests include innovation and knowledge management, e-commerce and e-partnership, performance measurement and total quality management. Dr. Zhao was a post-doctoral research fellow for two years at the Centre for Management Quality Research at RMIT before joining the School of Management. She is also a Visiting Professor at Qingdao University, China, and at Beijing Foreign Affair University, China.

Betty Zoppos is a Lecturer in the School of Business Information Technology at RMIT University (Australia), the School of Business and Informatics at Australian Catholic University, and the School of Information Systems at Victoria University, Melbourne, Australia. She teaches introductory-level Information System, Web-enabled Business Systems and Business Communications. Her research interests include e-commerce security issues, web design issues and e-payment systems.

Index

U

understanding resistance 73
unsolicited material 266
user identification module (UIM) 183

V

value chain 65
value-added processes 193
virtual organization 105, 106, 108, 114
virtual revolution 107
viruses 237
vision 61

W

Web markup language (WAP) 184
Western Region Economic Develop-
    ment Organisation (WREDO) 157
wire transfers 216
wireless application protocol (WAP)
    172
wireless application services providers
    (WASP) 180
wireless network devices 172
worms 237

NEW from Idea Group Publishing

- **The Enterprise Resource Planning Decade: Lessons Learned and Issues for the Future**, Frederic Adam and David Sammon/ ISBN:1-59140-188-7; eISBN 1-59140-189-5, © 2004
- **Electronic Commerce in Small to Medium-Sized Enterprises**, Nabeel A. Y. Al-Qirim/ ISBN: 1-59140-146-1; eISBN 1-59140-147-X, © 2004
- **e-Business, e-Government & Small and Medium-Size Enterprises: Opportunities & Challenges**, Brian J. Corbitt & Nabeel A. Y. Al-Qirim/ ISBN: 1-59140-202-6; eISBN 1-59140-203-4, © 2004
- **Multimedia Systems and Content-Based Image Retrieval**, Sagarmay Deb
  ISBN: 1-59140-156-9; eISBN 1-59140-157-7, © 2004
- **Computer Graphics and Multimedia: Applications, Problems and Solutions**, John DiMarco/ ISBN: 1-59140-196-86; eISBN 1-59140-197-6, © 2004
- **Social and Economic Transformation in the Digital Era**, Georgios Doukidis, Nikolaos Mylonopoulos & Nancy Pouloudi/ ISBN: 1-59140-158-5; eISBN 1-59140-159-3, © 2004
- **Information Security Policies and Actions in Modern Integrated Systems**, Mariagrazia Fugini & Carlo Bellettini/ ISBN: 1-59140-186-0; eISBN 1-59140-187-9, © 2004
- **Digital Government: Principles and Best Practices**, Alexei Pavlichev & G. David Garson/ISBN: 1-59140-122-4; eISBN 1-59140-123-2, © 2004
- **Virtual and Collaborative Teams: Process, Technologies and Practice**, Susan H. Godar & Sharmila Pixy Ferris/ ISBN: 1-59140-204-2; eISBN 1-59140-205-0, © 2004
- **Intelligent Enterprises of the 21st Century**, Jatinder Gupta & Sushil Sharma/ ISBN: 1-59140-160-7; eISBN 1-59140-161-5, © 2004
- **Creating Knowledge Based Organizations**, Jatinder Gupta & Sushil Sharma/ ISBN: 1-59140-162-3; eISBN 1-59140-163-1, © 2004
- **Knowledge Networks: Innovation through Communities of Practice**, Paul Hildreth & Chris Kimble/ISBN: 1-59140-200-X; eISBN 1-59140-201-8, © 2004
- **Going Virtual: Distributed Communities of Practice**, Paul Hildreth/ISBN: 1-59140-164-X; eISBN 1-59140-165-8, © 2004
- **Trust in Knowledge Management and Systems in Organizations**, Maija-Leena Huotari & Mirja Iivonen/ ISBN: 1-59140-126-7; eISBN 1-59140-127-5, © 2004
- **Strategies for Managing IS/IT Personnel**, Magid Igbaria & Conrad Shayo/ISBN: 1-59140-128-3; eISBN 1-59140-129-1, © 2004
- **Information Technology and Customer Relationship Management Strategies**, Vince Kellen, Andy Drefahl & Susy Chan/ ISBN: 1-59140-170-4; eISBN 1-59140-171-2, © 2004
- **Beyond Knowledge Management**, Brian Lehaney, Steve Clarke, Elayne Coakes & Gillian Jack/ ISBN: 1-59140-180-1; eISBN 1-59140-181-X, © 2004
- **Multimedia Security: Steganography and Digital Watermarking Techniques for Protection of Intellectual Property**, Chun-Shien Lu/ ISBN: 1-59140-192-5; eISBN 1-59140-193-3, © 2004
- **eTransformation in Governance: New Directions in Government and Politics**, Matti Mälkiä, Ari Veikko Anttiroiko & Reijo Savolainen/ISBN: 1-59140-130-5; eISBN 1-59140-131-3, © 2004
- **Intelligent Agents for Data Mining and Information Retrieval**, Masoud Mohammadian/ISBN: 1-59140-194-1; eISBN 1-59140-195-X, © 2004
- **Using Community Informatics to Transform Regions**, Stewart Marshall, Wal Taylor & Xinghuo Yu/ISBN: 1-59140-132-1; eISBN 1-59140-133-X, © 2004
- **Wireless Communications and Mobile Commerce**, Nan Si Shi/ ISBN: 1-59140-184-4; eISBN 1-59140-185-2, © 2004
- **Organizational Data Mining: Leveraging Enterprise Data Resources for Optimal Performance**, Hamid R. Nemati & Christopher D. Barko/ ISBN: 1-59140-134-8; eISBN 1-59140-135-6, © 2004
- **Virtual Teams: Projects, Protocols and Processes**, David J. Pauleen/ISBN: 1-59140-166-6; eISBN 1-59140-167-4, © 2004
- **Business Intelligence in the Digital Economy: Opportunities, Limitations and Risks**, Mahesh Raisinghani/ ISBN: 1-59140-206-9; eISBN 1-59140-207-7, © 2004
- **E-Business Innovation and Change Management**, Mohini Singh & Di Waddell/ISBN: 1-59140-138-0; eISBN 1-59140-139-9, © 2004
- **Responsible Management of Information Systems**, Bernd Stahl/ISBN: 1-59140-172-0; eISBN 1-59140-173-9, © 2004
- **Web Information Systems**, David Taniar/ISBN: 1-59140-208-5; eISBN 1-59140-209-3, © 2004
- **Strategies for Information Technology Governance**, Wim van Grembergen/ISBN: 1-59140-140-2; eISBN 1-59140-141-0, © 2004
- **Information and Communication Technology for Competitive Intelligence**, Dirk Vriens/ISBN: 1-59140-142-9; eISBN 1-59140-143-7, © 2004
- **The Handbook of Information Systems Research**, Michael E. Whitman & Amy B. Woszczynski/ISBN: 1-59140-144-5; eISBN 1-59140-145-3, © 2004
- **Neural Networks in Business Forecasting**, G. Peter Zhang/ISBN: 1-59140-176-3; eISBN 1-59140-177-1, © 2004

Excellent additions to your institution's library! Recommend these titles to your Librarian!

To receive a copy of the Idea Group Publishing catalog, please contact 1/717-533-8845,
fax 1/717-533-8661,or visit the IGP Online Bookstore at:
[http://www.idea-group.com]!
Note: All IGP books are also available as ebooks on netlibrary.com as well as other ebook sources.
Contact Ms. Carrie Skovrinskie at [cskovrinskie@idea-group.com] to receive a complete list of sources
where you can obtain ebook information or IGP titles.

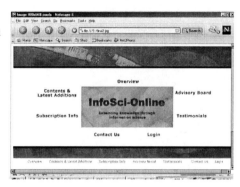